God
in Your
Body

*Kabbalah, Mindfulness
and Embodied
Spiritual Practice*

Jay Michaelson

For People of All Faiths, All Backgrounds

JEWISH LIGHTS Publishing

Woodstock, Vermont

God in Your Body:
Kabbalah, Mindfulness and Embodied Spiritual Practice

2014 Quality Paperback Edition, Fourth Printing

All rights reserved. No part of this book may be reproduced or transmitted in any form or by any means, electronic or mechanical, including photocopying, recording, or by any information storage and retrieval system, without permission in writing from the publisher.

For information regarding permission to reprint material from this book, please mail or fax your request in writing to Jewish Lights Publishing, Permissions Department, at the address / fax number listed below, or email your request to permissions@jewishlights.com.

© 2007 by Jay Michaelson

Page 239 constitutes a continuation of this copyright page.

Library of Congress Cataloging-in-Publication Data

Michaelson, Jay, 1971–
God in your body : Kabbalah, mindfulness and embodied spiritual practice /
Jay Michaelson.
p. cm.
Includes bibliographical references and index.
ISBN-13: 978-1-58023-304-0 (pbk.)
ISBN-10: 1-58023-304-X (pbk.)
1. Spiritual life—Judaism. 2. Body, Human—Religious aspects—Judaism.
3. Meditation—Judaism. 4. Cabala. I. Title.
BM723.M448 2006
296.7—dc22

2006028753

ISBN 978-1-58023-497-9 (eBook)
10 9 8 7 6 5 4

Manufactured in the United States of America

Published by Jewish Lights Publishing
A Division of LongHill Partners, Inc.
Sunset Farm Offices, Route 4, P.O. Box 237
Woodstock, VT 05091
Tel: (802) 457-4000   Fax: (802) 457-4004
www.jewishlights.com

In my flesh, I see God.
Job 19:26

Only the nonsensical is
at ease with the Absolute.
Listen to your angels
ripening your secrets.
Come to beautiful terms
with the god in your body.
James Broughton

Contents

Introduction

The Union of Body and Soul

This book is about embodied spiritual practice: how to experience the deep truths of reality in, and through, your body. To some, this may seem like a contradiction. Aren't spirit and body separate? Isn't a "spiritual" experience precisely one that is "out of body," in a special state of mind?

In the paths we will explore here, spirit and body are not separate at all. Nor is spirituality a special feeling, or a trance, or a vision, although such phenomena may accompany some spiritual practices. Rather, because Being is omnipresent, the experience of spirituality is nothing more or less than a deep, rich experience of ordinary reality. Realization is simply waking up. And the body, because it is always present here and now, is both the best vehicle for doing so, on the one hand, and, on the other, how holiness expresses itself in the world.

Jews are sometimes called the "people of the book." But as many scholars have observed, they are equally the people of the body. Consider the core practices of mainstream Jewish religion. Traditional observance of the Sabbath and holidays involves not beliefs or "spiritual feelings," but taking and refraining from certain physical actions. Jewish dietary laws are about foods, not sentiments; Jewish ethics is about action, not intention. Even Jewish prayer—built around the kneeling (*Barchu*), listening (*Shema*), and standing (*Amidah*) prayers—is based not upon some abstract soul or spirit, but upon the body. This body-centricity of the Jewish tradition is well known in academic and scholarly circles but, ironically, forgotten in many religious ones.

Even the Kabbalah, the vast body of Jewish mystical and esoteric literature, understands the greatest spiritual achievement not as transcending the body, but as joining body and spirit together. Symbolically, the Kabbalists imagined the six-pointed Jewish star as one triangle pointing upward—toward heaven, transcendence, and the emptiness of the Infinite—and another pointing downward, toward the earth, immanence, and the endless varieties of experience. The great goal of Kabbalah, which literally means "receiving," is not to privilege one triangle over the other—to flee the material world in favor of the spiritual one, or vice versa. It is the sacred marriage of the two.

This union has many iterations: body and spirit, earth and sky, experience and theory, the Presence and the Holy One, feminine and masculine, immanence and transcendence, form and emptiness, the many manifest energies of the world and their ultimate, essential unity. And the opportunities for consummating it are omnipresent, because there are no boundaries around the Infinite. Thus religion belongs in bed as well as in the sanctuary; and bodywork belongs in temples as well as on yoga mats. Sex, eating, bathing—these are not necessary evils in the Kabbalah. Rather, the body, about which there is often so much shame and so much fear, is the most practical place for spiritual work.

This integral vision is reflected in the kabbalistic concept of the four worlds,[1] which is used often in this book as an organizing principle for spiritual practice. Each of the worlds (a chart is in the Appendix) has a nest of symbolic associations and experiential elements, but perhaps their most important feature is that, because each world is important, the familiar hierarchies of spirit over body, and mind over heart, suddenly make no sense. As we will see, the worlds of *asiyah* (action), *yetzirah* (formation), *briyah* (creation), and *atzilut* (emanation) and the four souls of *nefesh* (fleshly, earth-soul), *ruach* (emotional, water-soul), *neshamah* (intellectual, air-soul), and *chayah* (spiritual, fire-soul) roughly map onto the familiar matrix of body, heart, mind, and spirit. But all are really a reflection of *yechidah* (unity). Thus the ideal is not transcendence alone, but transcendence with inclusion of the "lower" in the "higher." Forgetting the body in favor of the soul is like forgetting the foundation of a house in favor of the living room; it will not hold.

The values of integration, union, and balance affect how one studies this wisdom as well. On the one hand, intellectual theories give meaning and shape to experience. On the other hand, experience is essential: material, embodied experience—that which often wanders in exile, like a forgotten princess awaiting her redemption. Enlightenment is simply knowing the truth of what is, but knowing like the knowing of Adam by Eve. Secret wisdom, such as that of Kabbalah, is not secret simply because its formulae are not disclosed; with just a few years of education, you can learn their words. Rather, secret wisdom is such because it is experiential wisdom, and thus impossible to convey in words at all.

So, in this book we will speak of both theory and practice. For some, there may be too many words, too many concepts; for others, too much emphasis on subjective experience. Yet an integral spirituality, one that marries heaven and earth, must embrace intellect and the body, tradition and experience, analytical rigor and spiritual courage. Both sides are essential: the abstract ("God") and the concrete ("your body"). Theories of the body, pathways of the soul—these are wonderful maps and excellent recipes for wisdom. But the map is not the territory, and the recipe is not the meal.

"God"?

What is meant by the word "God"? And how does an *experience* in your body have anything to do with "God in your body"?

When I use the word "God" in an intellectual, third-person way, I mean what the ancient Hebrews called YHVH—What Is; Being; What Was, Is, and Will Be. Intellectually, for monotheists, God is *Ein Sof*, infinite, and thus must fill all creation; otherwise, God would go up until a certain point and then have a limit—and thus, not be infinite. Consequently, what appear, on the surface, to be computers, trees, and hamburgers are actually, in their essence, God. The *Ein Sof* is not a figure within or beyond the universe, a person who either does or does not exist; the *Ein Sof* is the ground of being itself. Forms that appear to be real are really manifestations of It. Or, to paraphrase a teaching from another tradition, God does not exist; God is existence itself.[2]

But what if you don't "believe in God" in this way? Feel free to set aside the word "God" and focus simply on waking up from illusion into reality. It's easy to see that ordinary experience is usually obscured by desires, conventions, and social constructions—walk into a room and see what you notice, how quickly your mind judges it as good or bad, and how much of our involvement with life is really involvement with the "small self," the selfish egoic inclinations. Even linguistic and social concepts construct our experience of reality. For example, if you're sitting in a chair right now, why are you not falling on the floor? Because of "the chair"? Or because of all sorts of molecular properties of wood or metal that derive from invisible forces of electromagnetism and gravity, and on and on and on? And who are "you" apart from the illusions produced by a well-functioning brain, like the images at the cinema that seem to be so whole? The sum of all these forces, beyond label, beyond self—this is what is meant by "Being." Nothing more.

So much for the plane of the mind. In the realm of the heart, when I speak of God in the second person, as "You," then the God-language of myth and anthropomorphism is not a symptom of fuzzy thinking but an expression of yearning. Not rational, but, then, neither is love—and would we be the richer for auditing out these "errors" from our experience? I find that when I relate to Being as God, I am able to better cultivate love, reverence, connection, personal relationship, gratitude, value, and ethics. The heart prays and cries and opens—and the object of these hopes, perhaps half-projected, I find echoed in the millennia of Jewish yearning for God.

So I invite you to stay with experience, rather than theology. Rather than starting from a position of "God exists, therefore I must be grateful to Him/Her/It," just use the body to experience gratitude, and see what happens. In the first chapter, for example, we will look at eating as a spiritual practice. Our bodies are hardwired to enjoy eating, and yet we often seem bored by it and distract ourselves with television, or reading, or conversation. With close attention to a few bites of our meal, though, amazing things can happen. The words *v'achalta, v'savata, u'verachta*—you will eat, you will be satisfied, and you will bless—suddenly make sense. The mind is quieted, the body is energized, and the food tastes more delicious than usual. Our attention is called to the miracle of eating: that you are turning lettuce into human, that your body knows exactly what to do to take what it needs from the food and discard the rest. All that's needed is time and attention. Try it and see.

Consider, too, the miracles we can't perceive. At this moment, there are more than seventy-five trillion cells in your body. How might that help explicate the Psalmist's joy: *ma gadlu ma'asecha yah*—how great are your creations, Yah? Or the midrashic idea, in *Bereshit Rabba* 12, that "The King of Kings counts every limb in your body, puts it in its proper place, and builds you to perfection, as it says 'is he not your father, who created you, the one who fashioned and established you?'" How would our sages respond to knowing that we each lose, on average, three million cells every second? How does this influence our understanding of God as *mechayeh meitim*, that which gives life to the dead?

Let theology follow experience. In chapter after chapter, our goal will be simple: through the body, to release the hold of the small, illusory, always-desiring self—the *yetzer hara*—and uncover our true natures beneath and beyond. Without any theology, without any doubt or belief—just to experience what is, instead of the illusions our minds are frantically creating. Ordinary reality is plenty.

The Idea of Practice

Practice, then, is the key: actually doing, actually experiencing. Of course, we all know about practice in the sense of football practice, practicing the piano, or practicing law, but what is meant by a "spiritual practice"?

On the simplest level, spiritual practice is what's called in the Jewish tradition *avodah*, the work humans do for God. That's what practices are: *doing* something for a contemplative, religious, or spiritual purpose. Ritually washing the hands, meditating, observing the Sabbath—all of these are actions with a purpose: perhaps a sense of spirituality, or the maintenance of a divine covenant, or connection with community.

On a deeper level, the idea of practice is quite subtle. First, practice is not dependent on preference; it contains preferences. For example, suppose you observe the Sabbath only when you are in need of a rest. In that case, Shabbat is so dependent upon mood that it is barely a practice at all. But if it is observed in a committed way, then the full range of emotional and intellectual life can be experienced through its prism, and effects can unfold that you could not have predicted in advance. So, too, with meditation. If you're meditating only until you feel like getting up, then, in a sense, you're not meditating at all, because the point of meditation is to see clearly whatever arises—including the strong desire to stop, the doubt that it's working, and, occasionally, redemptive, surprising moments of insight and revelation. A practice is done "no matter what" not for strictness's sake, but so that it can be a prism that casts light upon the mind.

Second, practices are best understood in functional, not mythical, terms. From the perspective of practice, the question is not where an act comes from (God, history, etc.), but what it *does*. Again, this function need not be making us feel good or "spiritual." Quite the contrary, the function of *kashrut* (dietary laws) for a traditional Jew may be to make her feel as if she is transcending preference and obeying divine command. For another person, the function of *kashrut* may be to sanctify eating according to a traditional method. For a third, it may indeed lead to a "spiritual" feeling. For all, though, the practice *does* something. With this practical orientation, certain otherwise immovable doubts (e.g., that God wrote the Torah, or that a personal God exists at all) become less crucial, because the way to judge a practice is not by its origination myth but by its fruits. What does a life of Torah and mitzvot (commandments) *do*? What does saying a blessing when you go to the bathroom *do*? None of this is to banish healthy skepticism or doubt. Rather, the idea of practice is to keep doubting—but keep *doing*, also, in order to obtain the evidence that you seek. *Na'aseh v'nishmah*, say the Israelites at Sinai: we will do, and by doing, we hope to understand. To once more have recourse to the culinary metaphor, reading a cookbook can be informative, but the practice is in preparing, and tasting, the meal. Approach practices with a mind of curiosity, and a little benefit of the doubt, and see what happens.

Finally, *avodah* can be anything, if done with intention. As the *Kitzur Shulchan Aruch*, a nineteenth-century summary of Jewish law, says:

> Our rabbis of blessed memory said, "What is a short verse upon which the entire body of the Torah depends? 'In all ways know God.'" (Proverbs 3:6) This means to know God even in the "ways" you fulfill your bodily needs, and to do them for the sake of God's name. For example: eating, drinking, walking, sitting, lying down, standing up, having sex, conversation—all the needs of your body can be for the service (*avodah*) of your Creator, or something that leads to it.[3]

Cutting and Pasting

In a way, embodied Jewish practice is simply a reunion. The mainstream Jewish tradition is already relentlessly embodied: the overwhelming majority of its commandments are performed with the body, its sacred myths are embodied (think of Abraham's circumcision, Isaac's binding, and Jacob's wrestling), and Jewish theology rarely negates the physical world in favor of some future one. Indeed, even the world to come is often seen as a resurrection of the physical body, beginning with the *luz*, the indestructible bone at the base of the spine.[4] Yet as we all know, contemporary Jewish practice can often seem very *dis*embodied—intellectual text study, prayers on the verge of glossolalia, and ritual practices whose material reality is eclipsed by symbolism, legalism, or myths of origination. However much we may aspire to be Israel, Godwrestlers, most of us are still Jacob (Yaakov), defined by, and often wounded in, the body.

Thus this book is a meeting between careful, mindful attention and a wise, embodied tradition that has lost some of its self-awareness over the years. Perhaps in a quieter time, with fewer distractions and technologies of amusement, it was easier to observe the miraculousness of the mundane. Today, however, we need first to interrupt the insistent momentum of contemporary life, to remember we are embodied beings not defined by our cell phones. It is for this reason that I have used many "technologies" of mindfulness in this book, and have tried to be open about their diverse origins. Many come from the

Jewish tradition. Many others come from Buddhism, Sufism, and other contemplative paths. This is not to dress up our spiritual practice in foreign or fancy clothing. On the contrary, it is to love God so simply and purely (with what the Hasidim call *t'mimu*t, simplicity) that we can learn from Torah, dharma, Kabbalah, even the wisdom of pop songs.

If this cosmopolitan approach is not for you, you obviously have the choice to try some practices and skip other ones. However, importing Buddhist technology of mind into Jewish ritual practice is not so different from past imports of Christian and Muslim prayer modes, eastern European cuisine, or the classical symposium (now known as the seder). Sometimes the techniques of Buddhism, with their rigorous science of mind and clear maps of consciousness, are the right "skillful means" to deepen Jewish practices such as the blessings on going to the bathroom, or the walking movements in prayer. Other times, the joys, myths, and metaphors of the Jewish tradition bring new life to the most ordinary of moments.

Relatedly, there is no pretense here that what is being offered is a fair, objective overview of all that Judaism, or Kabbalah, has to say about the body. Judaism says everything about the body—that it is evil, that it is beautiful; that it is a prison, and a temple; that it is a mirror of the Divine, that it must be repressed; that it is sacred, and that it is profane. The body is in many ways a cultural artifact, and Judaism is a culture, not a creed; its many conflicting ideologies reflect the three thousand years of Jewish civilization. There are very few topics on which there is only one Jewish answer—and many reasons to flee those who claim otherwise.

In my own process of *birur* (sifting), I have chosen to emphasize those aspects of Jewish and world wisdom that treat the body as a sacred site for contemplative practice—and not merely the practice of repression. I have made a choice: sources that simply regard the body as an obstacle to spiritual development, or an inconvenient accident of creation, are not greatly represented here. In part, of course, this results from my attempt to provide those seeking a body-affirming, body-involved spiritual practice with teachings and tools to help them on their journeys. However, it also reflects my sense that the deeper one penetrates into the core of Jewish religious teaching, the farther one moves away from the simple asceticism that shames the body's desires and relishes only the disembodied soul. Naturally, biblical and Talmudic texts are aware of the pitfalls of the body's appetites. But neither regard the body as, itself, a place of sin. On the contrary, as we will see, these texts tend to celebrate the body, see it as a gift (really, a loan) from the Divine, and direct its powerful energies toward enlightened living.

An Invitation

Embodied spiritual practice, simply, works. Letting go of the mind, letting the body lead, and as a result transcending the illusions of the small mind to access a deeper consciousness—we are thus turned toward the holy. This is how to "seize the day" and "suck the marrow out of life": to turn down the static of existence, and hear its subtle, softer music. *Hakarat hatov*, the sages called it: recognizing the good.

Jewish spiritual practice is an integral practice whose purpose is not to favor the body, heart, mind, or soul over the other parts of the self, but to join all four together, to experience life fully, richly, and deeply. Why obey the dietary laws if you could contemplate them instead? Why perform a physical circumcision if a spiritual one were good enough? Because the "lower" does not merely serve the "higher." The body, independent of the heart's stirring and the misgivings of the intellect, is the site of holiness; even if there is no apparent change in the mind, and no softening of the heart, transformation takes place within the field of the body. This is not consolation; it is liberation. By no longer evaluating experience according to "how it makes me feel," the grip of an important illusion is loosened: the illusion that you are your mind, and that reality only matters when the ego is affected. Thus the body is simultaneously the ground of traditional Jewish law, and the deepest of its esoteric truths.

"Man is of flesh, while the angels are of fire; but man is superior,"[5] said Rabbi Nachman of Breslov, the nineteenth-century Hasidic master whose startling, innovative, and often quite challenging teachings will recur throughout this book. Why? Because we have the opportunity not merely to transcend our bodies, but to unite them with spirit.

Of course, spiritual experiences can be very valuable; they offer glimpses of undreamt-of horizons and inspire the soul. But enlarging the field of significance beyond the bounds of preference—that is a mark of liberation. Beyond the circular spirituality of pleasant states of mind, even beyond mindfulness, lies the utter simplicity of the body itself: what one commentator has recently called "bodyfulness."[6] Just the body, breathing and touching and living in the world—with such simplicity are heaven and earth, hidden and revealed, Holy One and sacred Presence, united. Indeed, the marriage is already underway, and the wedding banquet is what you see before you now. Consider this your invitation.

*   *   *   *

1
Eating

You will eat, you will be satisfied, and you will bless YHVH, your God.

Deuteronomy 8:10

In almost every contemplative tradition, eating is regarded as a sacred act. From one perspective, consuming food is simply a necessity of the body—everyone must eat to survive. But eating can also be a deeply spiritual practice, with many layers of meaning. To the ancients, who did not know about ATP, proteins, and sugars, it was mysterious, and inspired gratitude, myth, and ritual. They saw it as a metaphor for the uniting of self and other, for receiving sustenance from a heavenly source, and as a primary social bond. Even today, there is something miraculous about turning lettuce into "me," and many layers of social and ritual meaning endure even in our generally deritualized society. Moreover, thanks to increased sensitivity to diet, nutrition, and practices of wellness, we more than any previous generation can explore how the sustenance of the body sets the conditions for the awakened soul. Naturally, such teachings fill many books. What will be our focus here, however, is something much simpler: the ways in which eating in general can focus the attention, calm the mind, and delight the heart and body. Precisely because it is a mundane, necessary act, it awaits and invites elevation.

It makes sense that a Jewish book about the body starts with eating. Jews have complicated relationships with food. On the one hand, the Jewish tradition celebrates eating and sanctifies its delights. On the other hand, there are all those fast days and all those restrictive dietary laws. Moreover, Jews really like to nosh—and sometimes not in the most mindful way either. Think of a traditional Jewish wedding—the carving board, the pasta bar, the mountains of pareve desserts—or our many meals spent arguing, shouting, even talking on the telephone. Who has time to sit quietly and be thankful?

Now, I don't want to put down eating on the run. I lived for many years in New York City, where doing so has become a kind of art. But it is possible, even in the midst of a rush, for a meal to be more than just the ingestion of proteins and carbs. To do so requires a practical, as well as theoretical, orientation. Put Kabbalah into a distracted and busy mind, and all you will get are more concepts. But in a quieted mind, true *kabbalah*—receiving of the Divine Light within—can take place. As the prophet Isaiah says, "Pay attention to Me, and you will eat that which is good, and enjoy the delights of your soul."[1]

V'achalta: Eating Meditation

The foundational teaching for this chapter is the Torah's injunction "to eat, be satisfied, and bless YHVH your God for the good earth"—in Hebrew:

$$\text{וְאָכַלְתָּ וְשָׂבָעְתָּ וּבֵרַכְתָּ אֶת יְיָ אֱלֹהֶיךָ עַל הָאָרֶץ הַטֹּבָה}$$

$$\text{אֲשֶׁר נָתַן לָךְ}$$

V'achalta, v'savata, u'verachta et Adonai eloche'cha al ha'aretz hatova asher natan lach.

Notice first how these words honor the act of eating. Eating is not a necessary evil, something we do because we have to sustain our bodies; it is holy. The Talmudic sages teach that the dinner table is like the altar in the Temple, and the meal we eat like the offerings that brought us close to God. (The Hebrew word for such offerings, *korbanot*, comes from the same root as *l'karev*, to be brought close. Rather than "sacrifices," a better translation might be "joiners" or even "unifiers.")

Second, notice the order of the biblical verse, as if only after one has eaten, and been satisfied, can one really make a blessing. Experience matters. And notice that the verse contains all four worlds within it: the body (eating), heart (satisfied), mind (the reason for the blessing), and soul (the blessing itself). But the body comes first.

Eating is simple, but eating in a way that really fulfills the commandment to "eat, be satisfied, and bless" takes a certain amount of subtraction—slowing down, quieting down, cutting down the noise of an impossibly rushed life. Technology has met nearly all of the material desires of a century ago, but it has left intact the spiral of desire itself, with a frenetic consumer culture all too eager to keep us spinning. We now have vastly improved means for unimproved ends. If we are not happy, we have more choices than ever of something to do, or get, or consume. Yet every philosophical and religious tradition, from epicurianism to Judaism to Taoism, stresses the opposite: slowing down desire itself enough to enjoy simple pleasures. Instead of the *yetzer*, desire, causing more and more suffering, all these traditions say that a person who is truly rich is happy with what is. Simple, even banal, when put into words, but not so easy to do in practice.

This is important not only for happiness, but also for truth. The beat prophet William S. Burroughs, not usually regarded as a spiritual teacher, said that he wanted to capture the "frozen moment when everyone sees what is on the end of every fork."[2] In other words, to see truth clearly, in all its beauty or terror—not a delusion, but rather its erasure; not a balm, but the unvarnished reality of experience. But how do we do this, literally or figuratively, when we're busy distracting ourselves?

Perhaps in a slower time it was easy to fulfill the mitzvah of *v'achalta, v'savata, u'verachta*. The pace of life allowed for more enjoyment—and besides, food was more scarce, and thus more precious. Today, however, to eat in this way requires what many contemporary teachers call "mindfulness," but what we might simply understand as seeing clearly whatever is actually happening, rather than being distracted by racing thoughts or the chattering of the television. The mechanics of this practice come from the Buddhist world, not the Jewish one, although there are Jewish injunctions to meditate while eating—for example, the *Darchei Tzedek*'s statement that "The main service of God is through eating ... and the *tzaddikim* [righteous ones] meditate as they eat, in love and fear of God, as with prayer."[3] Only by slowing down, however, can we really understand what the Jewish texts are saying. Experience first, and then the concepts can come alive. As the teacher and writer Eckhart Tolle said (on *Oprah*, no less), it's just about asking "What is happening right now—and can I be with it?"

To experience "what is happening right now" in your body, you can try this simple eating meditation for a whole meal, or five minutes—or even just a single bite. I find that a bit of fruit or vegetable is good, though I often teach this practice with a potato chip. Really, almost anything works. Here's how to do it:

1. First, spend a little time considering the food before you put it in your mouth. Use the kabbalistic map of the "four worlds" (see Appendix), which roughly correspond to body, heart, mind, and spirit, to help you. On the level of the body, you might gaze at the food with focused attention, or even, if appropriate, feel the food with your fingers. What does it feel like, or look like? Allow yourself the pleasure of being entranced by this object—most food is quite beautiful in its detail—as if you're giving yourself a miniature spiritual retreat, right now, at your lunch table. You might smell the food too, and notice what effects doing so has on your body.

2. "Check in" next with the heart. What desires are you experiencing? Are you hungry? Nauseated? Thankful? Do you think this practice might not be for you? Whatever the "feeling-tone" of this experience is, just note it attentively, without judgment; stay with it for a couple of breaths, and see if it shifts, or intensifies, or ebbs.

3. On the plane of the mind, consider for a moment all of the people involved in bringing this food to you. Farmers, truck drivers, factory workers, storekeepers—there are hundreds, if not thousands, of people whose labor created the simple occasion of this food arriving in this moment. Take a moment to consider them; imagine what they look like, how hard they are working to support themselves

and their families, the economic system that creates the conditions for their labor.

4. And, on the level of the soul, consider all the conditions necessary to have created this food: the four elements of fire, water, earth, and air; the genetic information in the plants or animals, part of the divine wisdom (*hochmah*); ecosystems and molecular biology beyond our understanding. Consider, in Vietnamese Buddhist monk Thich Nhat Hanh's words, all of the aspects of the universe that "inter-are" with this food. You are holding a small storehouse of the sun's energy, and water from a cloud. Allow the poetry of this simple piece of food to be felt, in your body. It's easy to be cynical or sarcastic. It's harder, and more rewarding, to cultivate a moment of sincerity. As the Talmud says, "The miracle of food that God provides is as spectacular as the splitting of the Red Sea."[4]

5. Then—finally!—place the food in your mouth. Before chewing and swallowing, experience the tactile sensations of the food on your tongue, the tastes, the feeling of your mouth watering. What happens to your body when you put the food in? Calibrate your sensitivity as finely and exquisitely as possible. See if the food tastes different in different parts of the mouth. Really give yourself a juicy, rich experience of this bit of food. You might keep your eyes closed for the duration of this practice, simply to focus your attention on what's going on in your mouth rather than on other things.

6. Next, bite into the food and chew, trying to omit any automatic movements. When chewing, know you are chewing. You probably know the joke about walking and chewing gum at the same time—this is the opposite. Do only one thing at a time, allowing the mind to slow down, focus, experience, and fulfill the act of *v'achalta*, eating.

7. Swallow after the food has been thoroughly chewed (you probably want to chew around twenty to thirty times). See if the flavor changes—some food really only comes alive after ten or more chews; some disappears. Finally, when you do swallow, see how far down your esophagus you can still feel the food. Just relax in the physical sensations of eating.

8. As your tongue cleans your mouth after this mindful bite of food, try to maintain the attentiveness you've cultivated; don't let it be automatic. We have a finite number of hours on this planet—why not be as awake as possible for each of them?

This is a very simple practice—there's not much Kabbalah, or many moving parts; just waking up to the body, fulfilling *v'achalta* with the same intensity our ancestors might have had. Now, if there hasn't yet been enough "God" for you in *God in Your Body*, remember that what we are doing here is setting the conditions necessary for an experience of God to be an experience, rather than just an idea—the theology will come soon enough.

I invite you to make eating meditation a regular part of your day, for forty days. See what five minutes a day, or one bite a meal, does for you, even if only for the duration of those five minutes. In my years of teaching this practice, people have reported deep relaxation, delight, insights into their personalities and needs, and immense gratitude to God—all from eating. One time, on a meditation retreat, I did this practice with a single string bean and had a sensory experience so intense and so beautiful that I was moved to tears. It was just an ordinary string bean—but my mind (and heart) was so exquisitely sensitive to the sensations of eating that it was a delightful experience.

The postmodernist and cultural critic Michel Foucault once said, "What we must work on, it seems to me, is not so much to liberate our desires but to make ourselves infinitely more susceptible to pleasure."[5] Meditation is just that: the process of becoming more susceptible. Then you can proceed to bless God.

V'savata: Experiencing Satisfaction

Rarely are we given so simple an opportunity to experience pleasure as after eating. Usually, meditation is not about having a pleasurable, or unpleasurable, experience; it is about being more present with whatever is happening, in all its fine detail. But in this case, because we are naturally wired to experience pleasure from eating, the sensations are almost always positive and can counter some of the negative, even tragic, ways in which eating disorders, health problems, or negative body images interfere with this simple joy. The natural desires of the body are gifts from God. As the Hasidic master Rabbi Zusya of Hanipol said, "The will of the Creator, blessed be He, then, is to 'enliven every thing' by means of eating. So I have to eat in holiness and purity, for I am doing His will by eating.... It is God who has brought you to this hunger and thirst. For the hunger is from God."[6]

There are three levels to the practice of experiencing satisfaction, which culminates in a traditional Hasidic contemplation.

The first level is simple. After you have finished eating, arrange your body in a comfortable position so you can sit still for at least a minute. Try to ensure that you're not hunched over, squashing your stomach as it tries to digest. You might even take an exaggerated pose of someone who's just finished a four-star dinner—have fun with it. Simply close your eyes, to enable concentration, and bring your attention to your stomach. In the words of one Thai Buddhist meditation teacher, "let your attention rub your belly." Don't feel you have to label the sensation or judge it—just watch it, as if it were a television program. As thoughts arise, let them drop away; return to the physical sensations in the belly, and to whatever "feeling-tone" accompanies them. Do this for at least a minute, longer if you like.

Next, see if anything arises for you emotionally. I find, when I do this practice, that a faint smile appears on my face; remember, we're hardwired to enjoy this. I don't have to scold myself to feel grateful: a beautiful, soft gratitude often arises naturally, as well as a natural compassion for those unable to get enough to eat. Just seeing that compassion arises on its own—that you don't have to "ought" yourself into it—can be a profound insight. Once, on retreat, I was aware of someone readjusting her posture during a meditation session—kind of a no-no. Immediately, without any prompting, I felt compassion for this woman. I hoped she wasn't in too much pain, and wasn't too distracted. I didn't judge or resent (like I do a lot of the time). And I realized that compassion was my natural state. Just turn down the distractions and *ahavat hashem* (love of God) and *ahavat re'acha ḳamocha* (love of the neighbor as yourself) naturally appear. It was a momentary but life-changing experience.

Finally, from compassion, principles flow. The traditional Hasidic eating meditation is to contemplate how the nourishment from the food supports different parts of the body, each of which is devoted to divine service. Try this. You might feel, physically, strength arising in the arms or legs, and imagine giving money to support the poor or going to visit the sick. Or you might notice a change in your heartbeat and connect that, in your mind, to opening the heart, or cultivating love, or improving your ethical behavior. As with the first two levels, spend enough time with this contemplation to inhabit it, mentally, perhaps drawing strength from the knowledge that two hundred years of Hasidic wisdom are behind it.

The Talmud says that "as long as the Temple was in existence, the altar was the means of atonement for Israel, but now it is every man's table that atones for him."[7] I doubt the Talmud had meditation in mind, but the sense of *ḳapparah*—translated as "atonement" but really meaning cleansing, or catharsis—can certainly arise as a consequence of it. This is the opposite of the narcissism sometimes found in "spiritual" circles; it's being honest with the truths of our experience, with the body at the center, and proceeding from those truths to work upon the self.

Eating is an everyday miracle. You don't need a special feeling in order to be spiritual—just more attention paid to the ordinary ones. And your own experiences can be a stronger basis for your religious or contemplative practice than any dogma or expectation. Sometimes, a sentence like "And you'll eat, and be satisfied, and bless the Lord your God" invites alienation right after the word "bless." That's because a concept is being used with which you may not agree, or of which you may have no experience, or with which you've been beaten over the head for decades. I invite you, then, to end the sentence with "bless." The important thing is to experience eating, satisfaction, and the blessing. Later, we can fill in the theological details. But start with the facts, as in this contemplation by the medieval Jewish sage Bahya ibn Pakuda, from his masterpiece *The Duties of the Heart*:

> Whoever contemplates the natural processes of the body—how when food enters it, it is distributed to every part of the body—will see such signs of wisdom that he will be inspired to thank the Creator and praise Him, as David said, "All my bones shall say: God, who is like You!" (Psalm 35:10) He will see how food passes into the stomach through a straight tube, called the esophagus, without any bend or twist; how afterwards, the stomach digests the food more thoroughly than chewing had; how then the food is carried into the liver through thin connecting veins that act as a strainer, preventing anything coarse from passing through to the liver; how the liver converts the food it receives into blood, which it distributes all over the body through tubes that look like water pipes and were formed specifically for this purpose.... Meditate, my brother, on the Creator's wisdom in structuring your body.[8]

The body, in its material miraculousness, is a gateway to the profound religious sentiments expressed by saints and poets. And the gate opens every day—in fact, every time we open our mouths.

U'verachta: Count Your Blessings

In the previous sections, we explored two different mindfulness techniques for waking up to the miraculous details of ordinary life. These practices are found in many world traditions, but they are not the primary Jewish ways to wake up. *Brachot*—usually translated as "blessings"—are.

Understanding *brachot* as a practice begins with the context of the *yetzer hara*, the "evil inclination," which is simply that aspect of our personalities that sees the self as separate, and the locus of all value, thus leading to jealousy, craving, attachment, fear, hatred, cruelty, and all the other ways the ego tries to protect itself. "Why are you unhappy?"

asked the twentieth-century teacher Wei Wu Wei. "Because 99% of everything that you think, and everything that you do, is for the self— and there isn't one."[9] The *bracha* is a way to shake off the delusion and selfishness of the *yetzer hara*. *Bracha*, like many Jewish spiritual terms, is a body word; it is related to *birkaim*, the word for knees. A *bracha* is figuratively getting down on your knees, in gratitude and supplication: I recognize that-to-which-I-am-kneeling as more important than "me." From a nondual perspective, kneeling is a way of saying, "Within myself, there is the part that is separate, and has its selfish desires, and there is the part that wants only the Good. Before I serve the self's needs, I am putting the separate, selfish part on a lower level than the Godly part." This is what a *bracha* does. It inserts a short pause ("You should not do anything else while you are saying a blessing," states the *Shulchan Aruch*) and interrupts desire, just for a moment.

Traditionally, *brachot* are recited before and after eating any substantial amount of food. The exact words depend on the type of food being eaten, but they all have the same beginning: *Baruch ata adonai, eloheinu melech ha'olam*. Let's take a moment to provide depth to each of those words, since they will appear in several of the chapters to come:

Baruch has the same root as the word *bracha*: to kneel, and thus to acknowledge. Consider using *baruch* as a pause, a moment to stop and take a breath. Let the mind clear a little, and remember that you are deliberately interrupting your train of thought to make room for a more attentive, restful consciousness.

Ata means "you." Jewish Godtalk rarely speaks of God as "It," in the third person; it prefers "You." As in the philosophy of Martin Buber, one can't say "You" to an abstraction; You must be present now. Look straight ahead, let the mind rest, and say "You" to what is in front of you now. Imagine it looking back at you with the same knowing gaze of another person. Theologically, this is It, God. Psychologically, it is You.

Adonai is a personalized rendition of YHVH, the divine name that is not pronounced. It literally means "my lord." If that relationship does not speak to you, you might substitute the letters *yood-hey-vav-hey*, or the abbreviation "Yah." Personally, I like the intimacy of *adonai*, with its first-person ending. This is something I'm saying; it's my Lord, as I understand It.

Eloheinu joins the personal to the communal; it means "our god." It is that which is being placed at the center, in priority over our particular needs of the moment, whether higher consciousness or primordial awareness or ancestral deity or tribal god. This is how we imagine the Infinite.

Melech ha'olam literally means "king of the universe," one way our ancestors thought of God. Today, as most of us have few (and often negative) associations with the word "king," I conceive of the king as the one who sets the rules; the ordering principle; the sovereign of all that is. When I say these words, I like to think of the laws of physics, the properties of nature that cause leaves to open and flowers to bloom, the forces of gravity and electromagnetism. It helps me remember that even when things are going in ways we don't like at all, they are unfolding just as they must, according to the laws of causality, physics, and so on. *Melech ha'olam* is an anthropomorphization of these principles.

If you are reciting a *bracha* as a spiritual practice, say each word slowly, taking a few seconds to allow for contemplation of these associations. Probably the results will be different each time. Sometimes they may be more heart-centered, sometimes more about the mind. Just focus the attention, not by straining or stretching, but by relaxing the parts of the mind that want to run off in a hundred directions at once. Let them go, and come to the words. The specific food blessings are:

בָּרוּךְ אַתָּה יְיָ אֱלֹהֵינוּ מֶלֶךְ הָעוֹלָם הַמוֹצִיא לֶחֶם מִן הָאָרֶץ

Baruch ata adonai, eloheinu melech ha'olam hamotzi lechem min ha'aretz.
... who brings forth bread from the earth.

בָּרוּךְ אַתָּה יְיָ אֱלֹהֵינוּ מֶלֶךְ הָעוֹלָם בּוֹרֵא פְּרִי הָעֵץ

Baruch ata adonai, eloheinu melech ha'olam borei pri ha'etz.
... who creates "tree-fruits" (most fruit).

בָּרוּךְ אַתָּה יְיָ אֱלֹהֵינוּ מֶלֶךְ הָעוֹלָם בּוֹרֵא פְּרִי הָאֲדָמָה

Baruch ata adonai, eloheinu melech ha'olam borei pri ha'adama.
... who creates "ground-fruits" (most vegetables).

בָּרוּךְ אַתָּה יְיָ אֱלֹהֵינוּ מֶלֶךְ הָעוֹלָם בּוֹרֵא פְּרִי הַגָּפֶן

Baruch ata adonai, eloheinu melech ha'olam borei pri hagafen.
... who creates "vine-fruits" (grapes, wine, etc.).

בָּרוּךְ אַתָּה יְיָ אֱלֹהֵינוּ מֶלֶךְ הָעוֹלָם בּוֹרֵא מִינֵי מְזוֹנוֹת

Baruch ata adonai, eloheinu melech ha'olam borei minei mezonot.
... who creates the varieties of grain.

בָּרוּךְ אַתָּה יְיָ אֱלֹהֵינוּ מֶלֶךְ הָעוֹלָם שֶׁהַכֹּל נִהְיֶה בִּדְבָרוֹ

Baruch ata adonai, eloheinu melech ha'olam shehaḳol nehiyeh bidvaro.
... that all exists in God's word (everything else).

For these last phrases, you might direct your attention at the specific food in front of you. Suppose it's an apple; you might envision the apple tree, growing from a seed, sprouting apples, just as its genetic information instructs. Or suppose it's a complicated processed or artificial food for which the last *bracha* is appropriate; know that God is even in the Cheetos, and that all the bizarre food technology we've created over the last few decades is still just manipulating God's *davar*, the physical and biological "word" that so reliably shapes the universe.

Even if it's just a pause in your day, a *bracha* can allow gratitude or joy to grow. *Brachot* are tiny islands of time, and since they are centered on the body, they are linked not to some abstract obligation, but to something actually happening. I also like to think of *brachot* as little acts of love. Being in love is beautiful, not only because we are loved by another, but also because we are able to experience love ourselves. It feels deeply nourishing to feel grateful, wondrous, or loving, and eating is an opportunity to feel all those things, albeit in miniature. The *brachot* ordained by our ancestors recognize this power. Try them.

Now let's turn to the *brachot* that are said after eating, which complement those said before. The Jewish legal tradition prescribes a series of *brachot*, some of them quite lengthy, to be made after eating. These *brachot* are detailed and beautiful in their language of thanksgiving, and I encourage you to study them. However, for many people today, reciting the full, prescribed *birkat hamazon* (grace after meals) is difficult; it has many Hebrew words, and it contextualizes our nourishment in the history of the Jewish people, and its yearnings, taking us far astray from the meal itself. Not that there's anything wrong with that—the entire blessing is a series of poetic contemplations of divine providence, replete with literary forms and poetic devices. No matter how many times I say *birkat hamazon*, there is almost always a phrase that jumps out of the liturgy and causes me to consider life anew. For our purposes, though, I would like to look briefly at two shorter versions of *birkat hamazon* that are quicker and more accessible to those with less knowledge of Hebrew.

First, in some communities, the following Talmudic "emergency blessing," originally intended for extenuating circumstances when you really have to rush, has been adopted for everyday use:[10]

בְּרִיךְ רַחֲמָנָא מַלְכָּא דְּעָלְמָא מָרֵיהּ דְּהַאי פִּיתָּא

Brich rachamana malka d'alma, marei d'hai pita.
Blessed is the Merciful One, ruler of the universe, provider of this food.

Try this simple phrase, perhaps sung, or repeated, mantra style, with your mind focusing on the words of the phrase and whatever emotions arise during its recital. Or you might slowly contemplate each word, as in the *brachot* before the meal, focusing on how you have experienced blessing, or mercy, or order in the universe, or how you've known the experience of eating. You might even come up with your own *kavvanah*—intention—for use with the phrase.

A second one-line grace after meals is the verse from Psalm 145:

פּוֹתֵחַ אֶת יָדֶךָ וּמַשְׂבִּיעַ לְכָל חַי רָצוֹן

Poteach et yadecha u'masbia' l'chol chai ratzon.
You open your hand, and satisfy all life according to your will.

Rabbinic tradition advises intensified concentration on these words of the psalm, so you might concentrate on each phrase in this way:

You open your hand—Use this anthropomorphic, embodied language to talk about the Divine: as you recite the line, think about a hand opening, from a tight, closed fist, to an open hand. You might even perform the motion with your own hand, and let yourself feel this opening: the coming in and out, the blood flowing. Expand the openness to what you see around you—breathing, opening—then to what you don't see, what's in the next room, or all the photons, radio waves, and microwaves surrounding you in the air. All this is what is meant by God's hand opening. Beyond your small plot of land on one continent of a small planet in a single solar system, the universe is constantly breathing, constantly opening and closing. Imagine if you could witness a billion flowers blooming, as they are right now. What reverence, compassion, wonder would they inspire?

And satisfy—*masbia'* has the same root as *savata*. Explore the sensations of just having eaten, as in the previous section, and perhaps bring your attention to what's right, or wrong, at the moment, following Eckhart Tolle's advice to "bring your full attention to the Now, and tell me what your problem is." You'll probably notice a remarkable secret: in the "now" there is rarely anything objectively wrong at all. Even if there is physical or emotional pain present, the actual sensations are much less painful than the story of the pain, or the wish that it weren't there. What is unsatisfactory, really, about what is happening right now?

All life—*l'chol chai* invites us to consider the provision of *masbia'* extends to all of life. It's impossible to visualize all of life, but use your imagination to approach it. Imagine a single field, or forest, or other natural place. Notice how myriad organisms are fed and nourished, how the ecosystem is in dynamic balance, how flowers are opening and trees are budding and the vital life energy of *eros* flows through all of them, drips from them. Take your time. Expand the field of vision, bringing in more and more creatures. Imagine, in the abstract, a world filled with humans, animals, plants, and other beings. Try to feel, in your body, the coursing energy of *masbia'*, in your blood, in your breathing, in your digestion, and try to imagine that sustenance expanding through the world.

Your will—*ratzon*: consider what it means to say that all the universe is really one field of matter and energy, one will, one Being. Manifesting as separate entities, yes, but entities that will eventually die and decay, and beings whose existence is dependent on others. We can try to separate ourselves from this net of interrelation—this is how the *yetzer hara*, the will to separation, leads us. But there's really only the one *ratzon*, the play of life unfolding and decaying and sprouting up again. All of what you traversed in your visualization is this one *ratzon* expressing itself, dancing with itself, putting on costumes. This is the first principle of Judaism: *Shema yisrael, adonai eloheinu, adonai echad*—Listen, you Godwrestler, YHVH, which we set as our god, YHVH is One. Teachings from the Kabbalah explain that the oneness of the *Shema* is not a simple oneness, like there is only one Empire State Building or one moon around the earth. Rather, the Kabbalah, especially as interpreted by Hasidism, insists that the One is actually all there is. All is One, and all is God. The name YHVH seems to capture some of this, as it contains within it the words Was, Is, and Will Be. YHVH is "What Is." And What Is is One.

These are easy words to say but hard ones to believe, because they contradict our obvious sense experience. But this is what the Baal Shem Tov, the founder of Hasidism, meant when he said that "when you eat, your thought should be that the taste and the sweetness of the food you are eating are coming from God's enlivening power and from the supernal sweetness which is the life of the food."[11] As you end with *ratzon*, see how it works for you. Perhaps you might sense this unity in a purely material way, as after all you've just consumed a lot of formerly separate entities and digested them into proteins and other materials. Perhaps it might be an emotional sensibility. Perhaps intellectually you might contemplate how your body, like the food you've eaten, is a temporary agglomeration of the same elements that make up everything else in the universe, and you are constantly rebuilding it, as you eat, from other things. Or even spiritually, you might think of all that makes you *you*—personality, career, family, identity, tribe—and notice that none of these things appeared out of nowhere; relationships depend on others, identities on groups and roles, and so on. If we look for the part of ourselves that is "me, and not connected to anything else," we won't find it. There's really only emptiness—and yet, someone is thinking these thoughts, right? So who is it? Who is doing all this knowing?

Try some of this *hitbonnenut*—contemplation practice—after you finish the word *ratzon*. Let yourself experience the dance from spirit to matter to spirit again, as in these lines from Rumi:

> A wheat grain breaks open in the ground,
>   then grows, then gets harvested, then is crushed in the mill
>   for flour, then baked, then crushed again between teeth
>   to become mind, spirit, and understanding.
>   Lost in Love, like the songs the planters sing
>   after they sow the seed.[12]

Transparent *Kashrut*

The most well-known Jewish practice relating to food is *kashrut*, the set of dietary laws. Along with the Sabbath and prayer, *kashrut* is perhaps the most demanding of Jewish ritual observances; it is a discipline that requires daily attention and can seem quite overbearing at times. However, *kashrut* is actually quite subtle and questions conventional assumptions about what spirituality is, and how the body acts within it.

Practically speaking, the vast majority of "keeping kosher" derives from three basic rules. First, only some animals may be eaten. Second, even those animals must be killed in a certain way. Third, even if the animals are killed the right way, their flesh cannot be mixed with milk. That's about 90 percent of it—but as anyone who keeps kosher knows, things quickly get complicated. For example, we would all agree that if a strip of bacon were fried in a pan, and an egg were fried right in the leftover bacon grease, then the egg would not be kosher, even though there's nothing intrinsically nonkosher about the egg. Well, what if a single drop of nonkosher gravy is dropped into a huge vat of kosher chicken soup? Generations of rabbis have busied themselves with such questions, and have created a huge, ornate body of rules and regulations as a result.

Why care about such rules? Today, Jews "keep kosher" for a variety of reasons. At one extreme is pure obedience: God wrote the Torah and commanded it. At the other end of the spectrum is observance purely for cultural or familial reasons: someone may have been raised in a kosher home and it just "feels right" to keep kosher, even though the specific rules may seem arcane. In between these poles are a thousand different rationales—everything from spirituality to animal rights to health. Some of these reasons are quite beautiful—when I eat kosher meat, for example, I feel as though there has been respect accorded to the autonomy of the animal, not unlike the Native American practice of apologizing to the animal before killing it. Of course, apologizing doesn't do the animal much good—but for us, it is a significant recognition of its ethical status.

However, many of the rationales for *kashrut* are clearly outdated today, in our time of strict food standards and humane methods of slaughter. Others seem problematic—for example, *kashrut*'s emphasis on keeping Jews distinct from other nations. And sometimes *kashrut* just seems to have no benefit whatsoever. Chicken parmesan is healthful and sounds delicious. I am sure I could eat it mindfully and healthily. *Kal v'chomer*—how much more so—foods that are themselves kosher but that I do not eat because of their having come in contact with nonkosher utensils.

Really, though, all the rationales, the good and the bad, are beside the point. The revolutionary principle of Jewish religion is that the body, itself, matters. Not just because it can calm the mind or make us feel good. And not just because of health. But really, for its own sake, even if it gives no emotional, intellectual, or spiritual benefit whatsoever. Actions, not intentions and not "spiritual" consequences, are themselves of religious value. Thus, rather than search for a "spiritual meaning" to the rules of *kashrut*, I prefer to see the practice as purely a matter of materiality. And rather than search for an intellectual justification for the particular laws (British anthropologist Mary Douglas's analysis in *Purity and Danger* seems to me the most lucid, though it has little application to a contemporary consciousness), I have learned to regard them as arbitrary—and yet critically important precisely because they *are* arbitrary, non-"spiritual," and devoid of emotional meaning. Why? Because it is a body practice, and performing it recognizes the value of the body, of the material world, on its own.

Often, we use the words "soul" and "spirit" to denote certain feelings—sensations we get at certain times, or certain places. In the kabbalistic model, though, the soul is not a feeling, not a faculty in addition to the body, mind, and heart; it is the point of connection between those aspects of the self and the reality of the One. Feelings are part of the picture, but the true "goal" of spiritual practice is to embrace all of the parts, on their own terms.

In this context, both *kashrut* specifically and Jewish practices generally take on a new cast. If we only perform those rituals that give us a certain feeling, then we are guilty of a form of idolatry: mistaking a certain feeling for God. But God transcends our feelings. God is in the fire, in the wind, in the still, small voices that nurture us at night—and in the physical body as well. Halacha, the Jewish "path," exists transsubjectively—that is, beyond the sensations it brings about. With *kashrut*, as with circumcision, technical Sabbath observance, and hundreds of other Jewish rituals, the religious discipline is on the plane of materiality.

Most of us, I think, are conditioned to believe that the body is merely a tool to affect some nonembodied spirit. There is a historical reason for this belief: it was one of the main sites of disagreement between Talmudic Jews and the early Christian Jews, led by Paul. Paul saw the body as flawed, fallen, and mortal; the soul, in contrast, was pure, capable of salvation, and immortal. How could circumcision of the flesh have any meaning, when circumcision of the heart was so much more important? Paul, Christianity, and Platonic dualism have so won the day that I think most of us take for granted that religion is a matter of heart and soul, and that religious practices exist only to bring about spiritual changes.

But the Talmudic sages disagreed. They argued in their "version" of the New Testament, the Mishna (literally, "Second"), that the significant sphere of religious life was the body, not the disembodied soul. This is why "pointless" embodied commandments such as *kashrut* are discussed in such intimate, endless detail: because the body is the point.

If we try to make each detail of legalistic Judaism conform to some higher "spiritual" purpose, most of us will get very frustrated. But if we approach the minutiae of *kashrut* as configuring the physical universe in a holy way—not because of how it makes us feel, but because of how it physically is, in itself—then we are liberated from the yoke of spirituality and we find ourselves in a place of honoring the physical bodies we inhabit. Your body is of importance; thus even the details of frying an egg are important as well, whether the ego feels it or not.

Rather than hunt for intrinsic meanings, or extrinsic justifications, we can see *kashrut* simply as a way to sanctify the ordinary. What I have experienced, when I am able to practice this way, is a different sort of love from the one I read about in books. It is an egoless love that inheres in the actual food I put in my mouth, in the actual stomach that digests it, and in the actual nutrients absorbed by my bloodstream. And it is an embrace that holds me even when I do not feel it, even when I do not want to be held. It is as inescapable as an Infinite Being should be: always with me, always touching every atom of my being, just waiting for me to wake up.

*   *   *   *

2
Prayer

A person should sway when praying for it is said (Psalm 35:10)
"All my bones shall say: O Lord, who is like You!" Doing this
is the practice of the pious.

Rabbi Yitzhak Abuhav[1]

After *kashrut*, prayer is perhaps the most pervasive Jewish ritual practice. Traditional Jews pray at least three times a day, and the contours of prayer shape the traditional Jewish life. Of course, in many circles prayer may not seem very embodied. We rise and we are seated, and that's about it. But think of a wild Hasidic *shteibel* (small synagogue), or a Sufi *zikr* circle, with mystics chanting and swaying, or a Southern church, with hand-clapping, dancing, rocking back and forth. Think of the energy, the vitality. The Talmud tells of a rabbi so devout in his prayer that he would start on one end of the room and end up on the other. And the Hasidim liken the movements of prayer to the motions of sexual intercourse. Prayer, says Bahya ibn Pakuda, is the service of the heart (*avodah sh'balev*), and the body heats the heart up.

In fact, prayer is the Jewish body practice that is hidden in plain view. Its component elements are named after body parts, its liturgy uses the body as a focus, and, when done in an ecstatic way, its manifestation is a highly energetic, embodied experience. It's not yoga in the narrow sense of a systematic series of precise movements. But ecstatic prayer is yoga in the wider sense: an embodied spiritual practice.

21

Embodied Jewish Prayer

The three most important prayers of the traditional morning and evening liturgy are the *Barchu*, the call to prayer; the *Shema*, the remembrance of divine unity; and the *Amidah*, the silent prayer. These are familiar words to those who know Jewish prayer—but have you ever noticed what they mean? *Barchu* comes from the same root as *birkayim*, knees. It is the kneeling prayer. *Shema* is the listening prayer. And *Amidah* is the standing prayer. In other words, three of the most important Jewish prayers are named after actions of the body.

An interesting fact, but what does it mean? First, it says something about how the body affects the mind. On a purely intellectual level, there should be no reason why a text should be any different when read sitting, standing, or kneeling. The text is the text. Yet there is a difference, which you can easily experience yourself. Choose a verse from the traditional liturgy, the Bible, or anywhere you like. Having first cleared your mind of distraction, perhaps with a meditation practice, try *davening* (the Yiddish term for praying) the verse in different body postures. For example, suppose you *daven* Moses's prayer for healing: *Ana el na, refa' na la*, which means, simply, "Please, God, heal her" (in this case, "her" could refer to a person, a place, or even your own soul). What happens when you sit absolutely still and slowly say the words aloud, listening in rapt concentration, allowing any intruding thoughts simply to drop away? How does it differ when you try kneeling—halachically speaking, it is permissible to kneel and perform full prostrations during prayer (see Rabbi Abraham Maimonides's *tshuvah* on the subject), and is specifically recommended by sages including Rabbi Nachman of Breslov, Rabbi Menachem Mendel of Kotsk, and, perhaps unexpectedly, the latter-day Torah scholar Rabbi Moshe Teitelbaum, who is reported to have kneeled regularly for the *Shema*. What happens to your heart when you do so? Try chanting the line over and over as you sway, dance, and move around, maybe even to music. What happens then?

Notice how different the same words feel, depending on how the body is positioned. Become a connoisseur of the minute fluctuations of your body. *Davening* is not reciting, not reading, and not worshiping.

It involves the yearnings of the heart, the words of the text, the realization of spirit, and the movements of the body. Now let's apply these ideas to the *Barchu*, *Shema*, and *Amidah*.

BARCHU

What are we doing when we kneel? As we saw in the last chapter, kneeling is an acknowledgment of subservience, either to another being or to an aspect of oneself. Because the Jewish tradition denies that some people should be subservient to others, Jews rarely kneel or even bow before figures of authority.[2] But the Barchu, which initiates the formal prayer service in the morning and the evening, enacts this drama in our bodies. Although today it is usually accompanied by only a perfunctory bow, imagine if, like the Muslims, we began our *davening* by getting on our knees and bowing our heads to the ground. This is far more intimate than recognizing authority. When I am in Child's Pose in yoga, or bowing to the ground on Yom Kippur, I often feel a curious blend of intimacy and power, immanence and transcendence, humility and presence. Like the phrase *da' lifnei mi ata omed* (know before whom you stand), which appears in many synagogues, I ask: What do I know? Who am I? What have I accomplished?

Soon, I'll get up, and remember my value and dignity and mission in life. But when I'm kneeling down, humility reigns. It's not rational; it's embodied, emotional, and primal, to pray in this way, to say, "God, there are so many times in my life when I want to kneel to You. I want to accept that You are there, that You are watching, that You are hearing my petition and my confession. I wish that I could have kneeling-consciousness before You always, and not get so lost. Allow me this time and space of the *Barchu* to pause my life's rush, to acknowledge and to remember."

There is nothing so whole as a broken heart, declare the Hasidim, and the *Barchu* can open it up. Even if you just go through the motions, merely putting the body in the position of kneeling can shift a part of the soul that may have seemed immovable—or invisible. Of course, you can't just read about it. You have to do the practice: quiet the mind, kneel with the body, and let your heart go where it goes. Try it in a private place, or for a half a minute in a synagogue, but try it.

As meditation teacher Lama Surya Das once told me, in his thick Brooklyn Jewish accent, "without practice—you got nuttin'."

SHEMA

If the *Barchu*'s kneeling-consciousness primarily affects the heart, then the *Shema*'s listening-consciousness works mostly on the mind. The connotation of the word *shema* is to pay attention. But listening is not just a metaphor. As I am writing this right now, I hear the traffic on Bezalel Street in Jerusalem, the rustling of the wind in palm fronds, my fingers clattering away on the keyboard. In theory, I am entirely focused on writing, but there's obviously a gap between theory and practice. What are we hearing but not listening to? What noise is interfering? How can we quiet down and pay attention?

The *Shema* is meant to be recited either seated or standing absolutely still, and spoken or chanted aloud. Many people today have the custom of saying each word of the *Shema* with a full breath, elongating the vowel sounds until the breath expires. This allows the mind to focus on each word, and provides the heightened physical sensation of hearing and reciting in unison. It helps if you've memorized the six words of the *Shema*'s opening line so you can close your eyes and really focus on the sound. *Shema, Yisrael*—formally translated as "Hear O Israel" but I prefer "Listen, Godwrestler"—seems to be directed inward: Okay, now pay attention. *Adonai Eloheinu*—YHVH, that which we set up as our god. *Adonai echad*—YHVH, all that is, is One. Some days, your mind may be ready to receive this radical teaching. Other days, it's wise to let the body lead. Close your eyes, join your voice with the voices of others, and physically feel each word. As with the *Barchu*, the physical act of listening counts. Worries, doubts, anger, tiredness may all be present, but just do the practice along with them, reciting each word for a full breath, hearing and feeling the vibrations of your voice. Who knows—a shift may occur.

AMIDAH

The third main prayer of the morning and evening service is the *Amidah*, or Standing Prayer—sometimes called *HaTefilah* (The Prayer) or the *Shmoneh Esrei* (The Eighteen), referring to the eighteen blessings within it, which in Talmud *Berachot* 28b are said to correspond to the body's eighteen vertebrae. It's the core of the liturgy ordained by the Rabbis, and it is the part of the service devoted to unity with the soul and with its Source.

There are several body movements associated with the *Amidah*, and we will get to them in a moment. But first, consider standing itself. Often standing can be uncomfortable so we shift position back and forth, actually generating more restlessness and energy with nowhere to go. It's a great practice to transform any time you're standing—for example, in line, or waiting somewhere—into standing meditation. Just stand upright, feet shoulder-width apart, knees slightly bent so that your weight is well distributed, as in yoga's Mountain Pose. Relax your body into this standing posture, as if you are sitting, and rest your gaze straight ahead. Thoughts and irritations will arise. Try to let them go. See if, after sixty seconds, you become more attentive, quieter, as if ready for whatever comes your way. Just like kneeling and listening, standing shifts mood whether we notice it or not. By noticing the shifts, though, our experience of the world becomes deeper and richer.

The *Amidah* posture is different from Mountain Pose, but the basic idea is the same: readiness, uprightness, standing at attention. In the *Amidah*, the practice is to stand straight upright: feet are put together, legs are absolutely straight, and the body becomes like a pinion uniting earth and sky. Think of our conventional associations of standing: "Stand up!"; "I stand for ... "; "Get Up, Stand Up." Recall the homology between the eighteen blessings and the eighteen vertebrae of the spine—and how we call people without integrity "spineless." All of these connotations suggest that standing with an upright spine is an emotional, mental, and even spiritual state—it's not just being on your feet. It's very Jewish, then, to have the *Amidah* be the time we get up, stand up, and face up to reality.

For newcomers to Jewish prayer, one of the most noticeable, and confusing, aspects of the *Amidah* is the various body movements associated with it. Those in the know semiautomatically walk backward and forward, bow, and move in all sorts of ways without cue or prompt. Really, the movements in the *Amidah* are not that complicated.

In addition to *shuckling*, the rhythmic swaying back and forth that helps get the blood flowing in prayer, the prescribed movements are:

1. Taking three steps back and three steps forward at the very beginning of the *Amidah*. These six steps correspond to the six Hebrew words for "God, open my lips and my mouth will tell your praises." The three steps forward are meant to evoke entering the presence of the Divine.

2. Bowing four times: at the first two *brachot*, and then at the beginning and end of the blessing for thanksgiving, *Modim*. (We'll look at the Talmudic methods for bowing later;[3] for now, let's just ponder its colorful, and presumably allegorical, warning that "if a person does not bow when reciting the *Modim* prayer, his spine will turn into a snake for seven years."[4])

3. When the *Amidah* is recited with a group, there are certain movements in the *kedushah* section, most notably standing on tip-toes three times for the recitation of *kadosh, kadosh, kadosh* ("holy, holy, holy"). According to mystical lore, this prayer is recited by the angels; the posture mimics their form and represents an embodied aspiration to be "higher" than we are.

4. When the *Amidah* includes a prayer acknowledging wrongdoing and asking forgiveness, it is customary to touch the heart with a closed fist two times, in the millennia-old gesture of penitence.

5. At the very end, it is customary to again take three steps back and three steps forward, also bowing left and right, to the *Oseh Shalom* prayer in which we ask for peace to be spread everywhere on earth, in all directions.

Notice how detailed and subtle Jewish prayer practice is, constantly involving the body. If you have a prayer practice, choose one or two of these movements each time you *daven* and really focus the attention on the movements of the body as you bend, stretch, or stand. See what happens. Jewish prayer is a rich set of tools for using the body to awaken the soul. We may have lost, in our noisy world, the natural quiet that made these movements so pregnant with meaning for our ancestors. But we can recapture that inner stillness with mindfulness, and from that still place, we can embody prayer anew.

Sweat Your Prayers—Hasidic Style

The mind can give words to its supplications, and the heart can cry its yearning, but how does the soul move in ecstasy, in joy, and in passion? Ecstatic prayer—that is, prayer that takes us out of our conventional selves—begins with the body. The notion of "sweating your prayers," made popular in recent years by Gabrielle Roth and others, is really an ancient one. Today we may think of Hasidim as conservative, black-clad pietists, but two hundred and fifty years ago they were a revolutionary band of ecstatics, and wild, energetic, embodied prayer was the center of their religious life. Consider Rabbi Yehudah Pesah of Lipsk, of whom it is said:

> His praying was with great *devekut* [cleaving to God] and a thunderous voice, like the roar of a lion, with great fervor and singing and dancing, with shaking and trembling, with bowing and prostrating—such that the hair on the bodies of all who were present when he prayed would stand up, when they would see and be overwhelmed, and be aroused to repent.[5]

Or these boldly erotic words, attributed to the Baal Shem Tov, the founder of Hasidism:

> Prayer is a form of intercourse with the Shechinah [Divine Presence]. Just as in the beginning of intercourse one moves one's body, so it is necessary to move one's body at first in prayer. Afterward one can stand still without any movement when one unites with the Shechinah. The power of his movement causes a great arousal, for it causes him to think: "Why am I moving myself? Because perhaps the Shechinah is actually standing in front of me." And from this great power, he comes to a great passion.[6]

Jewish prayer, especially Hasidic prayer, can be an ecstatic activity. If you've ever seen images of pious men bowing rhythmically to prayer—the Yiddish term is *shuckling*—you know what I'm talking about. If you've ever been to a Hasidic *tisch* (festive Friday night gathering) or wedding, then you *really* know what I'm talking about. In fact, the idea that Jewish prayer should shake your body around dates back two thousand years. About Rabbi Akiva it is said that "when praying alone, he engaged in so much kneeling and prostrating that if someone was with him and saw him in one corner of the room, when he walked out and came back he would find him in the opposite corner."[7]

If all this is true, then how did we get to the boring, life-negating, and body-twisting form we know today, sitting still in uncomfortable pews and standing ceremoniously while someone in a robe intones a somber tune? Well, it's a complicated story, but the short version is that most American Jewish prayer is pretending to be German Protestant. Lutheran prayer is meant to be edifying; you're meant to contemplate the words and music in a serene state, and cause your soul to be uplifted. It works, when it's done right, but it's not the point of most Jewish prayer. Most Jewish prayer is meant to be devotionalistic, pietistic, ecstatic, contemplative—it's all over the map, but it is always, always embodied.

How can this be put into practice today?

First, have an open mind. Often in my Embodied Judaism classes, I tell my students to "fake it till you make it." This is especially true for body movements during prayer. Try moving your body in a rhythmic way for a bit, either bowing or swaying. Maybe the rhythm matches the cadence of the words, or maybe it's your own "different drummer." It doesn't matter. What matters is that it comes from the heart and gets the body moving. It's probably best to start just with simple movements—don't rush to union with the Shechinah just yet. Find a rhythm that pushes the heart along.

Second, do what you need to do to get the blood flowing. You might clap your hands, following the advice of Rabbi Mordechai of Neshkiz, who said that "sometimes a person works to inspire himself while praying and claps his hands and makes other movements so as to push away foreign thoughts."[8] Again, fake it till you make it. Rabbi Nachman of Breslov, who believed hands to be the primary symbols of faith and prayer, is reported to have said: "We clap our hands during prayer, for by this the air of the place where a man of Israel prays is purified, and the air of holiness is drawn there, as in the Land of Israel itself."[9] You could even just raise and wave your hands, following this Hasidic source quoted by Yitzhak Buxbaum: "It is very precious to God that you raise your hands with spread fingers when you are praying from the depth of your heart."[10]

As you build up the energy, skeptical thoughts will inevitably arise. That's fine; just see them for what they are—"thinking"—and remember that this is not a thinking practice. Thinking is a gift from God, but it doesn't help you make love, it doesn't help you dance—and it doesn't help you pray in an ecstatic way.

Eventually, as you grow more relaxed and confident, don't be afraid to add more sensual elements to your prayer movements: perhaps a fluid swaying of the body, like slow dancing with a lover, or moving the head as if kissing a child on his forehead. Don't worry; if people are looking at you funny, they're probably jealous. Ecstasy is not a matter of intellect—it doesn't make sense. It's about using the body to inflame the heart (*hitlahavut*, the Hasidic term for ecstasy, means "being on fire").

Sometimes, as the Hasidim relate, a period of movement may naturally be followed by one of stillness. Says one source, "It is possible to pray in such a way that no other person can know of your devotion. Though you make no movement of your body, your soul is all aflame within you. And when you cry out in the ecstasy of that moment—your cry will be a whisper."[11] This stillness is a rarefied state, in which, as in sexual union, the state of oneness is such that movement is no longer needed to arouse it. Of course, *davening* is not all celebration. It's also begging, pleading, yearning, hoping. Traditional Jewish prayer, for example, includes a confessional known colloquially as *nefilat a payim*, or falling on the face (the actual practice is not quite so extreme: you just rest your head on your forearm). The range of prayers with the body is as wide as those of the heart. Let yourself explore them.

Hand gestures (hands over heart, open hands pleading, or others) and swaying the body—there is no rational reason why any of these should have any effect on our minds. But can you imagine an animated conversation without the body taking a role? Just as formalized body postures help cultivate mind-states in contemplative prayer, so expressive body movements help loosen the heart in ecstatic and petitionary prayer. Don't become trapped by the starched-shirt, rattle-your-jewelry approach to Jewish prayer. There is a time for rational reflection, and a time to cut loose emotionally. In innovative circles today, there are Jewish prayer services that involve full-body movement, contact improv, drumming, dancing, and body-centered awareness practices such as authentic movement. In some traditional Hasidic circles, Jewish prayer services involve jumping, swaying, dancing, and banging on walls. It's only in the mushy middle that we *daven* like disembodied heads. Whatever mode suits your personality, bring your whole self to prayer, letting the body lead you.

"Every Limb Will Praise You": Jewish Liturgy and the Body

Not only is Jewish prayer, in its essence, an embodied practice; not only is it rich with ritual movements; even its language is rich with body-centered imagery. Prayer language is not theology; it is *avodah sh'balev*, the service of the heart. So when we look at liturgy, we should see it as the poetry of holy longing, not "what Jews believe." Prayer was instituted to replace sacrifices, the ultimate irrational act of the heart, which in Hebrew are called *korbanot*, from the same root as *l'karev*, to bring near. Prayer, too, is meant to bridge a gap. Indeed, the fixed liturgy we know today was not codified or mandated until relatively late in Jewish history. Originally, the requirement was only to pray earnestly, from the heart, in whatever words the heart sought.

There are literally hundreds of Jewish body-prayer texts, but we'll look at just one group here: the morning blessings. The traditional Jewish prayer day opens with thankfulness for the body. The first words upon waking up thank God for the soul's return to the body. The first prescribed actions are using the restroom and washing the hands. And the first blessings in the Jewish morning prayer service, the *birchot hashachar*, or blessings of the dawn, thank God for the gifts of the body. Let's look at four of the blessings here. Each begins with the traditional Jewish blessing-phrase that we discussed in the last chapter: *Baruch ata adonai, eloheinu melech ha'olam,* usually translated something like "Blessed are you, God, ruler of the universe." Remember, though, that *baruch* is a body word—it doesn't mean that God is blessed; it means that YHVH is that-to-which-we-kneel. We are saying, in effect: my ego really wants to throw down a cup of coffee and rush off to work/school/carpool, but I'm going to kneel that part of me before the part that acknowledges that I am not the king of the universe—that there's a whole, miraculous world out there. Contrary to how many of us were taught in school, however, the *birchot hashachar* continue not by telling us about theodicy, but, as the Talmud explains,[12] by reflecting our own embodied experience every morning:

בָּרוּךְ אַתָּה יְיָ אֱלֹהֵינוּ מֶלֶךְ הָעוֹלָם פּוֹקֵחַ עִוְרִים

... *pokeach ivrim.*
... who gives sight to the blind (you open your eyes).

בָּרוּךְ אַתָּה יְיָ אֱלֹהֵינוּ מֶלֶךְ הָעוֹלָם מַלְבִּישׁ עֲרוּמִים

... *malbish arumim.*
... who clothes the naked (you get dressed).

בָּרוּךְ אַתָּה יְיָ אֱלֹהֵינוּ מֶלֶךְ הָעוֹלָם מַתִּיר אֲסוּרִים

... *matir asurim.*
... who releases the bound (you get out of bed)

בָּרוּךְ אַתָּה יְיָ אֱלֹהֵינוּ מֶלֶךְ הָעוֹלָם זוֹקֵף כְּפוּפִים

... *zokef kefufim.*
... who straightens the bent (you stretch and move your body)

We wake up blind, undressed, and immobile. Soon we are up, dressed, and moving around. Underneath what seems to be a set of claims about God's attributes is actually something much more transformative: that ordinary experience provides the occasion for blessing.

If you have a morning prayer or meditation practice, consider adding these blessings to it. You might also add a body movement for each—starting with your eyes closed and then opening for the first; wrapping yourself in a tallit (Jewish prayer shawl) or other special garment for the second; taking a step or two for the third; and getting a good morning stretch for the fourth. If you don't have a morning practice, consider adding these phrases as *kavvanot*—intentions—as you wake up each day. Just noting "opening the eyes ... stretching the body" is a start; adding gratitude is even better. It doesn't take long, it's exquisitely simple yet straight from the Talmud, and most of all, it works.

Or you might use these blessings at other times during the day. Diane Bloomfield, the creator of "Torah Yoga," has a whole sequence of yoga postures and visualizations based around the blessing of *zokef kefufim*, straightening the bent. When I lead Embodied Judaism sessions, we often focus on *matir asurim*, releasing tight places in the body so that the energies of the body can flow unimpeded. I'm not sure this is exactly what the authors of these prayers had in mind, but I do think it's a faithful translation of them into the shapes of our lives today.

These blessings are but a few examples of an entire literature of traditional body liturgy—and there is more being written every day. Of course, there are some who believe that religion should be confined to the great moments of life: birth, death, revelation, and so on. To such people, a blessing about ordinary sight or simply standing upright demeans the art of poetry. But Jewish prayer celebrates the ordinary, beginning with the body we almost always take for granted. As the beautiful *Nishmat Kol Chai* prayer understands, our arms do not soar like the eagle's, and our legs do not sprint like those of the deer:

> So, the limbs that You have set in us,
> The breath and soul that You have breathed in our nostrils,
> And the tongue that You have placed in our mouths—
> They will thank, and bless, and praise,
> And make beautiful, and raise up, and revere, and sanctify,
> and they will make You king.
> Every mouth thanks You.

Every tongue testifies to You.
Every knee bends to You.
Every spine bows to You.
Every heart is in awe of You,
And every innermost thought praises your name.
As it is written: All my bones say,
God, who is like You?

Often we're told that we're unbeautiful or imperfect, too skinny or too fat—or simply too ordinary to be miraculous. But such is not the Jewish way. In the Jewish tradition, that which is fallen, we uplift; that which is asleep, we wake up. And that which seems to be imperfect is usually just fine. We don't need to be reminded of God when life is tragic or triumphant. It's at all the other, ordinary times that the work of religion begins.

      *   *   *   *

3
Breathing

The world was created with breath—the breath of God. Divine breath is the sustainer of life. If breath is lacking, life is lacking.

Rabbi Nachman of Breslov[1]

Our sages said, let every soul (neshamah) *praise God (Psalm 150)—this means praise Him with every breath* (neshimah).

Or HaGanuz HaTzaddikim[2]

Let's review what's meant by "God in Your Body." The general view is that of the Baal Shem Tov, quoted by Rabbi Nachman of Breslov: "Woe is us! The world is full of light and mysteries both wonderful and awesome, but our little hand stands in front of our eyes and prevents them from seeing."[3] All around us, at every moment—even at moments when we are sad or in pain—there are miracles, not of the supernatural variety, but of the type so ordinary as to go unnoticed. And so they *do* go unnoticed, as our minds rush on to the next desire, leaning forward in time. We are trapped, according to Rabbi Nachman, by "our little hand"—our selfish inclination, the *yetzer*, which evaluates the world in terms of how well it is meeting our desires.

If we could only see clearly, Rabbi Nachman seems to be saying, much of the suffering we endure would have a different character. There would still be pain and the mission to improve the world, but we might not get trapped so often. As Jewish-Buddhist teacher Sylvia Boorstein says, in life, pain is mandatory—but suffering is optional.

35

What's needed, then, is, *hakarat hatov*, acknowledging the good. And the body is the best place to start; it is always present (until it isn't, when our preferences no longer matter anyway), and after all, God Himself, Herself, or Itself said it is *tov*, good. What's more, the most central Jewish ritual practices—prayer, eating, and the Sabbath and holidays (discussed toward the end of this book)—are all relentlessly embodied. All we need to do is pay attention.

Basic Breathing Meditation

Unlike diet and prayer, mindful breathing is not a primary practice of mainstream Judaism. However, in almost all of the world's traditions, including the Jewish one, it is a primary way to pay attention and begin the subtractive process of *hakarat hatov*: to quiet down and experience the pure being of Shabbat, of deep rest. We will turn to Shabbat itself at the end of this book, but first we need to lay the foundation for experiencing it in the body.

At first, it may seem odd to focus on breath—as beginning meditators know, it can be quite boring. But that is part of the point: to do less and notice more. This *neshamah*, the breath-soul, is in the kabbalistic schema, associated with the mind—and paying attention to breath quiets the mind. See for yourself, right now. Let your body be still and wait, like a crouching tiger, for your next breath to come. When it comes, watch it intently, again like a tiger. Observe the physical sensation of inhaling (chest rising ...) and exhaling (chest falling ...). That's it. Were you able to just focus on the breath—not thoughts about it, not an idea of "hmm, what will this do," but the physical sensation? Just one breath provides a pause in the constant stream of self-oriented thoughts and words—and, remembering Rabbi Nachman, that's all we need: just a short Shabbat in the stream of thought.

Shabbat has two aspects: the additive (that is, things you do only on the Sabbath) and the subtractive (things you refrain from doing). Likewise, meditation may be either "filling"—replacing thought with something else—or "emptying." Most indigenous Jewish meditation is of the filling kind, using contemplation to push thought out. It works very well in the midst of a noisy life. We'll start, though, with a very basic emptying meditation, derived from Theravada Buddhism, in which, rather than imposing a particular impression on the mind, simply "being with the breath" cultivates an attitude of equanimity, of witnessing whatever is going on, and simply being present with it. As we said earlier, the stillness engendered by such practices was natural for our ancestors, who lived in a quieter, slower, and less brightly lit world. Today, I see these foundational practices as setting the conditions that our ancestors took for granted, but that, for us, may be otherwise available only on rare occasions.

1. Find a quiet place to sit, where you won't be disturbed. Get into a comfortable posture in which you can remain still for several minutes. The first few times, you'll inevitably have to move; but as you progress you'll get better at knowing your body, and eventually should be able to stay still for the whole "sit." For some, sitting Indian-style works best—for others, sitting in a chair—with hands on knees or hands gently clasped. See what works for you. I usually do this practice with my eyes closed, which helps me focus inward, on the body. But you don't have to close your eyes—and if you find yourself falling asleep, open them.

2. Allow your body to really rest. Let gravity pull you down, and don't exert any effort. Make it a sort of game, to see how relaxed you can be without falling asleep. I like to scan through the body at the beginning of a sit, noticing and relaxing any tension that may have accumulated unconsciously. Perhaps the forehead is tensed, or the jaw; allow it to relax. Are my shoulders hunched? My hands rigid? As I work through the body, I am usually amazed at what I find. Just now, for instance, I noticed my toes painfully curled under my feet as I sit here writing. The mind may not be aware of these gratuitous tensions in the body—but the body knows. (The practice is worthwhile for this effect alone; try it at a dull meeting, or on a date.) As the body settles into stillness, you can actually feel the

sensation of being still. Just being is usually a somewhat pleasant feeling, like a little taste of Shabbat.

3. Come to the breath. You'll notice, in stillness, that there is a movement the body does all by itself, with no effort from you: the movement of breath. Often, as soon as I notice this, I start forcing the breath to come deeper, slower, or faster. Try not to do that—just lean back and let the breath arise and pass. *Kol haneshama t'hallel yah*—every breath praises God; it's not necessary to force it or make it special. As the contemporary breath teacher Carola Speads said (despite having pioneered several techniques of breath work), you don't have to learn how to breathe.

4. Find a spot in the body where the breath is easy to observe. This may be the rising and falling of the chest, or a sense of expansion and contraction, or even the sensation of breath entering and leaving the nostrils. The key is to tune into an actual physical sensation, not an idea or an image. Again, as you do this more often, you'll get better at it. Just treat it as though you're watching television and this is the show that's on. Watch the breath arise and pass effortlessly, as a physical sensation in the body. It's not that a skilled practitioner notices anything particularly special. Rather, as the Buddha says in the *Satipatthana Sutra*:

> Breathing in long, he discerns that he is breathing in long; or breathing out long, he discerns that he is breathing out long. Or breathing in short, he discerns that he is breathing in short; or breathing out short, he discerns that he is breathing out short ... Always mindful, he breathes in; mindful he breathes out.[4]

Just keep it simple.

5. As thoughts arise, note them and gently let them go. Don't yank your attention back to the body—be gentle with yourself, perhaps smile a bit internally, and come on back to step four.

Try this *avodah* for half an hour and see what happens. As you'll quickly find out, it's simple... but not easy. Welcome to meditation, where you let go of a hundred thoughts a minute, notice knee pain, and wonder if it is really for you. What's important to remember is what one of my teachers, Sharon Salzberg, often says: It's not what's going on, it's how you relate to it. Okay, thoughts are arising. Are you aware of them? Are you being gentle? Are you coming back, over and over, to watching the breath? Great.

On long retreats, watching the breath in this way can, believe it or not, lead to all kinds of insights about the self, God, and the universe. Indeed, it's the first step on "the direct path for the purification of beings, for the overcoming of sorrow and lamentation, for the disappearance of pain and distress, for the attainment of the right method, and for realization."[5] But don't expect such things from half an hour of meditation. In fact, don't expect anything at all. Don't try to improve. Don't try to achieve anything. You might notice, after a period of sitting, a bit more sensitivity in the body, or quietness in the mind. Or you might not. Surrender to however it's going—that, and not some idea of improvement, is the real practice. Remember that from a Jewish perspective, "however it's going" is how the *Ein Sof*, the Infinite, is manifesting, even if it seems difficult or unpleasant.

This is the foundation: using the body to open up and let God in. It's a way to receive, *l'kabel*—the root of Kabbalah. If Kabbalah were about improvement, or progress, or having a magical experience that's something other than this one, it would be called something else; but it's about receiving. The body is the gateway to this receiving, and the home to which the gateway leads. Don't try to have an out-of-body experience. You're in your body. Receive that. Develop a capacity to be so sensitive to the body that the breath becomes intricate, complicated, and absorbing. Lower your threshold for interest. Become a cheap date for God.

Adding God to Your Breath

The Hasidic masters suggest trying a new practice for forty days before evaluating it. When I try a new form of meditation, it usually takes me about forty seconds before I develop an opinion. The sit's going well, it's not going well, I should try this other practice, maybe I should eat breakfast first... whatever.

I mention this because there's a tendency to want to try all sorts of different breath practices like items on a salad bar, as if adding and mixing meditations will make the overall product better. It won't. So, while I'm about to describe a few additional breath-based meditation practices from the Jewish tradition, please don't try them all at once. Treat these and other practices you learn like precious chocolates in a box. You don't want to scarf them all down; you want to treasure each one, and give it space to be enjoyed.

Here's one kabbalistic bite of chocolate: if you find yourself having trouble concentrating on your breathing, you can add a visualization to focus the mind and cultivate a mind-state of presence. One such visualization is based on the Hebrew letters of the tetragrammaton: *yood*, *hey*, *vav*, and *hey*. The *yood* is like the body devoid of air, with empty lungs. The first *hey* is the inhale—just as it sounds. The *vav* is a body full of air, extended. And the second *hey* is the exhale. As you breath deeply, you can visualize your body in the form of these four letters, literally embodying the divine name. You can quietly chant the letter to yourself if that helps you concentrate. In so doing, you are learning through your body an essential kabbalistic truth: that the human exists in the divine image, that God lives through you. There's nothing magical here—this is just using skillful means to incline the mind in the direction of the truth. As always, try it and see what happens.

More complicated kabbalistic breath meditations are found in the writings of Abraham Abulafia, the thirteenth-century inventor of Prophetic Kabbalah (sometimes called Ecstatic Kabbalah). Abulafia created hundreds of techniques to lead to altered mind-states, which he believed enabled the flow of prophecy. Many of these involve pronouncing letters, or combining them, or working with free associations and streams of consciousness. One of his simplest practices, popularized by Rabbi Aryeh Kaplan in his books on Jewish meditation, involves a series of head movements and breath, combined with pronouncing the divine name.

The shortest version works by sounding out different Hebrew vowels together with the tetragrammaton. When you do the practice, you'll want to sit comfortably in a place where you will not be disturbed and allow your eyes to close. Begin with the first letter of the divine name, *yood*, and pronounce it with the vowels *oh*, *ah*, *ay*, *ee*, and *oo*. So it sounds like *yoh*, *yah*, *yay*, *yee*, *yoo*.

Each vowel has a corresponding head movement, which resembles the way the vowel mark is written in Hebrew: with *oh* the head moves up and back to center, *ah* to the left and back to center, *ay* to the right and back to center, *ee* down and back to center, and then *oo* forward, backward, and back to center. Move your head with the breath: on each inhale move away from center, then on the exhale, pronouncing the sound, move back. So, it looks a bit like this:

Inhale—move head upward

Exhale—move head back to center, pronouncing *yoh*

Inhale—move head to the left

Exhale—move head back to center, pronouncing *yah*

Inhale—move head to the right

Exhale—move head back to center, pronouncing *yay*

Inhale—move head downward

Exhale—move head back to center, pronouncing *yee*

Inhale—move head backward

Exhale—move head forward, backward, center, *yoo*

You then repeat that process with the letters *hey*, *vav*, and then *hey* again.

There are many layers to this practice. On the esoteric level, permuting each letter of the divine name with each vowel leads necessarily to pronouncing the ineffable name of God, somewhere within the permutations. On the more practical level, the complexity of this practice really focuses the mind, like a good puzzle. You can be thinking about mortgages, tests, and kids when you start, but in order to keep it straight, those thoughts just have to leave. And this is just the simplest level of the practice. As you progress, there are more and more complicated versions. A full Y-H-V-H sequence with each vowel preceding it (*oh-yoh ... oh-yah* ... , etc.) takes almost half an hour to complete. Or you can visualize the letters and vowels as you pronounce them. Another way is to combine divine names, such as YHVH and ADNY (*adonai*), and rotate through the vowel sequence with the two names. You can even do one name backward and the other name forward. As a parlor trick, these are not very interesting. But look closely at what Abulafia is doing: focusing the mind, and training the mind and body to work together, all in a system that expertly pushes distracting thoughts away.

The results can be amazing. Usually, when I finish it, I've really got YHVH in my head—I can imagine the letters of the name imprinted on whatever else I'm seeing: trees, people, traffic jams. And isn't it true that the trees and people and cars are just the skin of the Divine? Isn't that the simple truth we've been trying to experience?

There are many more advanced versions of this practice, and I encourage you to look at Kaplan's work and that of Rabbi David Cooper for charts, formulas, and techniques. (Abulafia's own books remain untranslated, and their complex symbolism and theological systems are quite difficult for beginners.) You can penetrate very deeply with it, whether you view it as a mystical incantation or as a skillful means for concentration. Just be sure not to go faster than feels comfortable; it's serious work, and not meant for spiritual daytrippers. If you decide to make it a practice, you'll find the journey enlightening.

These are just a few breath-based meditation practices that are easy to do. Of course, this is a lifetime practice, and there are dozens of other techniques, from *pranayama* to holotropic breath work, the various special breaths of yoga to Thich Nhat Hanh's mindful breathing with intentions and contemplation. Even just taking a deep breath, remembering to exhale fully, can help. What all of these practices have in common, from the simplest to the most complex, is a refutation of the simplistic opposition of body and spirit, and an affirmation that mindfulness of the body—grounding our attention in the here-and-now facts of our physical existence—is a path to God. Our spirits are tied to our bodies, nourished by them, and, in the Jewish conception, housed within them. Think about it: if God is everywhere, and you are always going to be in your body, why leave your body to experience God?

❋   ❋   ❋   ❋

4
Walking

Enoch walked with God, and was not.

Genesis 5:24

The spiritual journey is a strange one. Normally, we take trips to go somewhere—from point A to point B, from home to work, from New York to Puerto Rico. But on the spiritual journey, each step is the destination. The place we're trying to get to is right here, and the point is merely to arrive.

Walking is, for those of us who are able, such a natural process that we ordinarily take it for granted. But as we've seen already, spirituality is all about what's ordinarily taken for granted. In the Buddhist world, walking meditation complements sitting and watching the breath as a core meditative practice; it focuses the mind on the present instead of on the ever-inviting future—the journey instead of the destination—and it rests the body and gets the blood flowing, helping sleepy meditators stay awake. Walking meditation also allows an important truth to be learned firsthand: you can have a very still mind and a very fast-moving body. In the Jewish world, ritualized walking is confined to just a few movements during prayer—for example, at the beginning and end of the *Amidah*, as we saw earlier. But the core truth remains, translated into Jewish language: Wherever you go, God is with you. Walking meditation is like the core breathing practice: pure mindfulness of the body, with no special decorations.

Basic Walking Meditation

There are as many formal walking practices as there are ways to walk. I will begin with some basic ones, and, as before, use Buddhist technology to illuminate an embodied Jewish practice whose meaning we may have lost.

The first and simplest practice is basic walking meditation—simple, but not easy, because to walk mindfully means to give full attention to the physical sensations of walking, and there is actually a bewildering array of sensations and movement involved. One of my teachers, Joseph Goldstein, once challenged his students to explain how it is that we walk at all. Of course, we all know how to put one foot in front of the other. But it's actually a bit mysterious how the shifting of weight and momentum really work. To bring that level of attention to this ordinary task is the essence of this supposedly simple practice:

1. Find a spot where you can walk back and forth for at least a few yards, and where you won't be disturbed. Begin standing in one place, and as you step forward, make the physical sensations of walking the primary object of your attention. As thoughts arise, note them and let them go, returning the attention to your feet or legs. One step at a time; the journey is the destination. As you'll quickly notice, you have to move very slowly to observe closely. You can look a little strange, a bit like a zombie. Don't worry about how you look; you're just cultivating precise, moment-to-moment attention.

2 "Walking" will probably be too broad to really observe, so you can divide up the process into lifting the foot, moving the foot, and placing the foot—or another division that suggests itself. (Formal Buddhist walking meditation has up to seven different components of a single step.) You can gently label these motions ("lifting," "moving," "placing") if that helps you concentrate, but make sure you're actually feeling those sensations, and not just saying the words.

3. Try to walk only when you know you're walking. When you're caught in thought, pause; only start moving again once the mind is focused exclusively on the physical sensations in your legs.

4. Do the practice for a set period of time—fifteen minutes or half an hour, to start. When you get to a wall, turn around and come back. Turn ... lift ... move ... place ... and see what happens.

Chances are, all sorts of things will happen. You'll question why you're doing this. You'll get tired. You'll be amazed. You'll get very quiet internally. You'll start thinking of the shopping list. That's all fine, because remember, it's not what's going on that matters but how you relate to it. In addition to all those thoughts, you may notice some unique insights, or you may notice a lot of discomfort. That's fine too; staying with difficult mind- and body-states, just letting them happen, is the only way to really follow the dictum of *shiviti adonai l'negdi tamid*—to place God before you always, that is, not just in the pleasant times. With walking meditation specifically, you can really experience how the "in order to" mind, the mind of the *yetzer hara*, is always toppling forward with anticipation, not being *sameach b'chelko*, satisfied with what is already here. It's a little absurd; even if you're just walking back and forth, you might notice that you can't wait to get to the end ... so you can turn around and come back. It doesn't make sense, does it? But most of us act this way all the time. How much of what we do each day is just to satisfy this *yetzer*, to alleviate some minor suffering or perceived lack?

There are variations to the basic practice. For example, Thich Nhat Hanh suggests, in *Peace Is Every Step* and other books, lightly chanting intentions for peace or lovingkindness with each step you take. Or, you might take each step as though you were dancing, or add a short mantra to the rhythm of your walk. You might experiment with changing paces as you walk, starting at a normal pace and then, after five minutes or so, decreasing to the "zombie" pace so you can really pay attention to each movement. Find the right pace for you, between "too fast-can't notice" and "too slow-mind drifting." You might find that the slower you go, the more you can pay effective attention, and the less your mind will wander.

The most important element here is what computer programmers call KISS, or Keep It Simple, Stupid. Don't go spiritual shopping, spending your whole half hour deciding between different modes of walking. Pick one, and stay with it. Remember, if you change practices every time you feel uncomfortable, you never really practice because you never allow yourself to experience the full range of sensations that might arise. Set your clock, pick your practice, and let whatever arises arise.

Four Ways to Walk with God

Over time, you may reach a stage in your walking practice at which you experience "being walked" more than walking. Perhaps this is a way to understand the apotheosis of Enoch, who "walked with God, and was not, for God took him."[1] Of course, the Bible is here speaking in terms of metaphor, but the metaphor draws its language from embodied experience for a reason. Perhaps Enoch walked with God so perfectly that he was no longer present as a separate self. Perhaps he saw himself to be nothing other than walking itself, that is, a composite of a thousand separate elements, with no real independent essence at all—merely as "empty phenomena, rolling on." This is a rather high level of experiencing God in the body—but it is the essence of it.

One way to progress to this kind of awareness is by means of the four souls described in Kabbalah. When I was training for a marathon, I did my long runs as extended periods of walking meditation. First I would focus on the *nefesh*, on feelings in my legs. Later I would chant a mantra—*ein od milvado* (there is nothing beside God) or the *Shema*—and see what would happen to my *ruach*, the emotional soul connected with circulation, rhythm, and chant. Still later, I would focus my breath and concentration, like sharpening the knife of *neshamah*, the knowing soul. And sometimes, all of these conceptions would drop away and I would simply be Running—not Jay running, not Jay running in Central Park, and not Jay doing a spiritual practice.

Just Running, with *chayah*, the spiritual soul, giving a glimpse of *yechidah*, oneness. Here is how it works:

> *Nefesh* walking practice can be done anytime by transplanting the wisdom of basic walking meditation to a wide variety of walking states. For example, suppose you're running to catch a bus. Instead of doing what you usually do—fretting about the bus, cursing yourself for not leaving earlier—just focus on the physical sensations in the body. Bump, bump, bump, sweat, breath, pant, bump, bump ... the *nefesh* is doing its thing, even if your *neshamah* would rather spin stories about why it is that you never leave enough time to catch the bus. Maybe this is why God manifests in four worlds, so that there are always spare ones when one of them seems to be giving us problems.
>
> Arrive in each step. Stay with the *nefesh*: notice how your body feels, not why, not what's wrong. So often we run off in our minds to places that we don't need to be. The body, in contrast, is always present, always having an experience of "what is." If you're nervously awaiting a meeting, or an interview, it's there: breathing, lifting, moving, placing. If you're waiting, bored and angry at your friend for coming late, try just walking: lifting, moving, placing. This isn't a practice of thinking happy thoughts; it's a practice of returning from things as they aren't (i.e., the mind's various images) to things as they are. It's an interruption of fantasy by the Presence of the Real.

Ruach walking practice involves adding the emotional to the physical. It, too, can be done anytime, though it's rooted in traditional Jewish prayer. For example, at the end of the *Amidah* is the well-known line *Oseh shalom bimromav, hu ya'aseh shalom aleinu v'al kol Yisrael, v'imru Amen*: May He who makes peace on high, make peace upon us, and upon all Israel, and let us say Amen.[2] As we saw earlier, *Oseh Shalom* is recited while in motion: three steps back first, then bow to the left, then to the right, and then three steps forward, raising on tiptoes to reach up, finally bowing to point down. You'll sort out the exact choreography; the point is to move mindfully from stillness into movement, with the heart—the *ruach* soul—leading. I try to make those steps forward mindful, walking meditation steps, embodying my own wish for peace. And I let the movements of the body incline my own heart in this way. On the level of intellect, *neshamah*, there is no rational reason why this should work. But on the level of *ruach*, it works.

Outside traditional prayer, *ruach* walking might take the form of a mantra, or a phrase repeated over and over to the rhythm of walking. Unlike *nefesh* walking, this inclines the heart in a particular direction; it's not as transparent, but it can help shift a stuck mood or clogged-up mind. There are many phrases you can use; I like *ein od milvado* (there's nothing else but God), a touchstone for Hasidic theology, which also happens to fit well with the rhythm of running. Roger Joslin, in *Running the Spiritual Path*, suggests "Onward to the One." Other good ones include *rofeh kol basar* (who heals all flesh) from the *Asher Yatzar* blessing, or my own short couplet, "This journey is the strangest one / Each step is the destination."

Or *ruach* walking can be used to focus on touch. Try this, preferably barefoot: imagine that the truth really is true; that you are God walking on God. Imagine that your walk is really a caress of the delicate body of the Lover. Your body, as it steps, is touching the Lover—as it moves, it is slow dancing. Let judgment slide away, because this is what all the mystics say: that you are God loving God, or doubting or denying or touching or missing God; that you are, like Hafiz says, "a divine elephant with amnesia trying to live in an ant-hole."[3] See where this takes you. Don't push—but don't push back either.

Neshamah, the mind—the gateway to oneness, and also its obstruction. One of my favorite walking meditation practices is something I call "rushing meditation." Some of the great spiritual sages are often seen moving very quickly, yet not hurrying. How do they do this? By residing not in the mental space of rushing but in the mental space of noticing the body in rapid movement. The next time you find yourself having to move quickly, catch yourself before you fall into all the stories, just like in *nefesh* walking but this time, move not to the body but to the mirrorlike mind, which is perfectly perceiving, perfectly reflecting everything that is happening. The "everything" may well include a mind-state of discomfort or unhappiness, but notice how the mind perfectly reflects that too. As you walk, or run, move your attention to the mind itself, which is absolutely still even as the body is rushing toward the subway. Walk quickly, but move to the "witness" of the walking, perfectly knowing, just as leaves perfectly know how to turn colors in the fall and photosynthesize in the summer. Just as gravity "knows" to happen, and stars explode when the conditions are just right. Over time, this can become an extremely powerful practice; in Dzogchen schools of Buddhism, it's known as the "Great Perfection." Better than rushing for the bus, right?

Chayah/Yechidah;[4] unity. There's a Hasidic story about a rabbi who walked around with two notes, one in each pocket of his coat. One said, "The entire world was created for your sake." The other said, "You are dust and ashes." The conventional interpretation of this story is that the rabbi would look at one note when he was sad and needed a boost, and at the other when he was arrogant and needed to be more humble. But I would like to suggest that these two notes are saying exactly the same thing. Only once we really, deeply understand that we are nothing but dust and ashes (or the four elements, or carbon and oxygen and hydrogen) can our higher Self wake up and realize the entire universe has been leading to exactly this moment, in whatever shape we find it. So long as I'm identified with Jay, the small ego that gets what he wants sometimes and doesn't get what he wants more of the time, I'm trapped in alternating polarities of "for my sake!" and "dust and ashes!" But once I'm *really* dust and ashes, a whole new Self awakens—the Self that does the knowing. This is the true *bittul hayesh*, annihilation of the "self": not self-denigration, but lighting the small self afire, like an effigy, thus becoming so much more than the ego could ever have been.

We cannot describe this Self—but we can know it. The practice is the same as the *neshamah* practice, with one slight difference: here, there is no longer even the idea that "I" am walking at all. Dissolve into walking: be the sky, rather than the rushing motion of the clouds. This is the last barrier, the barrier of self, the illusion that "I" am separate from "You." In a real I-You moment, as Buber described, there is only the relational act itself: it is the love in which there is only one Lover. *Yechidah* is not really a soul; it is *awareness* of this reality, like Enoch, "who walked with God and was not." He was not—or, better, he was Nought; he became transfigured into the being Metatron, who speaks only as God.

It is not beyond you to experience these things. Start with the basic practice, a little at a time. Supplement your daily practice with Shabbat and retreats and let the awareness grow, like a small sapling growing into a tree. Each moment you spend not as "you" but as "You" is like a drop of water that will eventually fill the well. You will succeed, then you will fail again; you'll have a great experience, and then, if you're like me, you'll later get so caught in the small mind that you'll doubt the Great Mind even exists. It's all a bunch of delusion, you'll say. But your body will remember, and you'll find yourself, in the middle of polite company, suddenly dropping into a higher awareness. Let yourself drop. You have nothing to lose but yourself.

* * * *

5
Using the Bathroom

We do not like to look at the shadow-side of ourselves; therefore
there are many people in our civilized society who have lost their
shadow altogether ... and with it they have usually lost the body.
The body is a most doubtful friend because it produces things we
do not like; there are too many things about the body that cannot
be mentioned. The body is very often the personification of this
shadow of the ego. Sometimes it forms the skeleton in the cup-
board, and everybody naturally wants to get rid of such a thing.
Carl Jung[1]

When you go the bathroom, think "Am I not separating the bad
from the good, and is this not a unification [holy act]?"
Baal Shem Tov[2]

Yes, there is a blessing for going to the bathroom. And why shouldn't
there be? Because of our toilet training, and various social hang-ups,
we might be embarrassed about the excretory functions of the body—
but they are still remarkably complex, vital for our survival, and,
above all, occasions for gratitude.

I get a wide range of responses when I teach the *Asher Yatzar*, the
Jewish "bathroom blessing," which we'll look at in a moment. Some
people think it's beautiful to honor every part of life, admitting every
aspect of existence as a site for sanctification and blessing; after all,
mindfulness of the body extends to all the body's activities—that's
why there are so many chapters in this book. Others think it's just

55

ridiculous. Surely, though, while it is literally infantile to dwell too much on the details of urination and defecation (as seems a lamentable part of popular humor today), these functions of the body are perfect examples of miracles that go unnoticed until something goes wrong. After a person has been sick, incapacitated, or hospitalized, simply going to the bathroom unaided is an act of joy. Could we not, with embodied *hakarat hatov*, evoke a little of that gratitude every day?

What's more, using the toilet is often one of the few opportunities many people have to be alone, with nothing on the agenda but the body. If you're having trouble finding time to practice mindfulness, practice it at the times afforded to you—such as when you're in the bathroom. No e-mails, no kids—no studying Torah either, according to the Rabbis. Far from being a place of shame, the bathroom is an ideal site for practicing mindfulness of the miracles of the body, and for contemplating the blessings it bestows. As Bahya ibn Pakuda advised, "Dear brother, consider the wisdom of the Creator manifested in the composition of your body; how He set the organs in the right places, to receive the waste substances, so that they should not spread in the body and make you sick."[3] Or, as Rabbi Kalonymus Kalman Epstein writes in the *Maor V'Shemesh*, "Each and every member of Israel should view themselves as if holiness is dwelling within their inner physical organs."[4]

Asher Yatzar: The Bathroom Blessing
We find in the Talmud[5] the following text to be recited after using the bathroom:

בָּרוּךְ אַתָּה יְיָ אֱלֹהֵינוּ מֶלֶךְ הָעוֹלָם אֲשֶׁר יָצַר אֶת הָאָדָם

בְּחָכְמָה וּבָרָא בוֹ נְקָבִים נְקָבִים חֲלוּלִים חֲלוּלִים. גָּלוּי

וְיָדוּעַ לִפְנֵי כִסֵּא כְבוֹדֶךָ שֶׁאִם יִפָּתֵחַ אֶחָד מֵהֶם אוֹ יִסָּתֵם

אֶחָד מֵהֶם אִי אֶפְשָׁר לְהִתְקַיֵּם וְלַעֲמֹד לְפָנֶיךָ. בָּרוּךְ אַתָּה

יְיָ רוֹפֵא כָל בָּשָׂר וּמַפְלִיא לַעֲשׂוֹת.

Baruch ata adonai, eloheinu melech ha'olam, asher yatzar et ha'adam b'chochmah, u'vara vo n'kavim n'kavim, chalulim chalulim. Galu'i v'yadu'a lifnei kisei k'vodecha she'im yipateach echad me'hem, oh yisatem echad mehem, ee efshar l'hitkayem v'la'amod lefanecha. Baruch ata adonai, rofeh kol basar u'mafli la'asot.

Blessed are you, YHVH, our God, king of the universe, who formed the human being with wisdom, and created within him many openings, and many hollow spaces. It is obvious, and known before the seat of your glory, that if one of them were opened, or one of them were closed, it would be impossible to survive and stand before you. Blessed are you, YHVH, who heals all flesh and acts wondrously.

This is really one of my favorite *brachot* in the entire Jewish canon. Taking a moment, after using the restroom and washing your hands, to pause, to give thanks—it's a perfect interruption in a day of fretting and worrying. The language is wonderful too. There's a great rhythm to *n'kavim n'kavim, chalulim chalulim*, a form we don't have in English, in which the repetition of a word basically means "many." It's literally "openings, openings, hollows, hollows." The prayer even has some subtle humor. One Hebrew euphemism for restroom (itself a euphemism in English) is *bet kisei*—the place of the chair—which I see reflected in the reference to *kisei k'vodecha*, God's throne of glory. And of course the message is clear. The human body is complex and designed with wisdom. The slightest rupture and all of our plans, all of our pretension would fall apart. Have you ever tried to learn, or teach, when your body was disrupted? The "lower" supports the "higher;" it is essential for it.

We are so lucky for the body we often snicker about. One time, on a long meditation retreat, I was sitting in my room, perfectly content. The mind was blissfully quiet, and I thought to myself, "I could stay here forever. I don't need anything." Then I realized that I had to go to the bathroom—and that if I didn't go, I would experience a lot of physical pain, within a very short period of time. Maybe I could last an hour, or two, but at some point I would have to either get up and go to the bathroom or soil myself and endure the consequences. The point is: we're not nearly so independent of the body as we sometimes think. The toilet is the great equalizer, the great humanizer. And also a miracle.

It's interesting, in this regard, that the Talmud in *Berachot* 60b records a debate between the Rabbis as to what the blessing should actually say: one, Rabbi Sheshet, wished to emphasize the positive ("who acts wondrously"), another, Rav, the absence of the negative ("who heals all flesh"). The compromise was to say both phrases, recognizing both the presence of embodied miracles and their fragility. Far more aware than we are of the body's susceptibility to damage and disease, the Rabbis believed that angels accompanied them to the restroom, to keep them from harm. Could we cultivate such gratitude today?

Making *Asher Yatzar* part of your daily practice is one way to start. It's easily memorized, and easily photocopied onto a small piece of paper. You have occasion to recite it every day. And it only takes a moment—just long enough to cultivate gratitude and wonder based on the small miracles of the body.

Another option is to find your own language of blessing. This poem, *Asher Yatzar*, written by Rabbi Rachel Barenblat and published in *Zeek*, a journal that I edit, is a good example of how Jewish prayer shifts and evolves. I include it here in the hopes that her voice might inspire yours.

> Blessed is the breath of life
> who formed and animates this body:
>
> its myriad organs and tissues,
> protrusions, bones and sinews;
>
> winter skin so dry my calves rub bloody,
> flesh flushed with rhythm and heat;
>
> curve of hip distinguishing me
> from my mother whose pants need belting;
>
> breasts that sing, rubbed
> in concentric circles with shea butter;

nipples which will never know jewelry
because they flinch even at clip-ons;

nailbeds a reincarnation
of my grandmother's long fingers;

tiny dunes of bicep I have labored
to bring into being and maintain;

narrow feet which fit snug
only in the most expensive of shoes;

wrists and ankles I can encircle
with thumb and forefinger;

nose and mouth that together savor
venison, real vanilla, green tea;

hair so limp and fine I still use
Johnson & Johnson's baby shampoo;

all the weird, wet, noisy orifices
I need daily but can't understand.

How often do I remember
who sustains all of this, without ceasing?

If my bowels were to fail, or my kidneys,
pancreas, vision ... ? Doctors would stitch and sew,

but it wouldn't be easy
and You'd still have to prop me up

as You do today and every day.
Blessed are you, creator of embodied miracles.

Toilet Zen: Meditation for the Restroom

As we've seen, there are many ways to practice body-centered spirituality. One is the path of blessing, using our bodily experience to cultivate wonder. Another is simply to become more receptive to what is happening in life, using the body as an anchor. In a way, the two practices are like the two triangles of the Jewish star. Blessings, kabbalistic intentions, and contemplations elevate the body, the earth, to the heavens; they raise up our experience to God. Mindfulness brings heaven down to earth; it allows God to be experienced.

For many, practicing mindfulness on the toilet will be difficult, absurd, or even impossible. I especially encourage such people to give it a try; often where we laugh, or cry, the deepest of teachings are hidden. If we can acknowledge our discomfort, rather than be controlled by it, "toilet Zen" can be a wonderful, embodied spiritual practice.

The first step is to *subtract*—to not do. There are all sorts of Jewish prohibitions around what you can and can't do in the bathroom. Generally, you can't do anything—can't talk, can't study Torah, can't even think of sacred matters.[6] Let's extend that to thinking any thoughts at all. Instead of reading, Blackberrying, or talking on the telephone (come on, admit it), take the time as personal, spiritual time. You don't have to do this *despite* being in the restroom—you can do it *because* you're in the restroom. We are biologically wired, by God or evolution or both, to enjoy the process of excretion. It makes sense; the pleasure is an added incentive to tend to our bodily needs and not neglect or postpone them. All the awkwardness, the historically conditioned fears of dirtiness and contamination—let them arise if they need to, and then come back to the body.

So, as before: Stop doing other things, let the mind take a vacation, and then take notice of the sensations in the body as well as any feelings that come up with them. You don't have to push away feelings or thoughts; just note them and then return to the physical sensations. Let yourself fully experience this natural process, from beginning to end. At the end, "check in" with your body to note relaxation that wasn't present just a few moments ago. Throughout, cultivate an inner silence and a perspective from which you are just witnessing whatever is going on. Remember, the point of all this is simply to ask: what is going on, and how can I be with it? And the Jewish part is: what's going on is What Is—YHVH—and you can be with It if you open the doors of perception.

As with eating meditation, bathroom mindfulness leads to a natural arising of gratitude, which in turn enables a richer, deeper recitation of the *Asher Yatzar* blessing. Recall from Chapter 1 that when you eat mindfully, you enjoy more, and gratitude arises more naturally. So, too, in this case: when you are mindful, you can actually experience the pleasurable sensations of going to the bathroom (rather than stories in the mind), and thus experience gratitude more naturally. Give yourself a vacation from thought.

Every day we turn bread into human and perfectly sift out the refuse. We've got dissolving and filtering systems in our bellies more complicated than anything technology has constructed. And yet we're often too busy, or too ashamed, to be amazed by them. Toilet Zen doesn't make good conversation. But it makes a great three-minute retreat.

❈   ❈   ❈   ❈

6
Sex

I once heard a modest man bemoan the fact that it is human nature to have physical pleasure from sex. He preferred that there be no feeling of pleasure at all, so that he could have sex solely to fulfill the command of his creator ... and I thought that way myself ... Later, however, God favored me with a gift of grace, granting me understanding of the true meaning of sanctification during sexual intercourse: that it comes precisely from feeling physical pleasure. This secret is wondrous, deep and awesome.

Rabbi Baruch of Kosov[1]

Did you turn here first? Sexuality captures our attention, thanks to aeons of evolution and culture. Individually, it triggers us, inviting both judgment and excitement. Communally, our culture is obsessed with sex—not despite America's puritanical denigration of sexuality, but precisely because of it. The more liberation, the more condemnation; and the more condemnation, the more titillation. Sex is the sacrament that's been turned into sin—and from there, into innuendo, industry, and obsession.

So where, in this mess, can we find an embodied spiritual path that both embraces sexual expression and pursues the holy?

The first step is to become aware of attitudes of condemnation and comparison, both of which tend to define sexuality in terms of something it isn't or shouldn't be, rather than what it is. Our culture provides a toxic soil for nurturing healthy, spiritual sexuality, and years of cultural conditioning, guilt, and assumptions are not quickly erased—not because guilt is what we "really" feel "deep down," but simply because guilt, judgment, shame, and the rest are what most of us have been taught the longest. It's pointless to deny that, in our culture, religion and sexuality are opposed to one another, even though in the Jewish tradition they are anything but. So, what's needed is neither a denial nor an embrace of our culture's sexual hang-ups, but an openness, a curiosity, and a witness-consciousness as we explore how to know God through Jewish sacred sexuality.

Second, in approaching Jewish teachings around sexuality, the difference between what Rabbi Zalman Schachter-Shalomi calls "restoration" and "renewal" becomes very apparent. A person looking to restore some imagined past Judaism, in which everything was better than it is today, will hold fast to a literal reading of literal laws, even when this literal reading is amplified by generations of commentary far more stringent than the original text. A person looking to renew Judaism, however, looks to the teachings of the past and attempts to *translate* them into the present. The difference is in how we read. For example, in the case of sexuality, a restorationist must say that no sexual activity outside of (heterosexual) marriage can be condoned. Indeed, even within marriage, additional layers of law constrain sexual expression to procreative acts only. So, if our definition of "kosher sex" is limited to the proscriptions of Byzantine or Medieval Judaism, the band of acceptable sexual expression is narrow indeed. (Then again, it would also include polygamy, the dominant form of Jewish family relationship for the majority of Jewish history; most literalists are selective literalists.)

However, the alternative does not have to be rudderless hedonism, with no thought of spirituality, ethics, or holiness. Renewal, rather than restoration, takes seriously the impulses behind past laws and practices, even as it understands the historical contexts in which those impulses were expressed. For instance, there are at least two ways to read the Talmudic edict that a man must make love to his wife every day, unless under certain circumstances. One is to read the rule as being about husband and wife. Another is to translate the sex-positive injunction into the meaningful relationships we hold today.

Just as the Talmudic Rabbis required frequent, healthy sexual activity within their world, so should we in ours.

Obviously there is a tendency in this approach to shape our "translation" to be whatever we want it to be. That is why discernment and seriousness are required. Sometimes the result may seem more lenient; other times, as regarding polygamy or the Talmud's approval of marriage to nine-year-old girls, more strict. The key is to maintain a serious commitment to our tradition's sexual values, even as the containers for those values evolve. Of course, sages from previous generations would likely be shocked to have their ideas applied to unmarried partners, to gay people, or to any context outside a committed, dyadic relationship. But they would also be shocked by the Internet, cars, and television.

Sex Is Holy

Let's begin with first principles. The body has been wired for sexual pleasure—and if by God, then clearly God desired that sex be delightful. The question is what to do about it. In other chapters, we began with the body and then moved to the heart and mind. But because the pure sensations of bodily pleasure are, in our world, so clouded with concept and guilt, we must move in the opposite direction here. So let's begin with the mind: what does the tradition say about sex?

In the mainstream Jewish tradition, the common notion that sex is a necessary evil, or somehow opposed to religious sentiment, is almost wholly absent. On the contrary, the first commandment given to humankind is to be fruitful and multiply. And there is much more to sex than procreation—biblical heroes are intensely sexual beings, full of passion. The matriarchs Leah and Rachel use aphrodisiacs on their husband, Jacob, with no inkling in the text that passion, in and of itself, is wrong. Sarah's beauty is celebrated, Joseph's is renowned. Of course, when passion leads to ethical transgression—as when King David's lust for Bathsheba causes him to have her husband killed in battle—the Bible is unambiguous in its condemnation. But nowhere is there a notion that sex *itself* should be avoided.

This is not to say that sex in the Bible is simple. On the contrary, as scholars have noted, the Bible depicts sex as that which is *kadosh* (sacred, set apart, holy) and also that which can contaminate, even destroy. Fecundity and genealogy are central preoccupations, especially in passages that regulate priestly behavior. *Taharah* means both purity and pregnancy; *tumah* refers to both impurity and menstruation. Sex isn't simple, and it isn't merely kosher—it's powerful, magical, dangerous, holy.

So, too, in the Talmudic tradition, where sex is celebrated, feared, regulated, and endlessly discussed. First, most of the Rabbis frowned on celibacy. The Talmud in *Yevamot* 8:7 records Rabbi Eleazar ben Azariah as saying that "anyone who does not engage in procreation nullifies the Divine image." Yet Talmudic sex is much more than procreation. If the tales in the Talmud are any indication, our sages were passionate beings whose attitude toward sexual matters ranged from boastful pride (even about the size of their anatomy)[2] to extreme reverence for beauty and its power to bring about inspiration or calamity. The Talmud is not prudish; it recommends foods for good sex (*Eruvin* 28a and *Kiddushin* 2b), discusses multiple orgasm (*Niddah* 13a) and the length of time required for sexual intercourse (*Sotah* 4a), frowns upon wearing clothes during sex (*Ketubot* 48a), and explicitly permits oral sex (*Nedarim* 20a–b). It is also insistent that a husband provide his wife with sexual pleasure during "her time" (*onatah*), listing the required frequency of sex according to the occupation of the husband: every day for those with no job, twice a week for laborers, once a week for mule drivers, once a month for camel drivers, once every six months for sailors.[3]

Within the Talmud's various parameters, sexual love is celebrated and sanctified. One of the *Sheva Brachot*, the seven blessings recited after a wedding, celebrates the "joy" of bride and groom, which, if other uses of the term are any indication, refers to the physical ecstasy of consummating the marriage.[4] The Talmud saw love of God as reflecting sexual love:

> Said Rav Ktina: "When the Israelites were coming on pilgrimage to the temple in Jerusalem the priests were folding up the curtains and showing them the two Cherubs that were in the midst of lovemaking with each other and telling them: 'See your love with God, like the love of masculine and feminine.'"[5]

Most importantly, unlike the chaste Adam and Eve in the Christian tradition, rabbinic sources include sex in paradise.[6] In short, for the Rabbis, sex is neither good nor bad; it's powerful.

In the Jewish mystical literature, we find a more complicated, but perhaps even more erotically affirming, trend. One might think that the Kabbalah, concerned as it is with higher states of consciousness, would have an ascetic impulse. After all, the less energy is disbursed in sexual activity, the more it's available for study, meditation, and yearning for the Divine. However, although asceticism was present in some kabbalistic movements, the dominant trend is that sexuality is holy; that sexual union embodies, actualizes, and reflects the fundamental dynamics of cosmic and even theological processes; and that union must be actualized to maintain the flow of the *shefa*, the divine effluence. For the Zohar, the masterpiece of Kabbalah, God, creation, the balance of energies in the world—all are understood through the prism of the union of opposites, a union reflective of and expressed in sexuality.[7] This is no mere metaphor: the world of the Zohar is a dynamic universe in which energies are always combining, breaking apart, and then combining anew. Human agency, including sexuality, is an essential part of this process: the process of God itself. We are not meant to *return* to God by leaving the body behind—celibacy was condemned by the Zohar as a practice of the "Edomite kings" who ruled in the Land of Israel but died without leaving heirs. Rather, the Zohar says that we are meant to *imitate* God, who creates, manifests into separation, and unites the separate back into One. For the Zohar and other texts, sexual union reenacts the union of the high priest into the holy of holies; the union of heaven and earth; holiness and presence. Exactly how those energies are united will vary from individual to individual, since all of us contain both masculine and feminine aspects.[8] But in general, manifestation, separation, and union are not just the ways of the birds and bees: they are the imitation of God.

Although we are still only speaking theoretically, theory is important here because if we can really intend that our sexual expression be holy, then we have already done a large share of the work. Over my years of teaching, I've met so many people who assume they have to repress their sexual selves in order to be "spiritual." I've also met people who lead very liberated sexual lives, but who assume that what they're doing isn't religiously or spiritually okay and partition the two halves of themselves apart. To be honest, I have done all of these myself. But the facts are the facts. We may live in a sex-crazed, sex-condemning society, but the Jewish religious tradition honors sexuality as healthy, powerful, and embodying the action of God in the world. Pleasure is not sinful; the body is not a tomb. Sex is capable of holiness.

So, the first step toward building a healthy ethic of sacred sexuality is separating the religious fact from the fantasy. This is especially true for modes of sexual expression that, over the centuries, have been condemned by religious authorities. Take the example of masturbation, regarded in many yeshivas as the worst possible sin, but which is known to be biologically harmless, and indeed part of sexual health for those without regular partners—apart from the psychological frustrations of repression, storing seminal fluids for prolonged periods can cause nonspecific prostatitis, a disorder once called "priest's disease." And where does this "great sin" come from? The Kabbalah, to be sure, despises masturbation, because it undermines the creative process that we have just described. But the Bible never mentions it at all.[9] The infamous story of Onan, son of Judah, who "spilled his seed" rather than fulfill the mitzvah of levirate marriage after the death of his brother, is about familial obligations, not masturbation; indeed, as his "spilling of seed" was in the context of interrupted intercourse, he didn't even masturbate. Likewise in the Talmud and Kabbalah, the concern is not masturbation, per se, but *hashcha'tat zerah*, the wasting of (male) seed, a prohibition that applies equally to sex with birth control, oral sex, and a variety of other activities that carry none of the shame of masturbation.[10]

But how many people know these sources? How many know that the kabbalistic obsession with wasted seed stems from ideas about the proper flow of *shefa*, divine effluence, and not diverting any of it to places of shadow, and that it applies equally to any form of nonprocreative sexual activity? How many know that these laws and myths originated in a time when marriage came immediately after puberty? The Talmudic Rabbis believed any man left unmarried over the age of eighteen to be liable to constant sin; one rabbinic legend tells of a *beit midrash* being infested with demons because the young pupils were not married off and thus had no outlet for their sexual energy. Wasted seed is, first and foremost, *misdirected* seed, and comes at the expense of consummating a man's marriage.

Such subtleties, like those surrounding the Levitical priestly code and its prohibitions on cultic sexuality, are scarcely noticed amid the crude distortions of contemporary religious-sexual discourse. The results can be disastrous. Masturbation is an obsession in many yeshivas—who's doing it, who isn't doing it, how much penance you have to do for it, and so on. For some, atonement means simply reciting Rabbi Nachman of Breslov's *Tikkun Klali*, a collection of ten psalms meant to rectify sexual sin, and immersing in the mikva (see Chapter 12). But for others, this shame is nothing less than a plague. By not including healthy sexuality within the realm of *kedushah*, it is consigned to the zones of shadow, impurity, and guilt, blocking the experience of God in the body and tormenting the soul. Even "kosher sex" can be filled with shame in this way. Rabbi David Ingber, a brilliant young teacher of integral Judaism, tells the story of a man who had been celibate until his marriage at the age of twenty-eight, in keeping with his interpretation of halacha. So strong was the association of sex with sin that the morning after his wedding night, he awoke paralyzed with guilt and shame—even though he had just entered the *kiddushin*, the holy of holies.

So, again, the first step is on the level of the mind: *birur*, separating out what comes from the tradition and what comes from other sources. The second step is on the level of the heart: working with shame.

Shame distorts not just sexuality but the entire personality—even repentance itself. For many years in my own life, as I struggled with my own sexuality, Yom Kippur was about one sin, and one sin only. Everything else—ethics, honesty, prayer—seemed to pale in comparison. And I know, from having spoken with people from all walks of life—Jews and Christians, rabbis and heretics, gays and straights— that I am not alone. The demon varies; it may be a past incidence of abuse, or one's own sexuality, or something as trivial (to some) as

masturbation. But the results are strikingly similar: rather than enhance our connection with the Divine, sexual shame shuts it down.
And the societal mirrors the individual: our pathologically sex-ob-
sessed popular culture goes hand in hand with our puritanically terri-
fied religious one. Afraid to be adult about our sexual selves, we use
the word "adult" as a label for the most puerile.

The problem is not with guilt itself, but how it is understood.
That the feeling arises now and then is only natural—at times, even
healthy. The problem is how much weight it's given, due to the conventional geology of the self in which some things are "deep down,"
and others are just "on the surface," and when you feel something
deep down, you're meant to believe that it's real. Actually, this entire
geology is flawed—deep down inside what? "Really" know how? All
that's present, in pangs of guilt or shame, are beliefs with different
emotional tones, and the feeling of "deeper" does not mean truer. It
just means longer held. This may seem like a simple point, but for me
it has been revolutionary. Yes, shame arises—because I was told for
twenty years that my desires were hated by God. Now I neither deny
nor obey the voice of shame. I neither subscribe to ignorance-based
sexual taboos nor abandon the notion of sexual ethics as an ideal.
Rather, I try to look closely, carefully, and honestly at the values, and
consequences, in play.

To return one last time to the example of masturbation, context is
everything. In partnership, it may well be harmful; if it diminishes
desire for one's lover, certainly it is a poor substitute for intimacy. But
condemning it in all contexts simply because of its harmful effects in
one is like condemning every candy bar because you shouldn't snack
before dinner. Constructing a healthy sexual ethic requires knowledge
on the level of the mind, honesty on the level of the heart, and close
spiritual attention to the way such ethics develop and how they function in your life. With such attention, and celebration, sexual ethics
can enliven sensual expression, not deaden it.

Before we move on, let's close this section not with theory, but
with poetry, to remind us of what we're talking about—theory is useful, but it can sometimes objectify what it seeks to explain. In contrast,

the Bible's Song of Songs is one of the most sensual love poems in world literature. I invite you to read these lines as slowly as you like:

> Like threads of scarlet are your lips;
> Your mouth is lovely.
> Like a segment of pomegranate
> Are your cheeks amid your hair.[11]

> Let my beloved enter his garden,
> and eat its choicest fruits.
> I have come to my garden, my dear one, my bridge,
> I have gathered my myrrh with my spices,
> I have eaten my honeycomb with honey,
> And drunk my wine with milk.[12]

> My beloved is fair, and flushed,
> Distinguished among the multitudes.
> His head is the finest gold,
> His hair is curled, raven-black.
> His eyes are like doves by the water-courses,
> Washed with milk, set in fullness.
> His cheeks are like a perfumed bed,
> Like banks of fragrant flowers.
> His lips are like lilies,
> Dripping with flowing myrrh.
> His hands are rods of gold, filled with emeralds,
> His belly is polished ivory, inlaid with sapphire.[13]

There is no shame here, no denial of the body in these sensual celebrations of the human form. Even if read allegorically (as some insist on doing), the Song of Songs knows all vicissitudes of love and loss, and all the eroticism of the real. Indeed, perhaps we can hold both the literal and the allegorical together. Mystical love is not a matter of substitution or sublimation; when I am present with the body of someone I love, the arms and legs I caress are the arms and legs of God, if I am present enough to perceive them as they are. They are not other than those of my lover, and yet they are not other than divine. As the great Kabbalist Rabbi Isaac of Acco is said to have taught, "one who does not have sexual desire is like a donkey, and less. Because it is from what is felt that one discerns the divine service."[14]

Practicing Sacred Sexuality
So, in practice, what does all of this mean?

Unfortunately there is no Jewish *kama sutra*. There are books like the *Iggeret Hakodesh*, the thirteenth-century "holy epistle" that celebrates the different intentions people may have in sex, and gives men advice like "Do not hasten to arouse passion until her mood is ready; enter with love and willingness so that she 'seminates' first." But it's more common to find statements of values rather than techniques. The *Shulchan Aruch*, for example, holds that "the enjoyment of sex is one of the pleasures of Shabbat."[15] It does not provide tips. Still, from such statements, we can derive several principles of sacred sexuality.

First, sacred sexuality is *attentive* sexuality. Being present and focusing the mind are as important in bed as on the meditation cushion. Rabbi Baruch of Sassov, for example, teaches that at the moment of sexual union, you must not think of anything else. Of course, the rabbi's injunction notwithstanding, we all know that even the most mundane, inappropriate thoughts can come up during sex, as well as thoughts involving other people, thus threatening the bond of intimacy. In either case, these "foreign thoughts" (to use the Jewish term) take us out of the real (What Is—YHVH) and into somewhere else. Don't be afraid to use the same mindfulness techniques we reviewed in earlier chapters, here in a different context: notice the thoughts, let them drop, don't judge, and come back to the physical sensations of the body. Over time, focused concentration can lead to intense experiences of sexual release, and mindful awareness can tune us into the needs and desires of our partners.

Second, sacred sexuality is *not about the ego*. Because of its effect on consciousness, sex is an opportunity to transcend the self—but you have to do the work by letting go. If sex is about mechanically satisfying egoistic needs, the needs will only multiply. As Rabbi Yochanan says in *Sukkah* 52b, "a man has a small organ; if he leaves it hungry, it is satisfied, and if he satisfies it, it remains hungry." But when sex stops being about feeding a hungry organ, when it is about energy, love, and present experience, then what I need, what I want, what I'm accustomed to, and what I am owed all melt into a play of energies. For many men especially, sex is often treated like an express train to one destination, with one desirable result. But sexual energy is not a train, and intimacy has no tracks. What would it be like if each moment could be enjoyed as its own fleeting delight? What if there were no beginning, middle, and end to intimacy—only different tones of love? Truly giving and truly receiving entail a certain kind of surrender (within the bounds of safety and consent, of course) that mirrors the surrender of the self in prayer. For example, the small mind might say, "I'm not the sort of person to shout/moan/sigh during sex." But that small mind can be discarded, and just as we can *daven* with an open heart, crying and laughing and singing beyond tears, so, too, is it possible to access parts of our sexual being that our personalities might otherwise put out of reach. Don't check your theology at the bedroom door. Leave the ego on the floor with your clothes and see Who emerges.

Third, sacred sexuality is *magical*, and deeply erotic. Religion is not merely about the polite and the refined; it is also, centrally, about the deep, difficult, visceral realities of life. It's sometimes remarked that there are no atheists in foxholes, because when death is so present, rationality is abandoned in favor of a deeper, primal cry. That cry should be present in ecstasy as well. We've learned that the Kabbalah sees the act of sexual union as embodying the unification of masculine and feminine potencies within the Divine. Very well, but what would it be like to *feel* that in lovemaking—to know that your sexual expression, in whatever form it takes, is a sacrament, a magical act with theurgical possibility? Kabbalah is not Tantra, and it is not particularly egalitarian either. But the impulse of sacred *eros*, like other kabbalistic ideas, can be captured and experienced. Setting intentions, creating depth with your partner, eye contact, play and receptivity, sacred *yichudim* (kabbalistic union intentions), and joining sexuality with contemplation of the Divine can all help to realize the union of which the Kabbalists speak. What would it mean for you?

Fourth, sacred sexuality is *holy*. To designate sacred space and time, traditional Jewish sources advise everything from washing the hands before and afterwards, as with any sacred act, to stating intentions aloud, giving *tzedakah* (charity), even studying Torah or meditating. One way to sanctify sexuality is to recite a blessing, out loud with your partner or quietly to yourself, prior to sex. Admittedly, it is unusual foreplay, but it is recorded that Rabbi Tzvi Hirsh of Ziditchov taught his disciples that "before sexual intercourse, they should give thanks to God, in their spoken language, for the pleasure that He created."[16]

Fifth, sacred sexuality is about *how*, not *what*; quality, not quantity; emotional positions as much as physical ones. Whether you are circulating energy throughout your body with massage and holotropic breath work or just kissing your beloved good night, the closeness of love arouses the closeness of the holy, if you choose it. As the saying goes, it's not what you've got, it's what you do with it. It doesn't matter what positions you've learned from videotapes if the mind is absent or trying to avoid guilt. There is no place devoid of God, say the Hasidim; put that into practice.

Finally, sacred sexuality is *connected* to values. The content may vary, from the traditional admonition that sex must always be in a committed relationship, to a more liberal ethics of honesty, the quality of emotional connection, and the play of human energies. As the Ishbitzer Rebbe says, one can never know the individual contours of another's path to *kedushah* (holiness). But sex disconnected from ethics will increase the disconnection. If this seems too indeterminate, rely on the Ten Commandments. If sex involves jealousy, theft, dishonesty, or the use of another person, then the alienation inherent in those acts will be strengthened by its association with the power of sex. On the other hand, if sex involves love, celebration, joy, and play, then the freedom and connection those activities contain will likewise be strengthened. Is it honest? Is it honoring, not degrading, the body? Is it playful? Joyous? Does it unite the energies of the body with the heart and the mind?

These are just some general principles—the particulars will depend upon you. Remember, this doesn't have to be so serious. Maybe you've heard that sex is a "double mitzvah" on Shabbat. It really is—once for the sex itself, and a second time for enjoying the Sabbath. Thus we learn that enjoyment is part of healthy sexuality. So enjoy! The core of embodied spirituality remains the same, regardless of the shape or flavor of sexual practice: bring the attention to the body, and let the body wake you up.

*   *   *   *

7
Mirroring the Divine

Man is all symmetrie,
Full of proportions, one limbe to another,
And all to all the world besides:
Each part may call the furthest, brother:
For head with foot hath private amitie,
And both with moons and tides.

George Herbert, "Man"[1]

The human being is a little world that includes within itself all
the powers found in all the worlds.

Malbim[2]

Thus far we've explored a certain irony: how it is possible to encounter a higher state of consciousness by focusing the attention on the physical being of the body. Precisely the most mundane activities, like eating, breathing, and using the bathroom, are the best opportunities to enact the historic drama of creation, revelation, and redemption.

Now I'd like to step back and look at context: at some of the ways in which the body is regarded in the Jewish esoteric tradition. This chapter is a departure from the previous ones, because it is less about practice than theory; it is full of maps and models, concepts and coincidences. However, contemplation of these maps both complements the experiential elements and is a spiritual practice in its own right.

Contemplation as a practice is not about the thrill of the occult, which reduces Jewish esoteric literature to a cosmic treasure hunt. Kabbalah is about receiving, transforming, and uniting heaven and earth—it's not Dungeons & Dragons. It's for this reason that I've waited to introduce it; though what we will learn in this chapter are core Jewish mystical teachings on the body, they can become a distraction if they are seen merely as ideas. This is, unfortunately, how much of Kabbalah is taught today: as a complex technology of the occult whose terms and conditions are studied like notes for an exam. However, when put into practice—through study, contemplation, and experience—the web of kabbalistic symbolism can be transformative. A red jacket is no longer just red; it signifies *gevurah*, the forces of containment, reception, and constriction. A name is no longer just letters; it is a font of mysteries, correspondences, and even magic. Obviously, an endless symbolic matrix can lead to pseudoscience, divination, and delusion. But it's also possible to immerse oneself so deeply in the symbolic matrix that consciousness shifts, and the deeper realities of everyday existence become more real than the superficial illusions. As Emerson said, "a leaf, a drop, a crystal, a moment of time is related to the whole, and partakes of the perfection of the whole. Each particle is a microcosm, and faithfully renders the likeness of the world."[3]

Contemplating the Miniature World

Microcosm parallels macrocosm. Even before the Kabbalah, the idea that the human being is an *olam katan*, or miniature world, had developed in rabbinic literature as well as in sources outside the Jewish tradition, including Plato, Plutarch, and Philo. Plato's *Timaeus*, for example, depicts a part-for-part homology between body and world, and Philo saw the orders of creation contained within the human form. These ideas later inspired Renaissance alchemics like Marsilio Ficino, Robert Fludd, Paracelsus, and Jacob Boehme, as well as the poetry and theology of John Donne. And within the Jewish tradition, the sources are plentiful, mapping the body onto the world's processes, the Torah's commandments, and the ethical trajectory of human life. Consider this text from *Avot de Rabbi Natan*, a third-century commentary on the Talmudic *Pirke Avot (Ethics of the Ancestors)*:

Rabbi Yosi the Galilean says: Whatever the Holy One, blessed be He,
    created in the world, He created in humankind ...
Forests in the world, forests of hair in humans
Beasts in the world, microorganisms in man,
Caves in the world, and caves in human ears
Winds in the world, and the wind of the breath
A sun in the world, and two suns in our foreheads
Foul waters in the world, and mucus in people
Salt water in the world, and saltwater tears
The flow of streams in the world; in people the flow of urine
Walls in the world: lips; Doors in the world: teeth
A firmament in the world, the tongue in the mouth
Sweet waters in the world, saliva in human beings
Stars in the world, and the glowing of cheeks
Towers in the world, and the tower of the neck
Masts in the world, and masts of man—the arms
Pegs in the world, fingers on the hands
A King of the world; the head of the body
Grape-clusters in the world, and breasts in people
Advisors in the world, kidneys in man
Millstones in the world, intestines in the body
Factories in the world, the spleen in us
Pits in the world, the navel in mankind
Living waters in the world, blood in human beings
Trees in the world, and bones in human beings
Hills, the buttocks; Mortar and pestle, the joints
Horses in the world, human legs
The Angel of Death in the world, man's "Achilles' heel"
Mountains and valleys in the world; and the human form, standing
    and falling.[4]

What is the point of such literature? Surely it is that the body is not a
random collection of bones and sinews, but a reflection of holiness,
and cosmic order. If you contemplate these teachings, they can lead to
a powerful sense of interconnectedness. Usually the body can feel quite
separate and distinct from everything else; orienting consciousness
toward these symbolic homologies can help bridge the gap. Of course,

we may not believe in them literally, as descriptions of the cosmic plan. I'm not sure that was ever the point. They are more like poetry, or song, pregnant with meaning notwithstanding the strictures of fact. Notice how the harmonies of nature correspond to the harmonies of human anatomy; how, like today's scientists of chaos theory and fractal geometry, these rabbinic poets saw microcosm reflecting macrocosm. Notice how worthy the body is of our attention (one text in *Pirkei de Rabbi Eliezer* even notes how "the human being is made of four colors: red for the blood, black for the bile, white for the bones, and yellow for the nerves."). And notice, finally, how our bodies are not so distant from natural beauty as we sometimes may believe.

In Jewish tradition, the human body mirrors not just the natural universe but the sacred spaces and objects of Judaism. In this midrash, the body is analogized, part for part, to the *mishkan*, the holy tabernacle:

> "Gold" is the life-force (*nefesh*); "silver," the body; "copper," the voice ...
> "blue" (*techelet*) is the veins and "purple" (*argaman*) the flesh;
> "red," the blood; "flax," the intestines;
> "goat hair," the hair; "ram skins dyed red," the skin of the face;
> "tachash skins," the scalp;
> "shittim wood," the bones;
> "oil for lighting," the eyes;
> "spices for the anointing oil and for the sweet incense," are the mouth
>   which breathes and the palate which tastes ...
> "shoham stones and gemstones for setting," the kidneys and the heart.[5]

The Torah and commandments are likewise inscribed upon the human form. The Talmud famously maps the 248 positive commandments of the Torah onto the 248 limbs of the body, and the 365 negative ones onto the days of the solar year, for a total of 613.[6] Rabbi Eliezer Azikri, a sixteenth-century Kabbalist who wrote the gorgeous poem "Yedid Nefesh," categorizes all the mitzvot by the body part to which they correspond in his masterpiece, the *Sefer Haredim*. The heart, for example, has the mitzvot of faith, prayer, love of God, and repentance. The mouth speaks kindly, confesses, and refrains from false oaths. The legs walk to visit the sick, refuse to bow to idols, and stand before one's elders. The sexual organs honor circumcision, "family purity," and healthy sexuality. And these are but a few examples. As Rabbi Nachman of Breslov would later write, "each mitzvah corresponds to a different organ, limb, or vessel of the body."[7] If the self has fallen into greed, envy, or despair, even small teachings—such as the Vilna Gaon's that the ten fingers represent the first tablets of the Ten Commandments and the ten toes represent the second set; or the Malbim's that the two tablets mirror the cerebrum and the cerebellum—can bring it back.

So the body mirrors both the natural universe and the religious universe of Jewish law and tradition. It also, in many sacred texts, reflects the soul. Today we retain the notion that the heart, an organ that pumps blood, is involved with emotions. But in Jewish folk wisdom, other organs play intellectual, emotional, and spiritual roles as well. The kidneys, for instance, are often depicted as the seat of wisdom and advice, for better or worse. "Who put wisdom in the kidneys? Who gave understanding to the mind?" says God to Job.[8] "You desire truth in my kidneys, and teach me wisdom in my heart," says Psalm 51:8. And in the Talmud we find that "A man has two kidneys, one of which prompts him to good, the other to evil ... the kidneys prompt, the heart discerns, the tongue shapes [words], the mouth articulates."[9] Some contemporary sources update these ideas to our current understanding of the organs' functions. Tamar Frankiel and Judy Greenfield's *Minding the Temple of the Soul: Balancing Body, Mind and Spirit through Traditional Jewish Prayer, Movement and Meditation* (Jewish Lights), for example, notes that "kidneys filter and detoxify, cleansing the blood, separating what is good for our bodies from what is bad" and thus "symbolize the whole process of separating the useful from the not-useful."[10]

In this way, observing the body can become a contemplative practice—for the heart as well as the mind. For example, when the Talmud says that "the liver becomes angry; the gallbladder emits fluids to pacify that anger,"[11] I think of how I struggle with anger myself, and how, when I just allow it to arise and pass naturally, an almost chemical change seems to take place. It just needs time. Or consider this teaching from the midrashic anthology *Bereshit Rabba*, which sees in the body the simple truth that some things are up to us, and some are not:

> Rabbi Levi said: There are six organs in the body that serve man; three are under his control and three are not. The eye, the ear, and

the nose are independent of his will: he sees, hears, and smells even things he doesn't want to. The mouth, hand, and foot are subject to his will; he can speak decent things or slander and curse; his hands can fulfill the mitzvot of God or they can steal and kill; his feet can take him to the theater and the circus or to the house of worship and the house of study.[12]

It is Rabbi Nachman and his leading disciple, Reb Noson, though, who most developed the art of contemplating the body as a reflection of higher realities. In their writing digestion mirrors the process of purification and teaches patience as we wait for it to unfold. The heartbeat reflects the movement of *ratzo v'shuv*, fleeing and returning to God: "The pulse beats rhythmically. Sometimes the beat of the pulse draws a person to serve God; at other times it drives him away."[13] In general, as described in Chaim Kramer and Avraham Sutton's book *Anatomy of the Soul*, almost all of our psychic life is either actually or symbolically located in the body. Anger is rooted in the liver;[14] sadness in the spleen.[15] Speaking falsehood is a biochemical problem: "No one can speak absolute truth until he has cleansed his bloodstream of its impurities, which indicate falsehood. Conversely, no one speaks falsehood without first polluting his bloodstream."[16] And spiritual changes can effect physical ones:

> The festival of Shavuot is a cure for the lungs. The five lobes of the lungs correspond to the five books of the Torah. Each year on Shavuot, we receive the Torah anew. Thus, Shavuot is an especially beneficial time for one's lungs; at this time, we can receive "new life."[17]

As science, these maps may be of little interest. As a contemplative practice, however, I find that when I deeply immerse myself into them, consciousness shifts. Suddenly, a finger is not a finger; it's a commandment. In its very form I see the lighting of the candles, the washing of hands, and other ways to serve God. This path of symbolization is very different from bare mindfulness of the body; it unites the facts of reality with an entire conceptual matrix. But, like Rabbi Nachman, the Buddhist notices in the body the great truths of the wider world—impermanence in the changes of the body, suffering in its perceived inadequacies, and the emptiness of separate phenomena by means of its composite nature. Rabbi Nachman is obviously more involved with myth and symbol, but both contemplatives share that strange combination of a groundedness in actual experience and a transcendence of its conventional categorization.

Finally, the homology between body and world may also be reversed; if the body mirrors the universe, then the universe mirrors the body. This metaphor has a long history, from the "body politic" in Plato's *Republic* and Judah Halevi's *Kuzari* to recent "organismic" models of the cosmos and society. The notion that our differences contribute to the well-being of the whole is a useful metaphor for pluralism: the liver does not become "better" by being more like a heart, and the elbow should not be just like the spleen. Since uniformity is not what we see in our own bodies, and not what we should expect in the world, redemption comes not when everyone is just like me, or when we are all the same, irrespective of ethical or cultural differences. Rather, if the body is any indication, strength means differentiation—like the unity-in-multiplicity that is reading these words right now.

Sefer Yetzirah: The Book of Creation

Is the structure of the universe random or ordered? Ancient, mythical Judaism saw the forces of order and the forces of chaos as doing battle, with those of order emerging triumphant. Babylonian myths of the sky god slaying the primordial serpent, symbolic of order defeating chaos, are echoed in Israelite tales of the Leviathan, and perhaps even in Genesis, when YHVH creates order out of *tohu vavohu* (chaos) and light where darkness had been over the face of the deep. The word for "the deep" is *tehom*, and some scholars detect an echo of Tiamat, the primordial dragon whose slaughter allows the world to come into being. The belief underlying these myths is that the universe's structures, micro and macro, are ordered.

The *Sefer Yetzirah*, or Book of Creation, is the leading Jewish example of this idea. One of the oldest texts of Jewish esotericism, it dates back at least to the second century CE, and describes how the structure of the universe is created from the structure of language. Genesis merely says, "And God said ..." The *Sefer Yetzirah* spells out the words. Since all is created from the same matrix of letters and numbers, all reality shares the same fundamental construction. Consider the following charts, based on the twelve "simple" letters, the three "mother" letters, and the seven "double" letters (which have two pronunciations in Hebrew):

Letter	Sound	Zodiac	Month	Direction	Organ	Faculty
Heh	H	Aries	Nisan	East-Up	Right leg	Speech
Vav	V	Taurus	Iyyar	East-North	Right kidney	Thought
Zayin	Z	Gemini	Sivan	East-Down	Left leg	Movement
Chet	Ch	Cancer	Tammuz	South-Up	Right arm	Vision
Tet	T	Leo	Av	South-East	Left kidney	Hearing
Yood	Y	Virgo	Elul	South-Down	Left arm	Action
Lamed	L	Libra	Tishrei	West-Up	Gall bladder	Sexuality
Nun	N	Scorpio	Cheshvan	West-South	Intestine	Smell
Samech	S	Sagittarius	Kislev	West-Down	Intestine	Sleep
Ayin	(glottal)	Capricorn	Tevet	North-Up	Liver	Anger
Tzadi	Tz	Aquarius	Shvat	North-West	Stomach	Taste
Qoof	K	Pisces	Adar	North-Down	Spleen	Laughter

Letter	Sound	Element	Season	Body
Aleph	(silent/breath)	Air	In-between seasons	Chest
Mem	M	Water	Cold seasons	Belly
Shin	Sh	Fire	Hot seasons	Head

Letter	Sound	Planet	Day of week	Aperture of Body	Quality
Bet	V/B	Saturn	Sabbath	Right eye	Wisdom & foolishness
Gimmel	G/G	Jupiter	Sunday	Right ear	Wealth & poverty
Dalet	D/Dt	Mars	Monday	Right nostril	Fertility & barrenness
Kaf	Ch/K	Sun	Tuesday	Left eye	Life & death
Peh	F/P	Venus	Wednesday	Left ear	Dominion & slavery
Resh	R/R	Mercury	Thursday	Left nostril	Peace & harm
Tav	Th/T	Moon	Friday	Mouth	Grace & ugliness

Simply imagining a world in which the physical structure of the body was thought to mirror the astrological signs is fascinating, even if it is hard to comprehend as "science." But how to put the *Sefer Yetzirah*'s theory into practice has been a matter of debate for centuries, and the study of the text is a life's work. We don't even know what kind of book it is. Some regard it as a book of astrology. Some regard it as a guide to meditation—one practice based on it is contained in Chapter 14 of this book. Others consider it a guide to health. Indeed, for some, the Kabbalah offers far more insight into the universe's structure than does modern science. One physician friend of mine treated the renowned Kabbalist Rabbi Yitzhak Kadouri who was over the age of one hundred, prescribing various medications for a heart condition. The rabbi laughed and said that while he would take the medication, the true condition was far deeper than a physician could diagnose. Perhaps how each of us makes use of the *Sefer Yetzirah* depends on personality, or even mood.

I invite you to consider the charts above in any number of ways. You might inquire whether the processes of your body shift with the seasons, in the way the *Sefer Yetzirah* describes. You might read it purely as myth, and view your body in a similarly imaginative way. You might try to experience the four elements, not as scientific realities, but as perceptual ones; for example, you can learn to experience bodily phenomena as manifestations of earth, air, fire, and water, rather than as personal events that necessarily evoke emotional responses. Or, as with the contemplations in the previous section, you might simply appreciate the poetic ways in which the human body was conceived by our forebears.

As for the deeper mysteries of the *Sefer Yetzirah*, an exploration of them would take us far afield. If this path piques your interest, I encourage you to learn more from the books in the bibliography or on the website www.learnkabbalah.com, which I created for new students of Kabbalah. For now, I invite you to ponder the homologies between bodily organs and planets, sounds and emotions, and see what insights arise; the possibilities are only as bounded as creativity itself.

Embodying the Ten *Sefirot*

Why does the world have the texture that it does? Today, we might answer the question in terms of physics, chemistry, and biology, explaining how a universe of subatomic particles manifests as a world with tables, trees, and people. We might explain our emotions in terms of neurology, the colors of a sunset as particulate matter. Naturally, the Kabbalists of the thirteenth century approached the question differently. They did not know about subatomic particles, but they did have a sense that the entirety of the universe was but one impossibly complex entity—and they asked why it takes as many forms as it does. In their terms, what is the world, if the *Ein Sof*, the Infinite, is all there is?

One answer to this question was formulated in terms of *sefirot*, an untranslatable word that, in the words of Moshe Cordovero, one of the great Kabbalists, may be understood in this way:

> In the beginning, Ein Sof emanated ten *sefirot*, which are of its essence, united with it. It and they are entirely one. There is no change or division in the emanator that would justify saying it is divided into parts in these various *sefirot*. Division and change do not apply to it, only to the external *sefirot*.
>
> To help you conceive this, imagine water flowing through vessels of different colors: white, red, green and so forth. As the water spreads through those vessels, it appears to change into the colors of the vessels, although the water is devoid of all color. The change in color does not affect the water itself, just our perception of the water. So it is with the *sefirot*. They are vessels, known, for example, as *Hesed*, *Gevurah* and *Tiferet*, each colored according to its function, white, red, and green, respectively, while the light of the emanator—their essence—is in the water, having no color at all. This essence does not change; it only appears to change as it flows through the vessels.
>
> Better yet, imagine a ray of sunlight shining through a stained-glass window of ten different colors. The sunlight possesses no color at all but appears to change hue as it passes through

the different colors of glass. Colored light radiates through the window. The light has not essentially changed, though so it seems to the viewer. Just so with the *sefirot*.[18]

The energies of the *sefirot*—the colors of the glass, in Cordovero's metaphor—give shape and apparent form to the world we experience: the feeling-tones of fear, love, and harmony; physical manifestations of hardness, softness, warmth, and cool. For the Kabbalists, they explain how the world came into being, how the dynamic God of the Bible can coexist with the perfect God of the philosophers, and why, if the *Ein Sof* surrounds and fills everything in the world, we still have the experience of tables, chairs, people, and sky. Of course, explaining the *sefirot* themselves is not simple, as they comprise a nest of cosmological, theological, and literary speculation.[19] However, our focus here is more limited: on how the *sefirot* may be related to experientially, and form a useful part of embodied spiritual practice.

Experientially, the *sefirot* may be understood intellectually, emotionally, physically, and spiritually. For example, when you become angry, and then you relax, and then you feel in balance, you probably use a roughly psychoanalytical language to explain what has happened. Kabbalistically, however, what has happened is an excess of one sefirotic energy balanced by another and brought into harmony. Moreover, since microcosm parallels macrocosm, the world—not just the self—is made up of lovingkindness and judgment, as much as it is comprised of atoms. The philosophical God does not feel, does not change, and does not interact with the world of form. But the *sefirot* are prisms of feeling, dynamism, and energy—and by learning to perceive them, we can experience our lives more subtly.

Finally, the *sefirot* also exist on the plane of the body, which will be our focus here. As in the *Sefer Yetzirah*, the Kabbalah of the *sefirot* understands the structure of the human body to reflect the structure of the universe, and the Godhead. This, the Kabbalists teach, is literally God in your body: anatomy reflects and embodies divinity.[20] Here is the famous diagram of the *sefirot* as they are mapped onto the body:

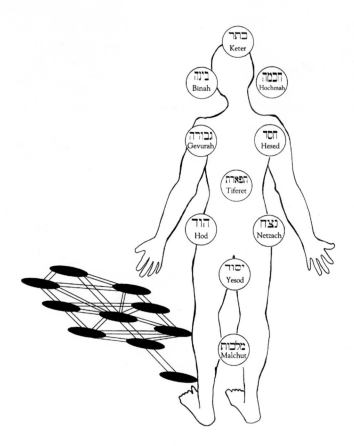

The *sefirot* are essentially in three triads, plus the tenth *sefirah* of *malchut*, which experiences separation from the other nine. From one perspective, the first triad is that of the mind; the second that of the heart; and the third that of the body. But since all ten *sefirot* exist on all four worlds, approaching the *sefirot* from an embodied perspective also means that the top three are "the mind of the body," the middle three are "the heart of the body," and the lower three are "the body of the body." Already you might begin to perceive how the *sefirot* work to fine-tune our perceptual apparatus, drawing ever more fine attention to the details of experience. "Spirituality," in its New Age forms, is often derided as vague, but the Kabbalah is anything but.

So let's take a closer look. The top triad of the *sefirot* is mapped onto the head. *Keter*, meaning "crown," stands for the transrational; it links the mind to that which is beyond. In the world of *keter*, there is only the *Ein Sof*, with the most subtle intention to expand into manifestation. *Hochmah*, meaning wisdom, is like a point: it has no dimension of its own, but it is the beginning point for everything else. In the body, it is mapped onto the right side of the brain. *Hochmah* is that "higher wisdom" that other traditions call primordial awareness; it is the first quality to proceed from Nothingness. This noetic quality of the universe—that every leaf "knows" when to fall in the autumn, that every atom "knows" how to organize itself—is, for the Kabbalists, the most refined quality of the manifested world. If you imagine the emanation of the *sefirot* in terms of the big bang, *hochmah* is the singularity with no size but with the laws of nature already instantiated. There is nothing there, but there is the divine wisdom that organizes all of creation. Finally, *binah*, meaning understanding, is a partner to *hochmah* and mapped onto the left side of the brain. The *sefirot* are often gendered (sometimes multigendered), and their interaction is often depicted as a series of erotic interchanges. In this case, *hochmah* is male and *binah* is female, the divine womb, the generative principle of the rest of the universe. *Binah* gives birth to the *sefirot*, and thus to the world of manifestation itself. She is the concealed, hidden, supernal divine mother; the ground of space and time, ready to give birth to the world.

From an embodied perspective, it's fascinating to observe that, centuries before neuroscience, Kabbalah had an idea of "right brain" (*hochmah*; point; intuition) and "left brain" (*binah*; reason), although, as usual in the Kabbalah, the genders of each are the inverse of what we Westerners might expect. Because they are located in the head, these centers of energy—if we may use the term loosely—are less obviously embodied than others. But consider how "the mind of the body" functions in daily life—how, for example, we can balance the rational wisdom of Western medicine with the intuitive wisdom of holistic medicine. Or how the principles must be balanced in spiritual practice; too much rationality and the tree of life is buried underground, but too little and it is blown over by the wind.

The second triad in the tree of the *sefirot* is that of *hesed, gevurah*, and *tiferet*, or lovingkindness, judgment, and harmony. I sometimes express the dynamic relationship between *hesed* and *gevurah* in terms of human relationship. We might suppose that all we want in the world is more *hesed*, more lovingkindness, but imagine a relationship in which one partner is *only* expressing *hesed*, doing everything for the other partner, not caring for his or her own needs, and trying all the time to help, nurture, feed, support, guide, and provide for the other. Quickly, such a relationship will become dysfunctional. Eventually, the other partner will form a dependence on the first one, or will feel smothered, or will yearn for self-expression and some degree of self-sufficiency. A relationship in which separateness is completely lost is not a healthy one. So even in the case of two lovers, *gevurah*—restraint, holding back—is necessary. Usually, our world does indeed need more love—not more judgment. But the point is balance, *tiferet*—harmony, beauty, and compassion.

In the body, *hesed* represents suppleness, *gevurah* constriction and strength. *Hesed* is yoga, *gevurah* weight-training. *Hesed* is relaxation, *gevurah* is work. And *hesed* is the right arm, *gevurah* the left. *Tiferet* is in the middle, the balance point, and the center of the body. Now, that *hesed* and *gevurah* are two faces of *tiferet* is easy enough to understand. But there is book knowledge and there is body knowledge—and the *sefirot* are the body divine. Kabbalistic wisdom can often be quite complex, but the deepest truths, for me, are usually very simple, even banal. Thus the crucial element is not what you know, but how you know it. Put another way, secret wisdom, in the Kabbalah, is not knowledge so complicated that only the few can comprehend it. Rather, secret wisdom is experiential wisdom, and it is not committed to writing because it can only be known firsthand.

So, I'd invite you to try this relatively simple meditation that I created based on the embodied nature of *hesed*, *gevurah*, and *tiferet*. I've led it many times on retreats and have found that students suddenly "get" the *sefirot* in a way they hadn't before. If the *sefirot* are feeling abstract for you, try learning them with your body. You can do it now, after reading these instructions:

1. Stand up, feet shoulder-width apart, so that you are comfortable and grounded. Clear your mind of distraction by

paying attention to ten breaths in a row; quiet down and settle back.

2. Then, bring to mind an image that, for you, evokes lovingkindness, warmth, and comfort. Perhaps it is a person, or a place—or maybe a memory of a particular time. Really try to stand in the presence of this image, experiencing *hesed*.

3. Now, use your right arm to express the sensation you are having. Don't worry if it seems strange; just give it a try, with an open, curious mind—and closed eyes. Move your arm, let it dance, or sway, or caress—whatever feels intuitive for you. If nothing's coming up, fake it. Stay with this for at least a minute, really allowing the right side of your body to express the sensation. Then, after a while, let it come to rest.

4. Next, the harder part: direct your attention to a source of difficulty and pain in your life. It may, again, be a person or a situation; perhaps it's an illness, or a disagreement, or a difficult time in your past or present. Be fearless: go into the pain and feel *gevurah*: tightness, constriction.

5. Express it with your left arm. Maybe you want to clench a fist, or push something away; maybe your muscles will tighten. As before, just follow the intuition, shamelessly, exaggeratedly, and with open curiosity. See how your left arm feels, and really stay with it for at least a full minute.

6. Now, without stopping the movement in your left arm, restart the movement in your right at the same time. Both arms are now moving, and you can allow your torso to move with them, mediate between them, dance with them. As before, don't judge; just let yourself have this experience. Devote the same attention to your spiritual development as you do to your intellectual or physical development. Feel these two energies, *hesed* on the right

and *gevurah* on the left, and notice that, whatever its source, the *experience* is real. You *can* cultivate this consciousness and express it in the body. Feel the suppleness, the love, the smoothness on the right, and the strength, the boundary, the constriction on the left. Go for it!

7. And then: clap your hands together, hold them there, and stand in stillness. With your body, know: Wisdom is not choosing the pleasurable over the difficult. Wisdom is in seeing the shadow as veiled light, uplifting it, integrating it. Stand for at least a full minute in this place of integration, being very attentive to the body and to thoughts and feelings arising in the mind. If you have a sensation of energy, notice it, follow it, be curious about it. If you're judging the practice, note that, but let go of it so you can see what it can teach.

It may take some time, but if you try this practice on a few occasions, I think you'll come to appreciate how the body can express the heart and reflect it back to us. That's what the middle triad of *sefirot* is: the heart in the body. Explore it.

The third triad of *sefirot—netzach*, *hod*, and *yesod*—are, from an embodied perspective, perhaps the most essential, since they represent the embodiment and actualization of all that has gone before. These are the principles that give clothing and form to the dreams of the mind and the yearnings of the heart.

Netzach means "eternity." It is the aspect of revelation that stretches horizontally through time, and it is the attribute of endurance—in the sense both of "God's mercy endures forever" and the more common usage of endurance through difficult times. *Hod*, its complement, means "splendor." It is the aspect of revelation that exists vertically, as a peak experience, or contact with that which is transcendence. It is the source of what Abraham Joshua Heschel called radical amazement: the shattering encounter with the numinous that engenders wonder. More simply, *hod* is inspiration; *netzach* is perspiration. *Hod* is in those moments we sing, shout, dance, and burn. *Netzach* is the rest of the time. *Hod* is in those perfect evenings on tropical islands, where the sun sets over the water and the night is filled with love. *Netzach* is the times you pick your lover up at the airport. To paraphrase Rabbi Zalman Schachter-Shalomi, *hod* is like a Ferrari; *netzach* like a Jeep. Or to paraphrase psychologist and teacher Jack Kornfield, *hod* is the ecstasy; *netzach* is the laundry.

In our culture, there is often a tendency to flee from *netzach* and embrace only the *hod*. Ours is an escapist culture, grounded in an economic system that endures precisely by providing lots of moments of mini-*hod* (the SUV "born to be wild") to distract us from our *netzach* reality (driving to the shopping mall). Even in the spiritual world, it sometimes seems that mysticism is about ecstasy, not laundry, and that love is about passion, not reliability. This is not the kabbalistic approach. We never want to value one *sefirah* over the other; we want to value the balance and dynamism between them. In relationship, a partnership that lacks *hod* lacks spice; it will ultimately be unsatisfying. But a partnership without *netzach* is a partnership with great sex but no stability. In the body, *netzach* can be felt in a steady diet, good exercise, putting one foot in front of the other; *hod* is the gourmet meal, great sex, and dancing. *Hod* moments give us the juice to keep going on; *netzach* is the going on itself.

In the kabbalistic schema, *netzach* and *hod* balance into *yesod*. If *tiferet* is the heart center, bringing together the various emotional energies to the core of inner balance, *yesod* is the sexual organ, bringing together the body's energies to the place of generativity (the Kabbalists did not have an idea of genetic material as we do, though it maps on quite well to *yesod*). In some charts of the *sefirot*, *yesod* is simply the phallus, and in many kabbalistic texts it does function in this way. But actually, *yesod* is the conduit between male and female energy, and as such includes both male and female anatomy. For a man, *yesod* can be understood as bringing together all the energies and projecting them out into the world. For a woman, it might be understood as bringing together all the energies so that their manifestation can be birthed.

This final triad is in the body and the physical world—not in what we hope or plan. For example, you may be feeling great *hesed*, but if it doesn't manifest through both *netzach* and *hod* to *yesod*—and out into *malchut*, the tenth *sefirah*, which corresponds to the actual products of your work—you haven't done anything. It's not the thought that counts—it's the deed that counts: the embodiment, the manifestation in *malchut*. *Netzach* and *hod* are the legs; without them, you don't get anywhere, no matter how wonderful your plans may be.

The *sefirot* are a web of associations, symbolic references, and divine potency. Each is a node of meaning, bringing together hundreds, if not thousands, of literary, cultural, physical, emotional, historical, theological, and magical concepts. When a Kabbalist hears the word "orchard," or "red," or "rainbow," he or she immediately associates it with the corresponding *sefirah*, and then with the dozens of other concepts that are likewise associated. Learning the *sefirot* is marinating the mind in a symbolic stew of divine interrelation, and engenders a uniquely kabbalistic mode of consciousness.

The *sefirot* can also be brought to our everyday experience. A week, for example, can be predominantly *netzach,* working, putting the body through its paces—or *hod*, vacationing and having fun. In your relationship with your partner, including your physical relationship, you may find yourself expressing more *hesed* or more *gevurah*, and you might consider ways to bring them into balance. The physical may be aligned with the emotional, or not. Your religious practice may need more intuition and spirit (*hochmah*), or more grounding in text and reasoning (*binah*). In your exercise practice, you may find yourself working in a slow and steady way (*netzach*) or pushing yourself in bursts of energy (*hod*).

There are myriad other maps of the *sefirot*—according to the Zohar, they are present on the face, on the hands, and even in the eyes, whose four colors correspond to *hesed* (white), *gevurah* (red), *tiferet* (black), and *malchut* (the iris's color).[21] It is easy to become bewildered by the complexity of it all. But if that happens to you, just come back. Feel the expansion of your chest when you inhale (*hesed*) and the contraction as you exhale fully (*gevurah*). There you are; there God is. It's as simple as that.

Looking in the Mirror

Human beings approach the infinite not only with the mind of the philosopher but also with the heart of the mystic and the imagination of the poet. From "Let us make humankind in our image" in Genesis through the anthropomorphism of the Kabbalah, Jewish texts imagine a symmetry between the human form and the Divine. Approached scientifically, such a notion makes little sense. But mythically, imaginatively, personally, it can give birth to poetry, and to insight.

What the Kabbalah teaches, above all, is that reality is deeper than appearance—and the more we see into reality, the more of its energies and forces we can bring into balance. And when mystics look into the infinite, there is a sense that something ineffable is looking back. In their attempts to describe the indescribable, humans in every culture have had recourse to their own experience, which is embodied, engendered, and ever-changing in form. And the deeper the exploration, the deeper the resonance of image. Some of the most powerful secrets of the Kabbalah, contained in the parts of the Zoharic literature called the Idra Rabba and Idra Zuta (the Greater Assembly and the Lesser Assembly), are conveyed in intimately, perhaps shockingly, detailed anthropomorphism, in passages that describe the hairs of God's beard and the shape of God's limbs. Like the *Shiur Komah*, the mysterious text containing measurements of the divine body, these texts can be shocking to those of us who were raised to believe that God has no form. But their insights are deep, psychoanalytically rich, and abundant in resonance and myth.

Studying such texts is itself a mystical practice, although they are difficult, obscure, and esoteric. Doing so invites the contemplation of how much, or how little, we really can know of the conditions of our lives. Ultimately, there is nothing we can say about God. But saying nothing about God leads us to forget why we wanted to speak in the first place. And so, we take up our mirrors, and try to reflect light into places that are dark.

• • • •

8

Exercising

Our physical demand is great. We need a healthy body. We dealt so much in soulfulness, we forgot the holiness of the body. We neglected physical health and strength; we forgot that we have holy flesh, no less than holy spirit.

Rav Kook[1]

Sweating is extremely beneficial, because it rids the body of polluting fluids ... Polluted fluids in the body cause depression; therefore sweating—that is, removing the pollution which leads to depression—brings joy.

Rabbi Nachman of Breslov[2]

If the state of the body affects the state of the mind, then it is obvious why a healthy diet and exercise are of great spiritual importance. At a bare minimum, maintaining the body's health enables us to focus, work, sing, dance, and pray. Notwithstanding the practices in many ascetically minded yeshivas today, which deliberately efface the body in favor of single-minded focus on study, learning Torah without proper nutrition is like reading with sunglasses on.

But exercise is of more than instrumental value. When the body is moved, stretched, and challenged, the self shifts. Rabbinic Judaism, reacting against the athletic cultures of Greece and Rome, tended to be ambivalent about exercise—although given that the rabbis were exceedingly careful about health, this ambivalence can only be understood in the context of a culture in which sport was part of a larger lifestyle, rather than part of an integrated approach to health. More recently, the notion of exercise as a spiritual discipline has a complicated modern history. In America, the advent of "muscular Christianity" in the nineteenth century brought with it the notion that serving the Lord meant strengthening the body. In the Jewish world, early Zionists like Max Nordau, reacting against the stereotype of the emaciated yeshiva student, created the idea of "muscular Jews," whose physical (and sexual) health would redeem the Jewish people from exile. Throughout, there have always been those who felt that exercising was part of a healthy lifestyle—and those who deemed it a waste of time.

More than anyone else, it is the great twentieth-century mystic (and first chief rabbi of Israel) Rabbi Abraham Isaac HaCohen Kook who is most famous for the notion that both the body and the soul must be prepared for redemption. Rav Kook himself embodied this ideal, cutting a striking profile of a Hasidic-garbed rabbi seen walking the land in tall, muddy boots. For Rav Kook, physical and spiritual were interdependent, both individually and nationally. On the national level, he believed that the "bodily" work of the secular Zionists enhanced the "spiritual" work of the religious:

> [T]he exercise that the Jewish youths in the Land of Israel engage in to strengthen their bodies in order to be powerful sons to the nation, enhances the spiritual prowess of the exalted righteous ... The one revelation of light cannot stand without the other.[3]

And individually:

> Natural reason cannot substitute for bodily strength. A person must endeavor to be full of life and bodily strength, so that reason can be operative in him with full potency in all its dimensions, in accordance with the principle of those knowledgeable in the ways of nature: a sound mind in a sound body.[4]

These were controversial ideas in the religious world of the 1930s and 1940s—and they still are today. To most Hasidic rabbis, the secular Zionists were heretics, and religious folk who imitated their ways, including by pursuing "a sound mind in a sound body," were taking a dangerous risk. Yet for Rav Kook, spiritual *tshuvah* (return, repentance) is incomplete without the physical:

> Our *tshuvah* will succeed only if it will be—with all its splendid spirituality—also a physical return, which produces healthy blood, healthy flesh, mighty, solid bodies, a fiery spirit radiating over powerful muscles. With the strength of holy flesh, the weakened soul will shine, reminiscent of the physical resurrection.[5]

But the body is not merely a tool of the soul. For Rav Kook, it is also the place where the soul's yearnings are fulfilled:

> The continual prayer of the soul is always striving to come out and reveal itself from its concealed place—to spread out into all the powers of the life of the spirit and into the power of the life of the whole physical body.[6]

How these ideas are best put into practice has been the subject of great debate over the years. For some, it means taking exercise as seriously as Torah study, and focusing on improvement of the self. For others, Rav Kook's teachings have more of a communal orientation, and call for hastening redemption not only spiritually, but also in the physical land of Israel—a religious view with sharp political consequences. Certainly this great mystic's ideas are complex, often troubling, and open to multiple interpretations. For our purposes, I think we can glean several principles from a personal reading of Rav Kook. First, that physical and spiritual are, and ought to be, interdependent; a spirituality without a physical dimension is as incomplete as brute physicality with no spiritual component. Second, that the body can be both a gateway to the soul and its canvas; creating a "spiritual exercise" practice both enriches and expresses the self. And finally, that the path of holiness is not renouncing physical manifestation in favor of Godly essence, but of continuing the divine work of extending the light of the infinite into the finite. That may seem to be a tall order for a morning workout, but let's see how it works.

Spiritual Exercise: Beyond the Mat

There is not, to my knowledge, an ancient Jewish system of exercise like yoga or T'ai Chi. Yes, there are a few movement practices from Abraham Abulafia, a system of embodied energies according to the Kabbalah, and plenty of rabbinic injunctions to stay healthy, but there is no practical science of bodily movement such as those in other traditions. Creating a Jewish or kabbalistic exercise practice, then, involves learning from other traditions and joining their wisdom to the teachings of Judaism. Certainly, there are plenty of options from which to choose. We've become accustomed, these days, to the shopping mall of spiritual exercises, a marketplace that now includes at least a dozen forms of yoga, T'ai Chi, Chi Gung, Pilates, gyrotonic, Feldenkrais and the Alexander Technique, a hundred martial arts from East and West, movement practices such as dynamic meditation and authentic movement—and, in the Jewish world alone, Embodied Judaism, Torah Yoga, *Torat HaGuf*, *Otiot Chayyot* (Living Letters), and countless other methodologies. All this in addition to the many new forms of exercise that lack an explicitly spiritual component but that provide one to those who seek it.

Hopefully, no one believes anymore that there's one magic bullet that will finally be "it," even if that is how some of these practices are marketed. Every practice has its strengths and shortcomings; the right one is only that which is best for you. In any case, what's most important is less the method then the benefits and mindfulness it brings about. Certainly, some modalities are more amenable, or at least more familiar, than others; a yoga class that places emphasis on meditation is more conducive to contemplative practice than a gym with testosterone-stimulating rock music. But my experience is that many forms of exercise can accomplish the task of strengthening the body, quieting the mind, and opening us to the subtle energies of ordinary mystical life—including those with rock music.

Of course, within the disciplines themselves, great importance is attached to the specific details: this chakra, not that one; the pose held this way, not that way. These instructions are important for reasons of attention, safety, and respect for centuries of inherent wisdom. But if we approach these techniques not as mythical-metaphysical dogmas but as practices—that is, as skillful means to get out of the *yetzer hara* and reorient in line with our deeper selves—then the language matters less than the attention to what it is describing. How can you transform an exercise routine into a spiritual practice? Let's look at what existing practices already have in common:

- Mindfulness of the body. The first stage of what the Buddha called "the direct path to realization" is as present in gymnastics and swimming as in walking meditation. The key is maintaining a continuity of awareness, out of thoughts and in experience. Simply being mindful of what you're doing—knowing that you're running, swimming, stretching—allows all kinds of insights to settle and arise. As Joseph Goldstein says, the four noble truths of Buddhism are all present in ordinary knee pain, because in it we can directly experience the impermanence, selflessness, and unsatisfactoriness of phenomena. Moreover, neurologists have found that the "Eureka!" phenomenon—scientific discoveries happening in bathtubs rather than laboratories—has a basis in brain chemistry, since it is when the brain is resting that neural connections are sealed. Everyone knows that a good run "clears the head"—the key is not to be too busy thinking, worrying, and distracting yourself. Just come to the body, and make it the object of attention.

- Focus and precision. Whether honing your downward-facing dog or moving energy through the chakras, spiritual exercises are focused and precise, not brutish. Precision, though, can be applied equally well in aerobic exercises, weightlifting, running, and most sports. With the focused attention of a basketball player at the foul line, the mind quiets because it has no choice. Set the intention to focus resolutely on precise, proper technique, and by concentrating the mind, you'll give it a rest from the thoughts that had depleted it.

- Visualization and other aids. Complementing bare mindfulness of the body or of technique is the skillful use of imagery. From the names of yogic *asanas* to the visualization of lines of energy within the body, mental images can affect the body, which in turn influences the mind. For example, you might proceed through the *sefirot* as you exercise the different parts of your body: *hesed* and *gevurah* as you work the right and left arms, *netzach* and *hod* on the legs. Or you might use a mantra or chant to create rhythm and focus the mind. If you get carried away with the map and lose the territory, come back to the physical experience and start again.

- *Kavvanot*. Exercise can be connected to prayer. Rabbi Nachman of Breslov is said to have spoken to his limbs on a regular basis, convincing each one to serve the Divine in its own distinctive way. What better time to do this than when you are working out? When working on arms, you might imagine how your arms can do righteous work in the world, or how they wear tefillin. You might recite the kabbalistic formula *l'shem yichud kudsha brich hu v'shechintei*, dedicating your work to the unification of the hidden Holy One and the manifest Divine Presence. Experiment with different *kavvanot* in this way, and uplift the sparks in your workout.

- Energy. No one really knows what the phenomenon of "energy" is, but with a little attention and practice everyone can experience it as a perceptual phenomenon. All those charts and diagrams work to call attention to conduits or "energy centers" where the phenomena can be felt. A session or two of kundalini yoga, acupuncture, T'ai Chi, Body Electric massage, or any number of other disciplines can teach you where to look. Then it's up to you to look; whatever these energies are, they are usually quite subtle, and easily ignored. Spiritual practice is like learning to appreciate wine; just as learning to detect the subtle notes of flavor in a wine enhances our experience of it, so, too, does an increased sensitivity to the energies of life increase our appreciation of it.

- Breath. Conscious breathing is present in almost every spiritual exercise form, and can be brought to "regular" exercise too. The next time you're out walking, notice what happens if you regulate your breath. Breathing once every four steps feels different from breathing every two. Breathing through the nose feels different from breathing through the mouth—try just breathing through your nose for fifteen minutes of walking, and see what happens to your perception and your gait.

- Nonjudgment. Remember, on this path, the body is not merely a tool for this or that mind-state; it is the journey and the destination. So, if you try all these techniques but end up not feeling anything "special" at all, that is okay. The body knows, the body learns, and the body teaches. Don't judge your practice too quickly; rather, keep at it for a while (the Baal Shem Tov recommends forty days before evaluating any new practice) and see what unfolds. This is what faith is really about: not believing in something someone tells you, but trusting in a process that you've seen work before, but that may, sometimes, be elusive.

- Anywhere. Drop the illusion that spirituality happens only in special places—a yoga mat, a synagogue, a retreat center. "God" may be a name we call the Infinite, and it may connote certain times and places. But the *Ein Sof*, the Infinite itself, is by definition everywhere. Of course, it is good and skillful to have a qualified instructor lead you in an hour-long session of practices honed for millennia. But what about when you're walking down the supermarket aisle? Can you not stretch to the top shelf mindfully, breathing, and grounded in the body? Advanced spiritual practice does not consist of ever more esoteric formulae. It is about applying the esoteric to an ever wider sphere of the mundane.

Let's apply these principles to running, perhaps the simplest form of exercise there is, and one with which, as a former marathon runner, I have some experience. Notice how tempting it is to distract oneself: with headphones, or conversation, or, in the gym, by watching television. Running in this way can still give you a good workout, but it won't cultivate much inner peace. Imagine if, instead, the body itself were the object of attention, and the mind were given a rest. From that attention would come a focus on precise technique and on regulated breath. The runner would keep her pace neatly and fall into a mindful rhythm. Her eyes might be straight ahead, keenly focused on the road. And from her mindfulness might come an awareness of circulation, or "energy," or even of subtle strains that may have otherwise escaped her notice.

Then she might add in a visualization, or a mantra. When I run, I sometimes chant *ein od milvado*—there is nothing beside God—or, if I'm well into a long run and needing some help, *ana el na, hosha na, hoshi'a na*, which means "please God, save us, grant us salvation" (it sounds much better in the Hebrew). Or sometimes, again deep into a ten- or fifteen-mile run, I'll imagine myself as a kind of hunter, or even as an animal, with focus dead ahead and determination moving each step. The inner stillness that arises is truly astonishing: the combination of fatigue and energy really silences the mind while maintaining an absolutely crisp and sharp perception.

These practices lead to experiencing "God in the Body" simply by removing the imaginary obstacles of mind, thought, and desire. There is nothing you need to "get" to be fully enlightened and united with God, just a lot of things to let go of—namely, the identification with your small self and its selfish desires. Running as an ecstatic practice is *bittul hayesh*, nullification of this illusory sense of self—and God appears wherever you let God in.

I invite you to bring in these intentions and orientations of mind to whatever exercise practice you have. And if you don't have one, get one. If you're walking in the mall, take a moment when no one is looking and ground yourself in the energies of the body: in the motions of steps and the rhythm of breath. If you're an advanced student of jujitsu, see if you can relate the practices you know to the general principles we've explored, and see how those practices are working for you in ways you may not have noticed. Not having a body practice is like never reading a book or marveling at a sunset; it's an incomplete form of living, and that's a shame, since you may only be here once.

A Four Worlds Workout

I'd now like to provide a taste of an Embodied Judaism workout that can be used either on its own or as a warmup for your existing work. The principle behind this practice is that we can experience the embodied energies the Kabbalists describe in their texts. As my co-teacher, Ari Weller, and I always tell our students, we don't have any way of knowing that what we experience is indeed what the Kabbalists are talking about. All we can do is take what they say about the four embodied souls, match it up with our experience, and see if there are places of congruence. If, when we stimulate aspects of our being that the Kabbalists describe as pertaining to the soul (freely borrowing, in our movement practice, from different traditions), and if there are perceptions that accord with the kabbalistic model—then perhaps we are getting close.

The model Ari and I use is that of the four worlds, which roughly correspond to the four "lower" souls: *nefesh*, *ruach*, *neshamah*, and *chayah*—the last of which gives a glimpse of *yechidah*, or unity. As applied to embodied phenomena, these words approximately represent the life-blood, the wind-spirit, the breath-soul, and the life-soul. In the self, they roughly align with body, heart, mind, and spirit. And in terms of the elements, they correspond to earth, water, air, and fire. This model is much simpler than that of the *sefirot*, and thus more suitable for an introduction such as this one.

As with any other spiritual exercise practice, begin by creating your environment. Treat your environment seriously; small things like lighting, space, and ambient noise will affect you (perhaps subconsciously), so take care to make your exercise space a sacred space, whatever that means for you. It's not enough to call something sacred—you have to actually create the conditions for sanctity. At the very least, you should have enough room to move around a bit, and you should be wearing comfortable clothing. If you're doing this warmup in the morning, do it before you eat breakfast, with the intention of experiencing whatever arises in the body for the next several minutes.

Nefesh: The Earth-Soul

We begin by stimulating the *nefesh* through massage, to literally get the blood flowing. The *nefesh* forms the foundation of the self, and cracks in the foundation make the whole structure unsound. We recommend starting in a seated position, sitting comfortably at the edge of a chair.

1. Start by rubbing your hands together, allowing the fingers to mesh with one another, creating friction, blood flow, and energy in the hands. If you like, after about twenty to thirty seconds, separate your hands about three inches apart and notice the tingling of the increased blood flow.

You might even feel a kind of energy in between your hands, as if they are being joined together. Go back to rubbing your hands together for another half a minute.

2. Close your eyes and bring your hands to the eyes, as if you're waking up in the morning, gently massaging into the eyeballs with the lids closed. Look for places beneath the skin surface that are sore, tender places that need attention. Massage into those places; throughout, we are loosening spots of trapped tension, allowing the *nefesh* to flow. You may feel very tired as you bring your attention to the eyes; that's fine, just massage gently.

3. Bring your index fingers into the tear ducts, massaging in that area, and then out to the outer corner of the eye, to the bony surfaces of the eye socket, gently massaging out there as well. Use eight fingers, everything but your thumbs, circling around the bony sockets of the eyes, making circles around the eyeballs—as if you're wearing a big pair of sunglasses and are tracing the rims. Aim for that blend of tranquility and alertness, being both relaxed and keenly aware of the body.

4. Still using eight fingers, rub gently up and down on the forehead, bringing the blood to the front of the head, then out to the temples, looking for any tender places there (if you like, you can visualize *hochmah* and *binah* residing at your holy "temples"), and then into the hairline, back onto the face—wherever your places of tension are, spend a moment there and massage.

5. Massage down to the jaw. This is one of the tightest places in the body, and it holds a great deal of tension. Try opening your mouth and pressing each index finger into the nook of the jaw just below the ears; you'll probably be surprised by how much tension is there. Massage it firmly as you open and shut your jaw. For the Kabbalists, all ten *sefirot* are found on the face as well as on the body, and the

mouth, where inside meets outside, is the place of the Divine Presence.

6. Next is the sinus cavity in between cheeks and the nose, alongside the nose itself (*af*—the seat of anger in Jewish lore). Gently rubbing with your index fingers, you'll notice that if you are breathing through your nose, the nasal passage will open up as you rub. Move to the ears, pulling on the lobes, massaging around the edges.

7. Now we're going to send vibrations to places we can't massage directly. Using your eight fingertips (thumbs out again), tap all around the head, sending the vibrations inside the skull, awakening the interior of the head. Take your time! Tap down the neck as well.

8. At the top of your shoulders, find the trapezius muscle, another very tight place in body. This is the part of your shoulder that you can't figure out how to drop, the thick muscle over and behind the collarbone. Ari and I like to say, "Squeeze that area like it's the handle on a piece of luggage." Massage as deeply as you like, maybe making noises, yawns, sighs—a sigh breaks up the body, say the Hasidic masters, and that is what we are trying to do: unstop the blockages to let the *nefesh* move.

9. Massage down the front of your throat (along the sides of the Adam's apple, if you have one), reaching the sterno-maschoid muscle—another spot that is often tight and constricted. Massage inward, and with your fingers, trace the sides of your throat down to your chest. Notice how much constriction we put up with every day without being aware of it; do you think this might have an effect on your emotional, spiritual, and mental well-being as well?

10. In the chest area, you have two options. You may simply tap around the chest with your eight fingertips, sending vibrations inside. Or, for a more vigorous exercise, clasp

your hands together and bang all around the chest, including the sides, making contact with the lower, fleshy parts of your thumbs. Make sure you're exhaling—what we're doing here sends vibrations into the lungs, which help eliminate breath stuck inside. There's a reason our ancestors beat their chests to expel energies of impurity; do this move for a minute or so, and you'll feel a little *kapparah* (cleansing) yourself.

11. At the bottom of the sternum is the solar plexus, where your "wind gets knocked out." Use your fingers to play it like a snare drum. This is a significant place in the body in many systems: *tiferet*, the heart center, the hub of the body.

12. Bend over and massage into the stomach; really stimulate the fleshy, earthy *nefesh* here. Then gently stimulate your lower back with lightly clenched fists—a bit like a Russian massage. Go to the tight places and loosen them.

13. Sit back up. Open your hands, and using the heel of the hand, strike along both sides of your right leg, from the thighs to the knees. Find the right level of intensity for your body. Repeat on the other leg. When finished, cup your hands and, with your fingertips, tap just under the kneecap, on the patella tendon. Gently tap all around the knees, then behind them as well.

14. Then, one leg at a time, you're going to make a "calf sandwich." Lift the leg slightly off the ground, with a bent knee and flexed foot. From both sides of the leg, gently press your calf under the heels of your hands all the way down to the bottom, then work the way back up. Behind the knee is the most tender place. Repeat for the other leg.

15. Finally, honor your feet. Usually we lock up (*na'al*) our feet in confining shoes or sandals (*na'alaim*), ignoring them except when they give us problems. With socks off, massage your foot using all of your fingers, including your

thumbs. Your toes can get a simple stretch too, in three directions: one front, the other back; one back, the other front; and split side to side. Go through each pair of toes like this, including, if you like, a gentle rubbing in the webbing of each toe.

When you're finished, sit comfortably and still for a moment. Scan through the body, noticing any changes that may have resulted from these simple actions. Focus on the physical, material essence of your body—blood, flesh, muscle, bone. Feel yourself as *adam*, the earth-creature. This is the *nefesh*, the life-blood in the body itself. Stay for a minute or two in a state of mindful awareness, noticing and feeling—just a human being doing its thing.

RUACH: THE WATER-SOUL

The embodied form of *ruach* is often difficult to understand because it does not precisely match up with a contemporary Western system. In addition to "spirit," *ruach* means "wind." So, you might think, it is connected to breath and air. However, it is *neshamah* that is the breath-soul. The *ruach*, drawing on the first lines of Genesis in which the divine *ruach* is described as hovering over water, is actually the water-soul, the seat of emotions, and the blending, as it were, of respiration and circulation.

One way to experience the *ruach* is by moving the body in imitation of it—undulating, like waves, or like the "wind over water" itself. The spine, which will be the center of this portion of the workout, is capable of four movements: extension, lateral movement, flexion/bending, and twisting. We will work through all four.

1. Extension. This movement is familiar: simply bend down to touch your toes (as close as you can, knees bending slightly) and feel the extension in the spine. Make room for breath, not by straining, but by gently expanding the range of your spine. And remember to breathe throughout, inhaling as you come up, exhaling as you go down. Repeat a few times.

2. Lateral movement. Still standing up, place your feet together and your hands over your head, fingers locked, palms turned up facing the sky. Make the link between *shamayim* and *aretz*, like the primordial human being joining heaven and earth. Then bend to the right, letting the left hip gently push out in opposition, opening up the left side of the body, and stay there for a few seconds. Then reverse. Now that you're warmed up, let's really get the *ruach* going.

3. Flexion. The movement here draws on a perhaps unexpected source: the traditional bowing motion as described in the Talmud in *Berachot* 12b. There we learn of Rabbi Shesheth, who, when he bowed, "used to bend like a reed, and when he raised himself, used to raise himself like a serpent." This has been understood by commentators to mean bowing down quickly, with all the vertebrae in the back bending, and coming up slowly, with the head leading. This motion can easily be integrated into your prayer practice, and serves as the basis for our primary movement here.

   Begin standing up, ensuring that the stomach is back and you are standing straight up (it may help to imagine an invisible string pulling you up from the back of your head). Exhaling on the way down, drop the head to the chin, and then bend each vertebra of the spine until you are fully bent over.

   Then, rising slowly, the head comes up first, followed by the spine, articulating each vertebra one at a time, like a snake. Inhale on your way up so that by the time you are standing up straight, you are coming up face to face with Presence, lungs full.

   This movement takes a bit of practice before it will feel natural, but see how you feel after doing it ten times, uniting the undulation of the body with the intake and exhalation of breath.

4. Twisting. This, too, takes a little practice, but it can give you a great, short workout even if you're sitting in your office. Begin seated, again extending the spine with the imaginary string atop the back of your head. Place your left hand behind you, palm resting on your sacrum (the spot by the "tail bone" where some commentators locate the *luz*, the bone from which resurrection takes place). Place your right hand on the inside of your lower left thigh, just above the knee, palm against your thigh. You'll notice you have to twist a little to make that happen— that's the point. During the movement, you're going to twist all the way to the side.

    The movement is simple once you get the hang of it: simply turn to the right so you switch hands—right hand on sacrum, left hand on right leg. Try it slowly a few times at first, twisting all the way to each side.

    Now add in breath. As if blowing out a candle, form your lips in the shape of an "O." At each end of the movement, when the hands are in place, you're going to exhale vigorously, like pronouncing the "wh" in "wheel," except the breath comes from the belly. Don't worry about inhaling—the body will take care of that by itself. Focus on the exhale each time you finish the movement.

    Increase your pace to a fairly rapid one—perhaps one breath each second, if that feels comfortable—and stay with this movement for about a minute. Try to really look behind you, letting your eyes lead your spine. Really get into this, working as vigorously as feels safe. Again, you can see what we are doing: uniting a fluid, twisting movement of the body with breath. *Ruach*: wind over water.

If you have back problems, as I do, these four movements can really help, especially mid-day. They are easy to do, once you get the hang of them, and they only take a few minutes. If you can close the door to your office, or get your co-workers used to your weird exercises, they can really give you an added dose of energy in the middle of a long day. They also invite the perception of an embodied consciousness that, if you are attentive to it, is really quite different from that of the *nefesh* and *neshamah*. Just test it out—see if you can experience for yourself these ancient perspectives on the embodied soul.

NESHAMAH: THE AIR-SOUL

The connection between breath and mind is present in countless spiritual traditions. In several Native American cultures, the diaphragm is called the place where heaven and earth meet. In *pranayama* and many forms of yoga, special breathing practices such as the popular *ujaya*, or ocean-breath, are used to cultivate ecstatic, contemplative, or other energized states of mind and body. And, as we saw in Chapter 3, the Kabbalah places great emphasis on the "breathing-soul" of *neshamah* and on exercises to stimulate it. Here, I suggest three additional practices, that flow naturally from the *ruach* portion of the workout.

1. First, become mindful of breath itself. In a workout context, follow a different path from ordinary meditation and take deep, full breaths at the beginning of your practice. Fill your belly shamelessly with air, feeling the diaphragm expand downward. Exaggerate the breathing so that it feels as though breath is entering places it rarely visits. And then, again following the advice of the Hasidic masters, exhale with a sigh—"breaking up the body"—and pull the belly back. Squeeze the last bits of stale air from the bottom of your lungs, tightening your muscles to do so. Do this four or five times, creating a softness in the belly and focusing the attention inward. Many teachers suggest a few of these breaths at the beginning of every period of sitting meditation. This builds attention and momentum, and acts as a gateway to what comes next.

2. Next is three-part breathing. This breathing is like filling a glass of water. When you pour water in, the bottom gets

filled first and then the water rises to the top. Likewise, to stimulate the *neshamah* in this way, you first inhale into the belly, then into the chest, then into the collarbone. Practice mindful three-part breathing for two minutes, inhaling and exhaling completely, and see to what extent you can regulate the filling of your chest with air. At the end of two minutes, pause and experience whatever bodily sensations and mental formations (clarity? quiet? noise?) are arising.

3. The third and final step is the "fire-breath" popular in kundalini yoga. In this breath, the belly acts not like a water glass but like a pump, pushing air out of the body. In twentieth-century guru Osho's "dynamic meditation," a vigorous form of embodied meditation practice, this form of breathing is practiced for fifteen minutes. We suggest trying it for just three to five minutes at first... and with plenty of tissues at hand. Simply stand up and blow air out the body through the nose (hence the tissues) in a vigorous way. Focus entirely on the exhalation—as in the *ruach* practice, your body will inhale by itself. Try to exhale from your belly, not your chest, pushing the air out from below as with a pump. Chances are you'll find that even one minute of this practice can be very strenuous; don't push yourself. Rather, if you become tired, focus on technique: ensuring that the exhalation is coming from the belly, focusing your gaze, letting go of thoughts. Set a fixed time for this practice and stick to it so you don't question it along the way; it's much easier on the mind this way. At the conclusion of the fire-breaths, stand still and notice, looking at your body and mind with an attitude of curiosity. See if perception is different, and, as before, see if this short bit of breath work has created a mood different from other stages, like a distinct flavor, or a timbre of sound.

As with the other portions of the workout, I find that just a few minutes of breath work can lead to significant shifts in state of mind, making it exceptionally useful for when you're stuck in a difficult mind-state. There are many ways to deepen the practice: holotropic or "cosmic" breath work; adding *kavvanot* or letter permutations from the sources we looked at earlier; and lengthening the duration of the workout. With practice, these forms of breath work can lead to deep insights about the self, ecstatic states, even, some would say, heightened awareness of the Divine. Considering that all we're really doing is oxygenating blood and working out some muscles, the transformation can be astonishing.

CHAYAH/YECHIDAH: THE SOUL'S ROOT IN UNITY

At Embodied Judaism classes, Ari and I finish with a series of vigorous, ecstatic movements that stimulate the transrational life-soul, *chayah*, and approach the consciousness of *yechidah*, or oneness. These ecstatic *chayah* movements are complicated, and I won't try to convey them here, but the kind of dancing we'll explore in the next chapter can take you to the same place, transcending the dualisms of our everyday consciousness. Ultimately, though, *yechidah* is so transparent that it is nothing but the experience of the world as it is. The difference lies only with the identity of who is experiencing it. So really, *yechidah* practice is just experiencing whatever is happening—as in, right now—with the doors of perception opened wide enough to let it in. Try it at the end of a workout, before going back to "regular life." With endorphins flowing and the mind quieted down, you can get a taste of unity.

Remember, secret wisdom isn't secret because it's a complicated formula that can't be spoken. It's secret because it's experiential, and thus cannot be conveyed at all. In all the foregoing practices, the point is always the same: living in the body; grounding perception in its present, vibrant experience; and letting the constructions of the egoic mind slowly relax. For all the systems and concepts, the core is very simple. But as you deepen in your practice, your consciousness will transcend words.

9
Dancing

Where does the real poetry
Come from?
From the amorous sighs
In this moist dark when making love
With form or Spirit ...
From the heart saying,
Shouting,
"I am so damn alive."

Hafiz[1]

Praise God's name in the dance.

Psalm 149:3

Sometimes religious practices are so familiar that we don't notice they're centered on the body. And sometimes, embodied activities like dancing—ecstatically, elegantly, joyfully, intimately—are so familiar that we don't notice their religious potential. Of course, everyone has danced at a wedding, and most have danced at concerts or clubs. Some have danced in churches and synagogues; a few even in the streets. Yet how many have joined these physical acts with the spiritual aspirations of King David, Miriam, and the other holy dancers of the Bible—or their Hasidic descendents? How many have approached it as what it is: a quintessentially Jewish, ecstatic mystical practice.

Like almost everything else that matters, dancing makes little sense rationally. Surely, though, a life without dancing would be duller, and sadder. Luckily, the kinds of spiritual, ecstatic dancing we will look at in this chapter do not require special skills, or special settings. Embodied spiritual practice is as at home at a late-night rave as at a separate-dancing wedding. It can be Apollonian or Dionysian, elegant or rough—as long as it brings the soul and body together, it marries heaven and earth. When that happens, when the body fills the soul with energies of the Creator, profound movements of the spirit can occur.

Ecstatic Dancing, Sacred and Secular

I have a small statue of a Buddha that my mother brought me as a gift from Thailand. I don't venerate it as an icon, but I do like the Buddha's image, sitting serenely, slightly smiling, hand pointing toward the earth, the witness of his meritorious acts. Ari Weller (my colleague whom we met in the last chapter) felt a little uncomfortable with this "idol" of mine, and bought me a tiny statue of a Hasid dancing. Now they sit next to each other, the meditating Buddha and the dancing Hasid, and they say much about how spiritual and contemplative practices feed one another. The Buddha sits quietly, witnessing the arising and passing of emotions, not identifying with their ebb and flow. The Hasid dances. He celebrates when he's happy, he mourns when he's sad. His path is, by design, rockier than the Buddha's; he is less equanimous, more prone to desire. But he dances better.

Jewish spiritual practice is poised between the stillness of the Buddha and the wild dancing of the Hasidim, as well as of our biblical ancestors, and their prebiblical roots. Perhaps "poised" is too quiet a word; the practice itself is a dance—between reflection and celebration, decorum and abandon. On the one hand, Jewish tradition is critical of too much religious enthusiasm, like that of Nadav and Avihu, Aaron's sons who brought "strange fire" to the altar and were consumed by it. On the other hand, it celebrates *some* enthusiasm, as in Saul, who danced with prophets, and David, who danced half-naked before the Ark of the Covenant. The fault lines are still present today. The Hasidim dance, stomp, sing, and bang on walls; and the "neo-Hasidim" gather in drum circles—but their opponents are suspicious. Too much energy, too much excitement—where will it lead?

I invite you to find out where it leads for yourself. Dancing has the capacity to teach at least as much as books, if we're able to undo the tangles, let down the guards, and give up trying to do it right. This "not trying" takes a little practice, though, and a fair amount of effort. Sometimes you'll look like a fool, but, as William Blake said, if the fool would persist in his folly, he would become wise. For me, wisdom comes when I really let go, and the rhythm dances itself, the music moves the gestures, and the "I" that is watching it all unfold is no longer the neurotic "I" that wants to impress people by dancing right. That is embodied spiritual practice, in its essence: letting go of the mind, letting the body lead, and, as a result, transcending the illusions of the small mind to access a deeper consciousness.

There is a very long tradition of ecstatic, sacred dance in the Jewish tradition. There are eleven different verbs for "dance" in the Hebrew Bible, with meanings ranging from swaying to ecstasy to spinning in circles. Just as the Eskimos know a lot about snow, it would seem our ancestors knew a lot about dancing. Some evidence:

> Miriam the prophetess, the sister of Aaron, took a timbrel in her hand, and all the women went out after her with timbrels and with dances.[2]

> And it came to pass as they came, when David was returned from the slaughter of the Philistine, that the women came out of all the cities of Israel, singing and dancing, to meet King Saul with drums and joy and music.[3]

> Then shall the young maiden rejoice in the dance, with young and old together, for I will turn their mourning to joy.[4]

> To everything there is a season ... a time to mourn and a time to dance.[5]

Some dancing was celebratory; some, like that of Tu B'Av, was erotic; and some, as in these selections from the books of Samuel, was ecstatic:

> You will come to the hill of God, where the garrison of the
> Philistines is, and it will come to pass when you are near the city,
> that you will meet a troupe of prophets coming down from the
> high place with a psalm-harp, and a drum, a flute, and a harp,
> and they will be prophesying. And the spirit of YHVH will come
> upon you, and you will prophesy with them, and be turned into
> another man.[6]

> And David danced with all his strength before YHVH—and
> David was wearing but a linen *ephod*. So David and all the house
> of Israel brought up the ark of YHVH with trumpets and the call
> of the shofar.[7]

From where we sit, thousands of years later, all this prerational ecstasy
and music can seem, to some, primitive, or pagan. Clearly, though,
these are "kosher" practices; indeed, when David was rebuked by
Michal, Saul's daughter, for his immodesty (and, perhaps, his crossing
of gender lines, since the vast majority of biblical dancers are women),
Michal herself was stricken with barrenness—a sure sign, in the biblical literature, that God does not agree. Really, the "error" of paganism
comes not from the ecstatic, embodied practices themselves—which
are essentially about accessing energies and modes of consciousness we
might normally not encounter—but from the error of ascribing those
energies to "foreign gods," that is, projections and imagined entities.
It's the theory, not the practice, that's the problem.

Rabbi Ohad Ezrachi, whose own path has led him from the
Hasidic world and kabbalistic yeshivas to ashrams and Tantric practice, likes to say that monotheism is an advanced form of religion—
but first you need the beginner's version. First you have to know that
there is a spirit in the tree, and in the sky, and in the water. Then you
can say that they are all the same Spirit. Often we skip the first step,
asserting or denying that there is one God but not actually experiencing how God manifests in different forms. Indeed, we can get so worried about mistaking the forms for separate realities that we recoil
from anything that might lead to their discovery. It's funny how immediate the anxiety is, even though the religions of ancient Canaan are

no more than a dim historical memory. For many people, just the sight of twenty drummers sitting in a circle and some dancers gyrating in the center evokes a generalized anxiety. But behind the anxiety is a real concern that we might really think the energy of the dance is a different god from the energy of sitting, *davening*, learning, or making love. Our God is a chameleon-god, ever shifting in the way we perceive It—so our fear of confusion is forgivable.

But very righteous people have done this for thousands of years. After the biblical period, the dances continued, as in this account from the Talmud of the autumnal Simchat Beit Shoeva festival:

> Whoever has not witnessed the joy of Simchat Beit Shoevah has seen no joy in his life. Pious men and businessmen danced with torches in their hands, singing songs of joy and praise, and the Levites made music with lyre and harp and cymbals and trumpets and countless other instruments.[8]

Indeed, one year, the great Talmudic sage Rabbi Shimon ben Gamliel is reported to have juggled eight lit torches, and when he prostrated himself, he dug his two thumbs into the ground, bent, kissed the ground, leapt up, and stood on his feet.[9] So much for reserved, rationalist rabbis.

In later times, dancing became a staple of eastern European Jewry, whose repertoire included such steps as the *koilich tanz* (in which women hold bread and salt to wish prosperity to a marrying couple), the *klapper* (clapping) *tanz*, a dozen circle dances like the *redl*, *frailachs*, *karahod*, and *hopke*, and many, many more. "Through dancing and body motions, joy is aroused," teaches Rabbi Nachman of Breslov,[10] while his leading disciple said, "Whoever did not witness Rabbi Nachman's dancing never beheld goodness in his life."[11] According to Rabbi Yehudah Loew ben Bezalel, "When the physical body is only in potential, not action, it is incomplete, because what is not in action is weighed down by nature, especially the body. So when a person dances he experiences a greater joy, because the nefesh [life-force] is made perfect in this way—and that is where joy is found."[12] And the great mystical ethicist Rabbi Moshe Chaim Luzzatto held that physical movement, whether in dance or in the performance of a commandment, can stimulate the stirrings of the soul:

> "My soul thirsts for You, my flesh pines for you."[13] The person in whom this desire is not sufficiently kindled, ought to physically arouse himself. As a result, the desire will become a part of his nature, for external, physical movements will stimulate internal ones ... If he will do what is within his ability to do, eventually he will also acquire what lies beyond it, and he will discover inner joy, yearning, and desire, as a result of the deliberate intensity in his movement.[14]

Today, thousands of Hasidim can be found trance-dancing for hours on end, every Friday night, seeking the *ruach hakodesh*, the Holy Spirit. According to one Hasidic tradition, "the dances of a Jew before his creator are prayers."[15] I've danced in huge Hasidic synagogues on Simchat Torah, at Bar Yochai's tomb on Lag B'Omer, and at many a wedding and *tisch*—and it seems to me that more than a few of the ecstatic dancers there have reached the heights of *devekut,* which, after all, is the point.

Of course, very unpious people dance like this as well. Far from the halls of the Hasidim, but often on the same night of the week, thousands of people reenact ancient rites of ecstatic dance. Tribal music plays, with repetitive drumbeats and recurring melodic motifs that sound like chant. Lights like spinning torches flash to the beat. Sexual energy is in the air, with somatic substances sometimes used to enhance its effects. But this isn't West Africa; it's West Chelsea in New York. Really, though, the tribal dance culture that exists in most major cities around the world is scarcely different from the tribal dance cultures that exist in indigenous societies—except that the heart has been removed, and the sacred confused with the secular.

Yet there is holiness there, and we can learn to experience it. Ecstatic dancing is a play with manifestation. Yes, it carries dangers—misappropriating its energies to fill some emotional gap, or misascribing its energies to figments of the imagination. But to see the One in the faces of the many—this, according to the Hasidic masters, was the true gift of Moses's sight. How do we do it? Practically speaking, there are a number of ways to use ecstatic dance on an embodied Jewish spiritual path.

First, enter it as with the intention of spiritual practice. Like eating, or going to the bathroom, dancing is itself mindfulness-neutral. You can dance the night away, talking all the while, and not have a moment of mindful, spiritual awareness. Not that there's anything wrong with that. But if you want the benefits of mindfulness practice, you have to set the intention. Suppose you're at a traditional wedding, with Jewish circle dances. You might set the intention to leave your thoughts at the table and fulfill the one mitzvah you have as a wedding guest: bringing joy to the married couple. Or suppose you're at a nightclub. There, you might set the intention not to hunt desperately after suitable partners, but to go into your own space, letting the music, lights, and atmosphere create an inner journey. Wherever you are, you might set an intention to create "inner silence," where you just dance, without thinking or commenting or judging.

Second, find the right context and boundaries for you. I understand that, for some, the idea of spiritual practice in a dance club may seem problematic. For others, though, it may be deeply liberating to utilize the secular rituals of nightclubs for sacred ends. Some may wish to try ecstatic dance only in certain ritual contexts, like Simchat Torah and Lag B'Omer, when they can connect their dancing to myth—to the Torah, or Shimon Bar Yochai, or something else. Others, however, may go in the other direction, preferring an environment where there are *no* layers of meaning over the dance itself. I encourage you to find the right context for yourself. If a drum circle in the desert is too far too fast, *shul* on Friday night is fine.

But, and this is a third instruction, do stretch your boundaries just a little every time—ratchet up, notch by notch, the level to which you're willing to take your dance. Once again, this may require you to "fake it till you make it." When you're sitting down, or standing on the side, you're building inertia. To get over that hump, you have to just take on faith that the body will change your mind. Right now you don't feel like dancing, but if you move a little, you will. Once you see this for yourself a dozen or so times, it won't be taking it on faith any-more—it'll just be a bit of trust. Push yourself, a little.

Fourth, allow the mind to play with whatever symbols and im-ages come its way during the dance. In Hasidic dancing, for example, there is often symbolism of circles—with the imagination lubricated by the energy of dancing, these might bring to mind the changing sea-sons, or the life cycle, or the water cycle, or a bicycle; let yourself play with these associations, not taking anything too seriously, not going off on philosophical investigations, but allowing the mind to dance just as the body is. See what comes up; again, you might be surprised by the insights that occur.

Finally—and perhaps in contradiction to the last suggestion—learn how to turn the mind off entirely. This is such a crucial skill, and it is probably the reason dancing is a euphemism for sex in pop music. The brain is our most complex, useful, and awe-inspiring organ. But sometimes the rational mind needs to take a rest in order for the trans-rational faculties to become active. One nice adage about spiritual practice says that just as dancing is ridiculous to someone who can't hear the music, so spiritual practice may seem ridiculous to someone who can't hear its tones, timbres, and rhythms. To such a person, spir-ituality is delusion. But with deep listening—which requires quieting the mind enough to allow spirit to be perceived—what had seemed to be fantasy becomes, instead, an intimation of the deepest reality. So, yes, dancing is ridiculous, but it is also profound—and in just that pair of facts lies an important Torah of the human soul.

The Quartet and the Mosh Pit

Ecstatic dancing is only one kind of spiritual dance, and I want to say a brief word about another before moving on. Some dance is the very opposite of "letting yourself go"—it is a precise, attentive positioning of the body, as in some forms of Indian dance, ballet, and disciplines of mindful movement. In these practices, the self is forgotten not by effacing it through ecstasy, but through focusing the intention on the movements and stillness of the body. The mode is Apollonian, as de-scribed by Nietzsche in *The Birth of Tragedy*, emphasizing precision, refinement, decorum, and edification; sophistication, delicacy, and taste, just as Apollonian spirituality cultivates the mind, edifies the heart with ethical wisdom, and maintains the body in a dignified and honored state.

If the Apollonian is a string quartet, then the Dionysian is a mosh pit. It values the nonrational, the orgiastic, the expressive—it's Allen Ginsberg's "Howl" to the Apollonian Robert Frost, the rhythms of African dance to the choreography of a Viennese waltz. The Dionysian is commonly confused with the merely barbaric, but this is not the case. Jackson Pollack, for example, is sometimes seen as a mere splatter-artist ("My kid could do that!") but actually approached painting as a ritual practice. The "whirling dervishes" are actually quite deliberate in their every move, even as they dance their way into ecstasy. And having been in more than one loud musical band in my time, I can tell you that creating good Dionysian music is very different from "doing what you want."

The Dionysian, like the Apollonian, has specific purposes in mind: inspiration, energy, excitement of the spirit, celebration of the body. It is the Dionysian mode that is dominant in most rituals involving intoxicants, as in the Dionysian rites themselves. When the sages say "there is no joy [*simcha*] without wine,"[16] they are aware that, while substances such as wine can lead simply to blind revelry, they can also gladden the heart and enliven the spirit.

We are not meant to choose sides between these two polarities of human experience. Both are capable of holiness, as well as of idolatry, and both exist in every spiritual tradition of which I am aware. The joy of living is to experience the full range of human life, from delicate French cuisine and wine to pizza and beer, formal dance to a freestyle frolic. There is a wide range of faces to the Divine, and the more we expand the range of those faces, the less idolatrous our images of God become, and the more delight enters into our lives. To deprive the soul of human experience is an impoverishment of the life you have been given.

❖　❖　❖　❖

10
Fasting

The righteous eats to satisfy his soul, but the belly of the wicked is lacking.

Proverbs 13:25

Isn't what the Torah prohibited for you enough? You have to prohibit yourself other things?

Yerushalmi Nedarim 9:1

The practice of fasting evokes many of the worst associations with religion: asceticism, self-denial, fear of the body and its pleasures. Some readers may even wonder why there's a chapter on fasting in a book about body-positive spirituality. Isn't fasting about unhealthy desires to punish the body, or get beyond it? Isn't it the antithesis of body-centered spirituality?

These are fair concerns, but as with so many supposedly outdated religious practices, fasting has transformative potential. First, experiencing God in the body is not a matter of seeking pleasant experiences and deifying our desires to have them; it is about the whole range of embodied experience, both as a means to shift consciousness and on its own terms. Second, in my experience—and, by choice, I am writing much of this chapter on a Jewish fast day—denying the body food and water, for a limited period of time, enriches all the levels of the soul, and is a powerful tool in contemplative life. Third, I love that the body can be so powerfully placed in the service of God. As scholar Carolyn Walker Bynum has written of Medieval female mystics, the point is "not rebelling against or torturing [the] flesh out of guilt over its capacities, so much as using the possibilities of its full sensual and affective range to soar ever closer to God."[1] Let's look first at how fasting works in practice, and then turn to the Jewish context.

The Benefits of Denial

Purely on the level of *asiyah*, the world of action and materiality, occasional fasting can be good for the body. It is a healthy way to clean out the system of toxins that have accumulated. Now, although I know nutritionists who recommend a liquid or total fast once every few months, I am not one myself and am not prescribing anything. However, in my own experience, fasting does make me *feel* as though my body has been cleansed. There can be, at the end of a fast, a powerful sense of catharsis. Sometimes I feel like I've sweat out the garbage from the industrialized food I've been eating, and I've cried out the accumulated grime of the emotions I've been ignoring. It is a primal, embodied act that makes as little sense as does love, passion, or beauty.

On the emotional plane of *yetzirah*, fasts are like vacations from the pursuit of pleasure. Sometimes the appetites and desires of the physical body really can become our masters, rather than our servants; without getting carried away, it's useful to think about fasting as correctives at such times. As a lifestyle, denying ourselves the pleasures of the world is antispiritual and anti-Jewish: God lives in manifestation, and our souls are attuned to wonder. But as an occasional practice— my practice is to fast on the six days a year prescribed by halacha—it's a welcome break. It's as if I say: This day, I'm not worried about feeling good. In fact, I'm going to let myself not feel good. Supported by my community, I'm going to set aside these six days a year for reflection, introspection, even outright mourning. I don't flip a switch (one day happy, the next sad), but I do invite in whatever emotions might ordinarily be beneath my cognitive radar. Also on the level of *yetzirah*, fasting can help cool overheated emotions. For example, "the main value of fasting lies in breaking the force of anger," says Rabbi Nachman of Breslov, who over his life had both strongly ascetic and antiascetic beliefs. It "has the power to resolve conflict, both physical and spiritual. When a person is unable to pray or do what he should to worship God, this is 'conflict.' Fasting helps to calm the heart and devote one's will to God alone and make peace."[2]

The most profound effect of fasting, though, is on the level of the mind—of *briyah*. For those who have difficulty meditating, I recommend fasting. Denying the body food reduces the amount of energy available to the brain, and so it becomes increasingly difficult, as the day wears on, to think in the usual, linear ways. You lose track of lists, you get frustrated trying to plan—all the routine activities of the thinking mind get disrupted. The momentum of thought decreases, and you become quite satisfied just to be here now. This, of course, is just what meditation does also: it slows down the train of thought so that we can actually see the world (internal and external) more clearly. Fasting makes meditation easier; if meditation is like biking up a steep slope of thought, then meditating while fasting is like biking downhill. It's easy to let go of thought—you can't think straight anyway. Sit for forty-five minutes toward the end of a fast day and see how much easier it is, as the quantity and intensity of distracting thoughts markedly diminish. You slow down. You start appreciating the beauty of a single breath, or textures, colors, or fabrics. Your mind enters a somewhat altered state.

It's no wonder, then, that fasting has been part of contemplative, prophetic, and even magical practices from the Bible to the present day. It's not that the altered state *is* enlightenment or *devekut*. Rather, in a concentrated mind-state (known in Sanskrit as *samadhi*), it's easier to see what you're looking for. It's important to remember that the mind-states are only a context; they are not actually the goal, which is to see the Light in *everything*—in whatever mind-state you're in, in whatever place you're in; to uplift every spark, not just the ones that have a pleasing flavor or appearance. It's also important to remember that none of this is magic; it's simple, and biological. But as long as these provisos are borne in mind, fasting and *samadhi* can show you the way.

Try to fast for one day, and meditate somewhere toward the end, and you'll see for yourself that fasting is not (merely) about denial, magic, and self-mortification. It is essentially a shamanic practice, capable of enabling inner journeys that would otherwise be very difficult. Thus fasting leads even to the fourth plane of reality, *atzilut*, not because the concentrated mind is itself the ultimate reality, but because, in a concentrated state, the mind can visit territories otherwise beyond our ken. And yet, of course, these lands are nowhere other than here.

Fasting in Context: The Five Minor Fasts

In Jewish law, fasting is tied to context, and thus raises the question of whether the "real" meaning of a religious practice inheres with the *gashmiut* (materiality) of the practice itself, or in the context provided for it by rabbinic Jewish thought. Fortunately, it's not necessary to resolve the question once and for all. Judaism is not a systematic religion; it wasn't invented all at once, and structured in a unitary, logical way. Rather, it evolved over millennia, across vastly different historical and social contexts, and involves aspects of religion, culture, tribe, and nation. Examining a single practice, like fasting, is like taking a geologic core sample: there are multiple layers of sedimentation, each with different content and meaning.

The Bible generally regards fasting as a practice that works on the heart, usually as an individual expression of grief, prayer, or meditation. Yom Kippur is the most important of these spiritual fasts, and is discussed in detail below. But fasting also appears as a mourning rite (II Samuel 1:12, 12:16–23), as part of revelation or prophecy (Exodus 34:28, I Samuel 28:20), as preparation for an important event (Judges 20:26, I Samuel 14:24, Esther 4:6), and as part of petitionary prayer (I Samuel 7:5, II Samuel 12:16) or repentance (Jonah 3:5, Jeremiah 36:9). There is also evidence of a little-discussed discipline of women voluntarily fasting (see Numbers 30:14 and the apocryphal Judith 8:6), and many later examples of fasting as a preparation for visions (e.g., Daniel 10:2, and several apocryphal books). And there are instances of fasting as, essentially, magic (Judges 20:26, Joel 1:14, Jonah 3:5–10). In all these contexts, fasting is regarded for what it does, not what it signifies or observes.

Later, however, the individual effects of fasting became secondary to its historical and social significance. For example, in the "Zechariah fasts" that were later made part of Jewish law, it may be interesting that fasting changes mind-states, but the primary theme is the destruction of the Temple in Jerusalem. As Eliezer Diamond has shown in his book *Holy Men and Hunger Artists*, many Talmudic Rabbis often took up fasting as an ongoing discipline, but as Diamond also shows, mourning the destruction of the Temple was almost always provided as a rationale. Perhaps the Temple was but a pretext for an ascetic practice the rabbis wanted to take on; there is certainly evidence for that view, and fasting remains to this day a common practice among the pious. But today, if you look at a traditional Jewish explanation of why we fast, what you'll learn about the fasts are not their effects but their historical reasons. The five Temple-related fasts are:

1. The 9th of Av, which commemorates the destruction of both the first (in 586 BCE) and the second (in 70 CE) Temples in Jerusalem. It is the saddest day of the Jewish calendar, filled with mourning.
2. The 17th of Tammuz, three weeks earlier, commemorates the breaking of the gates of Jerusalem by the Romans in 70 CE, after a long and bitter siege.
3. The 10th of Tevet, in the winter, commemorates the breaking of Jerusalem by the Babylonians in 586 BCE.
4. Tzom Gedaliah, the day after Rosh Hashanah, commemorates the end of Jewish sovereignty, shortly after 586 BCE, after hundreds of years. The specific event it recalls is a Yitzhak Rabin–like assassination of a Babylon-installed Jewish governor by a Jewish zealot.
5. The Fast of Esther, the day before Purim, actually commemorates two events: Esther's fast before she asked the king to annul his genocidal decree, and the fast immediately before the battle with those who sought to destroy the Jews. The connection between the events of Purim and the destruction of the first Temple is tenuous, but the rabbis insist on it, noting that the story is basically one of diaspora and vulnerability.

Personally, I have struggled for decades to connect in a meaningful way with the destruction of the two Temples. True, these catastrophes are the halachic basis of all the public fast days except Yom Kippur.

True, they were massive upheavals that caused widespread suffering and death. And, true, the Temple was no mere building; it was seen as the connecting point between heaven and earth, the earthly dwelling place of the Divine Presence, and the geographical, political, and spiritual center of the Jewish people. The tears of exile, from the Crusades to the Holocaust, all flow from the wound of its destruction.

But in my own life, the *effects* of fasting are far more interesting to me than the reason the fast may have been instituted by Rabbis two thousand years ago. The mind is shifting; perception is opening—these are steps toward redemption, not merely acts that bemoan our evil. So, I approach the five Temple-related fast days by expanding the metaphor of the Temple's destruction to embrace the principle of separation itself. Then I see my fast not merely as mourning, but also as the path to healing.

Why, then, fast on these days, rather than when the inspiration is present? First, I draw strength from the knowledge that, around me as I write this, hundreds of thousands of people are also fasting on this communal day—even if my reading of the day's significance is different from theirs. Jews have never agreed on why we do anything; we have four new years, and three names for the Passover holiday. Yet community is built by doing. That I can *daven* next to someone whose theology and ethics are absolutely antithetical to my own, and that he can answer Amen to a blessing I recite can be a more enduring bond than that of creed. Second, and relatedly, is the aspect of humility in spiritual practice. Every year, I learn from the tradition, even if my relationship to it is no longer as orthodox as it once was. Perhaps I'll explore the social meaning of fasting—what depriving the body might have meant in a culture where food was not taken for granted. Or I'll ponder what it means that ignoring the needs of the body is, itself, a sign of mourning. Every year, there is something new.

Third, I approach the five Temple-related fast days in the spirit of practice, and practice requires form. If we only do the practice when we feel like doing it, it isn't a practice. If you get up after ten minutes of meditation because you're not feeling like meditating, then, in a way, you're never meditating. The container is meant to be fixed so that whatever transpires inside it can be as fluid, and open, as possible.

So I fast when the fast days fall. Sometimes, there is a wonderful congruence between observance and life. Other times, as when I recently observed Tisha B'Av while traveling through Norway, there isn't. Allowing the fast to proceed, whatever its shape, allows its effects to be seen in a variety of shapes and colors.

It's true that, in the Jewish tradition, it is also permitted to observe a "private fast" for personal reasons: to focus on a decision, to mourn a loss, to engage in a spiritual practice, or to mark any kind of personal occasion. Like those in every other tradition, Jewish mystics know that fasting focuses the mind, opens the heart, and prepares the spirit for union—and so they practice it often. Still, I like the regularity of the set fasts, that they come and go on their own accord, and force me out of wherever I am into wherever they want to take me. That is, for me, the essence of practice: it exists beyond the ego.

So, before moving to Yom Kippur, let's look at a few practical ways to make the Jewish fasts part of your embodied spiritual practice.

First, as with every practice, once you've decided to do it, surrender to it. Don't fight the fast. Don't dwell on what you're lacking or count the minutes until you can eat. Just notice. Treat the starved state of the body as another state of being. What does it feel like? What is arising in the mind as a result? Don't jump, immediately, to aversion, as in "I'm hungry ... I hate it ... I want to be full." Again, "to see the Light in everything" includes places that don't seem light, or body-states that aren't as pleasant as relaxing on the beach. If we don't include uncomfortable places in our spiritual practice, then we're just taking narcotics. Can you make room for presence with a bodily sensation you might ordinarily label as unpleasant? Can you love God in this? If you can, then your practice becomes "practice" in a different sense—you're practicing for when it's even harder to accept, even harder to yield and surrender. Feel the sensations—but don't jump to associations and judgment. Build yourself a space of freedom, where you can be with any shape of the Divine.

Second, don't try to have a normal day. Doing so will be both frustrating and counterproductive, because the precious insights and moments of presence that come with a fast will just disappear. It'll be a shame—you'll be missing out on some of the best fruits of the practice, all the while frustrated because you can't think straight. Now, if there's no alternative, then the point of practice is still to do it regardless; don't skip the fast because you can't devote all afternoon to meditation. But if you do have the ability to slow down, quiet down, and listen—what a gift.

Third, if you notice a strong thought or feeling arising, I encourage you to explore it. Sages in the Jewish tradition frequently use a fast to aid discernment, because it helps you cut to the core of your indecision. Are you facing a life decision? Are you unsure what to do? Fasting is conducive to finding direction—not to making practical, logistical plans, but to deciding which plan you want to make. Or, to take another example, perhaps you've experienced a loss that you haven't had time to mourn; on a fast day you might let the tears flow. Find a safe space, and let them lead.

And finally, notice, notice, notice. I am "led" by fasts to places that are often achingly beautiful. I find myself more loving, more accepting, more grateful. Sometimes I'm overwhelmed with humility, as I see how much the "I" that I'm so proud of is dependent on daily nourishment. Just one skipped meal, and look what happens to this supposedly self-sufficient ego! Usually we encounter the fragility of life in tragic circumstances, but fasting provides us a similar experiential insight in a safer, quieter way. As Isaiah famously says, fasting without heart is no guarantee of piety. But with intention and attention, it can lead to precisely the compassion the prophet demands.

As we saw earlier, all this intention-plus-fasting is simply a meeting between careful, mindful attention and a wise, embodied tradition that has lost some of its self-awareness over the years. If you can hold doubt in abeyance, just for a day, and if you can pay attention to what unfolds as a result, then you can open yourself to the paradoxical gifts of denial.

Fasting as Catharsis: Yom Kippur

Yom Kippur is the best known of Jewish public fasts, and the only one tied to individual rather than communal ideals. On Yom Kippur, the process, context, and trajectory is different from other fasts. It is, alone in the Jewish calendar, a "Day of Death," a time when all the normal teachings around the body are, for one day, reversed. On this day, the sanctification of ordinary life and the celebration of the body and the world are undone, so that layers of self can be meticulously scrubbed away.

As always, there may be a yawning gap between the ideals of Yom Kippur and its reality. Ideally, one spends no time beautifying the body: men wear a *kittel*, the death shroud, and no one wears makeup, or even looks in the mirror. In actuality, Yom Kippur is, for some, the time for the most expensive new dress and sharpest suit and tie. Ideally, Yom Kippur is a day of abstention from "small talk." But in practice, it becomes a day to meet and greet at the synagogue. Ideally, the embodied practices of Yom Kippur lead to an emotional and spiritual catharsis, an emotive prayer and confession that comes from the vulnerable, open heart. But in practice, many Jews spend the day sitting bored and bewildered while a cantor or choir sings a stultifying tune lifted from Protestant liturgy.

Wherever you find yourself on Yom Kippur, though, you can use the fast to your advantage, because the body is always there to ground you—and when it's fasting, it's pretty hard to ignore. If you stay focused, not counting the minutes until the shofar blows but really undertaking the journey of Yom Kippur, then not only will the mind enter some of the states we spoke about in the last section, but the heart, too, will begin to open. Depending on where you are, you may not have the opportunity to cry out to God with your voice—but you can with your body.

The myth of Yom Kippur is problematic for many; do we really believe in a Book of Life in which all our deeds are inscribed—even in a metaphorical way? Do we think that the unrepentant are punished? These are challenging ideas. In reality, however, the entire story of Yom Kippur—the sin, the forgiveness, the catharsis—is a psychological drama projected onto theology. All of us have done things that we regret. Yom Kippur is the day to release them. The point isn't whether you'll be good enough to be written in the right Book; it's about getting in there, looking at the dirty stuff, and then being washed clean. The myth is secondary. The psychological drama is primary.

Speaking psychologically, then, *tshuvah*—return to one's deepest self—is not an intellectual process. It may make no sense to spend hours in *shul* banging one's heart with one's fist, but yearning, crying, and begging are not meant to be sensible. Don't spend time worrying over the literal words of the Yom Kippur liturgy. The important thing is to do the practice of *tshuvah*, with your body leading and your heart following. Do the fast, the bowing, the banging on the chest; do the standing, and notice as the body gets exhausted. Really, what is liturgy anyway but the verbal expressions of inchoate yearning? It's not theology; it's poetry.

Seen in this way, Yom Kippur is a journey. Over the course of twenty-six hours, you have the opportunity to turn off the regular world and reenact the drama of *kapparah*, cleansing. And the soul-searching and the catharsis are two sides of the same coin, because you can't release what you don't first discover and accept. The phases will vary. You might move from apathy to remembering to regret, and then to reconciliation and release. Or you might drift in and out of the day's emotions, focusing more on resolutions, concerns, and pleas. Wherever the journey goes, though, the body is the central vehicle. The Torah instructs Israel: *v'initem et nafshotechem*—impoverish your souls. What does this mean? On the level of *asiyah* it is denial of food and drink, as well as of sex, bathing, and wearing leather shoes. But these denials lead to opening the heart, and allowing the mind to see clearly.

One of the embodied highlights of the Yom Kippur day is the *Avodah* service, which reenacts the climactic moment of the ancient Temple ritual. The Talmudic account of the priestly ritual is interesting, but I like the *Avodah* most because, where I *daven*, everyone gets on their knees and bows right down to the floor, multiple times. Perhaps because there is little intellectual justification for the bodily reenactment of the Temple worship, many temples and synagogues have abandoned it. But the *Avodah* service comes about midway through the day, just when, for me, things are getting difficult, and productive. Bowing down, truly giving up the body and subjugating the ego to the deeper parts of the self, is often just the push that breaks me open.

And later, the endless standing of the *Neilah* service, right at the end of the day. Some years, the whole day will pass uneventfully, but then I'll finally "get it" right at *Neilah*. Something will open, whether a current of release, or a sudden relevance of a few words of the confessional. And then I'll find myself moving around, shouting the final *selichot*, and leaving the doubt behind. It's not that I've become convinced of dogma; it's that I've remembered that the dogma isn't the point. Let the body lead, and just do the work. If it's yielding fruits, great. If not, have a little faith, or at least curiosity. Eventually, at some point, the body will take you somewhere.

Kapparah, the root of Yom Kippur, means cleansing—catharsis, if you like. It's what's done to the Temple after it is defiled; getting into the muck and grime and scrubbing it away. You're not meant to feel good, or have an "easy fast." Rather, you can use the body's duress to get into the dirty stuff, whatever that may be for you. May you have a difficult Yom Kippur—one of searching, discovery, and release.

❀   ❀   ❀   ❀

11
Washing

You should bathe your face, hands and feet every day in honor of your Creator.

Shabbat 50b

Cleaning the body restores purity to the soul.

Rabbi Elijah de Vidas[1]

The body does not cater to our desires. It decays, it becomes dirty, and, though less likely than might be expected for such a complex machine, it sometimes breaks. Thus, even apart from the unreasonable demands we place on our bodies, and the unreachable ideals by which we measure them, there is an intrinsic struggle between the nature of the body and the ego's desires that it conform with expectations.

The most common way in which we experience this conflict is in the ordinary, daily maintenance it requires. We prefer that the body not smell, so it needs to be washed. We want our skin and hair to have certain appearances, so they need to be moisturized, conditioned, and arranged. These are universal desires; grooming practices can be found in every culture on the globe, and even most animals clean themselves in some way. And while we, in our age, may have taken body maintenance to a bizarre extreme, there is obviously a hygienic basis for washing and cleaning the body that makes doing so as fundamental as eating, sleeping, and sex.

In religious cultures, washing takes on additional levels of meaning. Religious Jews wash their hands in a ritual fashion several times a day, reciting a blessing each time. Catholics symbolically wash themselves in holy water. Muslims wash their feet upon entering a mosque, in facilities designed for ritual use. The bodily act becomes a site for connection—to myth, spirit, or covenant. Washing the body may seem like a very trivial thing, but it is precisely the trivial that is most amenable to sanctification.

Is Cleanliness Next to Godliness?

Biblical Judaism is highly concerned with the cleanliness of the body. The Bible, which has only two or three references to the afterlife, and only a few sentences about the creation of the world, there are dozens of detailed instructions for when, and how, the Children of Israel are to bathe, wash, anoint, and otherwise beautify their bodies. The Torah, as Mary Douglas and Howard Eilberg-Schwartz have separately observed, is practically obsessed with irregularities of the body; the book Leviticus alone discusses, in vivid detail, skin diseases (Leviticus 13 and 14), venereal diseases (Leviticus 12 and 15), and bodily deformities (Leviticus 21:16–23). And ordinary bathing, cleaning, and care of the body are critical components of biblical *kedushah* and *taharah*, holiness and purity.

The American adage that "cleanliness is next to godliness" may have been merely a convenient way to convince children to wash behind their ears, but it certainly had a basis in biblical Jewish religion. For our ancestors, cleanliness really was next to godliness; or, more precisely, it was a prerequisite for it. They could not approach the sacred spaces of the tabernacle or the Temple if they were "unclean," and the requirements for washing increased in proportion to the sanctity of the moment: at the holiest day of the year, the high priest would have to immerse in a ritual bath no fewer than five times.

What do we make of these practices today? To begin, it's useful to imagine some of the context: a world without plumbing, without epidemiology, and in which the smells and fluids of life were never far away. Westerners are often shocked when they visit the market streets of the developing world, with their overpowering odors, rivulets of blood from the butcher shops, and, sometimes, open sewers. But even those places are immaculate compared with everyday life in the ancient world. As with so many of the practices in this book, the body's needs were more acutely known then than now. Thus, if we are to derive meaning from these practices today, we have to prepare the mind and heart in a way that was unnecessary for our ancestors. They knew directly the power of the cleansing bath; we need to practice in order to experience it.

There are some today who would prefer to get rid of the whole thing. They observe that in the Jewish tradition dirtiness is not mere filth, but *tumah*, sometimes translated as "impurity." For some, this seems like neurosis, or a fear of the natural products of the body. For others, the whole discourse of impurity reeks of primitive superstition. Fair enough—but I'd like to invite an openness to *tumah* and *taharah* without the negative associations of "pure and impure." The most important context in which these categories occur, menstruation, is discussed in Chapter 12. In general, though, I want to suggest that *tumah* and *taharah* can be felt, and can be useful ways of looking at shifts within the body. An act as simple as washing the hands can create a liminal space, a gateway through which we pass from an ordinary state into one ready to receive holiness. Of course we know more about hygiene and bacteria and how disease is passed than did our Bronze Age forebears, but they may have known more about the soul.

In this light, the discourse about care of the body may be seen not as neurosis but as an affirmation of the body's importance. Today, there is a persistent notion that the more "spiritual" you are, the less you pay attention to your physical appearance—to grooming, fashion, and care of the physical body. Why? Because the spiritual is "otherworldly"? The Talmud in *Shabbat* 114a holds the exact opposite; it says that a *talmid hacham* (outstanding student) who wears soiled clothing is *mit'hayev b'nafsho*—he is liable for the worst punishment, because he brings shame upon Torah learning by presenting a decrepit appearance.

The body and its beautification matter spiritually because the body is not a curse, not an impediment, but, in fact, a gift from God. Bahya ibn Pakuda writes, "In skin and flesh have you clothed me, and with bones and sinews have you sheltered me."[2] And that "clothing" is seen, throughout the Jewish tradition, as a garment of both beauty and sanctity. Celebrations of the body's beauty occur throughout the Bible, from the perfume in the Book of Esther to priestly bathing and dressing practices, the anointing of the Messiah to the jewelry worn by queens. There are Jewish prohibitions on defacing the body (which, in traditional understanding, includes the applications of tattoos) as well as any practices that harm the human form (piercings, apparently common among ancient Israelites, are permitted[3]). Grooming is a sign of religious affiliation—hence the prohibition on shaving the sides of the head, a law that is the source of the Orthodox custom of men growing beards, and of *payot*, the long sidecurls that were an eighteenth-century innovation and are familiar among ultra-Orthodox Jews today. There are Talmudic passages about mascara (*Shabbat* 109a), about measurements of the face (*Sukkah* 5a), legs (*Yevamot* 103a), and limbs (*Nedarim* 32b), and about the volume of the body (*Eruvin* 48b, *Sukkah* 8a). Even the points of a man's beard are said to reflect the thirteen attributes of divine mercy. The body matters, whether as a gift (or loan) from God, or simply as reflecting the Divine image, as in this rabbinic tale:

> When Hillel the elder took leave of his disciples, they asked him "Rabbi, where are you going?"
>
> He replied, "I am going to perform a *mitzvah*."
>
> "What *mitzvah*?" they inquired.
>
> "I am going to bathe in a bathhouse," he replied.
>
> "Is that considered a *mitzvah*?" they asked.
>
> "Indeed it is," he answered. "Look the fellow who is in charge of the statues of the emperor in the theaters and circuses cleans and shines them every day. I am created in the image of God, as it says, 'For God made man in God's image.'[4] Surely, I should be meticulous about my cleanliness."[5]

This same rationale—that humanity is made in God's image—underlies the *Shulchan Aruch*'s requirement that Jews wash daily "in honor of the creator."[6] Perhaps the phrase "cleanliness is next to Godliness" has a whiff of the puritanical. But how one cares for the body, how one dresses and cultivates one's physical appearance, reflects how one approaches the physical world as a whole. Is life in this world, in this body, merely a predicament, a prelude to something better? Or is it a colorful, sensual, and all-too-transient gift, which we would best approach with the love and reverence usually reserved for the cathedral?

Washing as a Spiritual Practice

Putting these values into practice requires a translation of *tumah* and *taharah* into meaningful categories today. First, we can understand *tumah* as a physical state that results from contact with death. *Tumah* exists whenever that which is capable of life has died—a person; semen or blood, which had the capacity to create life; even everyday dust, most of which is comprised of dead skin and other organic matter. *Tumah* is a natural state of being, but it is one in which the ideal trajectory of life has been inverted. And so, before entering a sacred space, a transformation is necessary.

Water is seen as effecting that transformation. The Jewish tradition shares with many other cultures the belief that water cleanses not only physically, but spiritually as well. As we will explore in even more depth in the next chapter, immersing, washing, and bathing in water shift consciousness, and move the body from one state of being to another. Two of the most common daily occurrences of this transformation occur in the morning, upon awakening from sleep—which the tradition sees as "one-sixtieth of death"—and before eating, which is regarded as a sacred act. During sleep, our rabbinic forbears imagined that the soul journeyed outside the body, and that it was only through the grace of God that it returned. Indeed, the first words uttered by a pious Jew in the morning thank God for returning the soul to the body. Thus, the notion is that when we awaken, we have a bit of death still clinging to us—today we might associate it with shed skin cells, or the germs in our mouths, all of which we wash away by showering, washing our hands, and brushing our teeth. Either way, washing the body prepares it for the life of the day.

Likewise when preparing to eat a meal—and, according to some customs, between eating and reciting *birkat hamazon*, the grace after meals.[7] Today, many people wash their hands before eating because we know that all sorts of microorganisms are picked up by the hands from surfaces they touch in the world. Washing with soap and water is good hygienic practice. Spiritually, it is connected to the notion we explored in Chapter 1: that the dining table is like the sacrificial altar, where one elevates the sparks of plants and animals to the plane of consciousness. To be mindful of this sacred act requires a transition from ordinary life into a state of holiness. By way of analogy, have you ever found yourself running late to a meeting, and when you get there, you're still rushing even though you've made it, now, and the rush should be over? Spiritually, you're still in instrumental mind, still denying this moment in order to get to the next, and still a bit dirtied by the instrumentalizing, life-denying dust of the everyday.

The practice is not complicated. Ritual washing involves filling a cup (or a special decorated laver) with water, then pouring the cup first over the right hand, then the left, then right and left again, and then again a third time. There are typically Talmudic debates over exactly how much water is needed, and what vessels can be used—but this is the basic idea. Afterwards, a blessing in the standard form is recited:

בָּרוּךְ אַתָּה יְיָ אֱלֹהֵינוּ מֶלֶךְ הָעוֹלָם אֲשֶׁר קִדְּשָׁנוּ

בְּמִצְוֹתָיו וְצִוָּנוּ עַל נְטִילַת יָדַיִם

Baruch ata adonai eloheinu melech ha'olam asher ḳid'shanu b'mitzvotav, v'tzivanu al netilat yadaim.

Blessed are You, YHVH, our God, king of the universe, who has sanctified us with commandments, and commanded us regarding the washing of the hands.

As you wash, pay attention to the feeling of the water, both the physical sensations and any emotions or thoughts that arise. Use the moments of silence to notice the physical cleanliness, or cultivate a sense of readiness for what comes next. The body is always there—wherever the mind may be wandering, the body is remarkably enlightened. The point is to "be here now," right? And isn't the body always doing just that?

Between washing and eating, it's customary not to speak. The reason is that there is meant to be no interruption between the two acts—you can dry your hands, of course, but the theory is that it's one continuous motion from washing to eating. You can use this time to allow the physical transition to percolate through mind and heart. Instead of trying to communicate with others (which can often be a bit comical), or feeling awkward in the silence, enjoy a precious island of silence to transition and "arrive" where you are.

You may also want to go out of your way to pause in the moment after washing. One Hasidic rabbi suggests, "after pouring the water over your hands, raise them to the level of your face ... palms inward. Then, slightly cupping your fingers, and with your hands touching, reach out like someone who wants to receive something—this symbolizes the reception of purity."[8] In addition to providing a beautiful opportunity to turn inward, this custom also literalizes the blessing over handwashing, which literally means "on the raising of hands."

You can also extend this practice beyond the formal ritual washing of the hands to your already-existing morning ritual of taking a shower. Oftentimes I'm so busy in the morning that I race into the shower, scrub the parts of the body that need scrubbing, and spend the whole time worrying about what I have to do next. But the shower, like those moments before eating, can be an island of solitude and peace in an otherwise frantic, crowded, and noisy morning. It's usually a pleasant environment: the body is naked, the water is warm and rushing. What a pity to spend these pleasant moments worrying about the future or the past. So, if you have the opportunity, enter the shower as if entering a sacred space. It might be useful to call to mind a few basic reminders, that this is the place of transformation, or of honoring the body. Or you might hum a *niggun* (wordless tune) or sing a tune, such as the Reclaiming Community's "Born of water, cleansing, powerful, healing, changing, we are... Born of water ... ," also a powerful chant before entering the mikva. Whatever works for you, the point is simply to get the mind to arrive in the shower, instead of wandering off somewhere else.

If you can't shower this way every day, then at least try to do so before Shabbat. The *Shulchan Aruch*, the great codification of Jewish law, says that "It is a mitzvah on *erev* Shabbat to wash your whole body with hot water; but if it is not possible, then at least wash your face, hands and feet. It is also a mitzvah to wash your hair." I love how the *Shulchan Aruch*, not known for its flexibility, is so accommodating here. Do your best; if only once a week, fine; if only partially, fine. Try.

Finally, it's possible to experience "spiritual cleanliness" on each of the four worlds we've spoken of before. As a purely embodied phenomenon, all that's needed is attention to the sensations of water, washing, and so on, to ground the mind back in the present moment, and cut the circuits of thought that might otherwise drive it more than a little crazy. Cleansing the body often, mysteriously, opens the heart, inviting a range of emotional responses, from renewal to grief to joy— even in the small act of washing the hands before a meal. Intellectually, there is the conceptual edifice of Jewish law, and the scientific understanding of what is actually happening when the body is washed. And spiritually, the states of *taharah* and *tumah* can be gateways to shifting consciousness. Some days, you might inhabit the realm of the spirit; others, just the body. Sometimes you might not really be present for it at all. But the idea of a practice is that you do it anyway so it can contain the range of experience. And all this from a little soap and water.

Washing is perhaps the simplest of all the practices in this book, but nearly every religious and mystical tradition sanctifies it, and recognizes its power. Why search for complexity?

* * * *

12
The Mikva

Wash, wash me clean—mend my wounded seams
Cleanse my tarnished dreams.

k.d. lang[1]

Human beings are called children of the earth, *b'nei adam*, but our bodies are mostly water. We breathe air, and are warmed by the sun, but we still retain some primal memory of when we floated in the womb, insulated from the bruises of life. All of us dance in *eros*, yet experience, too, the death wish, *thanatos*—which reflects our nostalgia for the womb.

All religions still in touch with the body and the earth recognize the power of water to renew, cleanse, and create a sense of rebirth. In the ancient Near East, immersing in fresh water played a central role in cultic life, from the Children of Israel at Sinai to the Baptism of Jesus. And recently, immersing in the mikva—the "ritual bath"—which had been the practice only of Orthodox Jews, and which had become regarded as primitive and superstitious (not to mention misogynist), has undergone a surprising renaissance. Many Jews today have adopted the Hasidic practice of immersing in the mikva before each Shabbat, or even every morning. Women have begun reclaiming the mikva, even the core practice of immersing at the end of the monthly menstrual cycle. And the mikva is used to mark all kinds of transitions, beginnings, and endings, and is becoming, in some circles, as central as it once had been to our ancestors. As we will see, there are many layers to the mikva's symbolism, and many ways to make a mikva practice part of an embodied spiritual path. Yet perhaps what is most powerful about the mikva is its simplicity: bodies immersing in water, connecting with memories more ancient than memory.

Waters of Rebirth

Transitions are sacred. In between one state of being and another, in the liminal space where one is neither what one was nor yet what one is to become, there is a temporary approximation of Godliness: pure being without label, form, or differentiation. Before, there is identity, fixed in shape and meaning. Afterward, there will be a new identity, different in content but equally defined. But in between, in the moments of transition and change, there is a namelessness that recalls the ineffable.

Moments and spaces of transition touch the realm of the unseen, and thus contain danger as well as possibility. Most religious life takes place within defined bounds and regions. Remove the definitions, and a sort of spiritual anarchy takes place that carries within it the seed of disarray. Thus we place a mezuzah at every doorway, a talisman containing a sacred text. We honor shifts in our bodies with ceremonies of designation and demarcation. And we ritually mark a transition, as if to acknowledge what might too easily be forgotten.

The mikva is a shrine to transition, marking the movements from taboo to permitted, from profane to sacred. And it marks transition by embodying it. Suspended, naked, in the waters of Eden, we are stripped of signifiers of identity or role. We entered the world in this way, naked and alone, and we will leave the world in this way as well. Thus do we move from one state to the next.

But the mikva also shelters, nurtures; its waters are waters of life that can return us to a state of innocence. It is possible to enter the mikva thinking of errands, irritants, and all the mundane detritus of quotidian existence—and exit unable to remember why they mattered so dearly. One person may enter a cynic and emerge a believer. Another may begin with clouded eyes and end with a vision of clarity. Poke the mikva with the sticks of rational inquiry and you will find little there, other than the bruises inflicted by criticism. As with love and desire, there is little reasonable about the sacred. But enter the waters with a broken heart and you may find a wordless healing.

Let's first explore the mikva in Jewish textual tradition. It derives from biblical verses in which the Children of Israel are described as "washing themselves"—in one instance, in a "fountain for purging." Given the significance attached to each of the occasions (for example, the revelation at Sinai), the Talmudic sages took this to mean something other than an ordinary bath, and understood it in terms of Leviticus 11:36, which states that both property and people "shall be *tahor* only [by means of] a spring, a pit, or a gathering of water." From here, the Rabbis developed the halachic requirements for the mikva, a word that on its own simply means "gathering," as in a gathering of water.

According to halacha, the mikva is used at the end of a woman's menstrual bleeding, when a person converts to Judaism, and before marriage. In addition, in a practice not widely observed today outside the Orthodox world, new dishes are immersed in the mikva prior to their first use (they, too, must be "converted" and sanctified for divine use, since eating is a sacred act). In the time of the Temple, the high priest immersed in the mikva prior to commencing the sacrificial rite on Yom Kippur. And today, mikvas are used to commemorate new jobs, Sabbaths and holidays, births, divorces, completions of cycles of study—all moments of transformation, at which the mikva is both the marker and the enactor of change.

The mikva itself must conform to a number of specifications, all of which are pregnant with symbolism. It must consist of a natural water: a spring or lake, or rainwater gathered in a cistern—though nowadays, many mikvas consist of built structures whose water "kisses" the natural water, so the water in which you immerse can be cleaned and heated while still maintaining a connection to the actual mikva. The minimum amount of water in a valid mikva is forty *se'ah* (roughly two hundred gallons), a number that symbolizes wholeness, the completion of a cycle, and the readiness for rebirth—as in the forty days Moses spent on Mount Sinai, the forty years the Israelites wandered in the desert, the forty days of the flood in the story of Noah, and the forty days between conception and an embryo taking human form. Forty is the number of liminality, where a person is in between, neither "before" nor "after." Forty is also the numerical equivalent of *mem*, the first letter of the word mikva and the first and last letters of the word *mayim* (water), which in the Kabbalah is the element most often gendered feminine, signifying the eternal present, without history or trajectory; in a sense, all that ever is. *Mem*, the middle letter of the Hebrew alphabet, is the letter of transition and change; midway between *aleph* (past) and *taf* (future)—letters that, together, spell *emet*, or truth. Aryeh Kaplan notes that according to the Bahir, the mysterious kabbalistic book that appeared in the twelfth century, the shape of the letter itself—which in its usual form is open but is closed when found at the end of a word—represents the womb, open during birth but closed during pregnancy.[2]

In kabbalistic and Hasidic practice, the mikva has long held a central place. The Ari, Rabbi Isaac Luria, would immerse in a natural spring near Safed every day—the spot is now a pilgrimage site, and perhaps the most famous mikva in the world. Two and a half centuries later, Rabbi Nachman of Breslov commended the mikva as a rectification for sin, especially improper sexual behavior, and would call immersing "the first step" in turning from error. Indeed, Rabbi Nachman offered all sorts of promises, recommendations, and advice for mikva practice—to remain underwater until breath has run out, to go at least three times a week, and so on. His essential theme, though, is that immersion in the mikva is the mystery of being contained in water, where the illusory differentiation that comes from ordinary life on land is temporarily suspended.

Finally, mikvas are uniquely gendered places. Traditionally, they were "women's spaces," in the same way that pre-egalitarian synagogues were "men's spaces," even though men have also used them for centuries. They are places of healing and yielding, not of acquisition, activity, or production. A mikva's warm waters invite associations of the womb, while a cold, natural mikva may demand surrender. All these symbols—water, the womb, rebirth—are feminine ones, as is, for some people, the mikva's focus on the body. Of course, it is problematic to ascribe any particular characteristics to particular genders; it's easy to be overdeterministic, to think that typological "male" and "female" equal actual men and women. Still, to miss what is archetypically feminine about the mikva deprives men of an opportunity to explore that part of themselves, and takes from women one of the few

Jewish spaces that was traditionally theirs. A mikva is not masculinized when men immerse in it. It remains the womb, the ocean, the mother, and the Divine Presence—and it promises rebirth.

Solitary Mikva Practices

At the center of every mikva practice is the elegantly simple action of immersing the body into water. As with most of the other embodied practices in this book, it is possible to go through the motions with the body alone. However, it is also possible to deepen the practice, with attention and intention.

First, nothing should be between you and the natural waters of the mikva. It is proper to remove not only your clothes, but also jewelry, Band-Aids, nail polish, and makeup. Most people shower before entering as well. As you prepare, practice silence (or at least avoidance of small talk), paying attention to the sensations of the body, and taking your time. Try to notice how you feel on all four levels, and accept whatever sensations arise.

Second, you may wish to set intentions (*kavvanot*) for your immersion. Because the mikva marks transition, one *kavvanah* might be what you would like to let go of, or welcome in, as you immerse. If before Shabbat, maybe there is something from the week you would like to stop thinking about; if after menstruation, perhaps you want to look ahead at the month to come. Or the *kavvanah* may be simply what you are seeking right now: renewal, cleansing, rebirth. Or you might select one of the longer *kavvanot* written by contemporary ritual-makers. There are dozens of such texts, but we will look at two that are representative. One simple, beautiful *kavvanah* comes from Rabbi Nina Beth Cardin:

> *El Maleh Rachamim*, God full of mercy, with an overflowing heart I approach the waters of the mikveh, gathered from the rain sent here from the heavens. Let these waters rush strong against my body, washing away all sadness and sorrow, all worries and fears. Let them refresh my soul and restore my strength.
>
> God, as my cycle begins anew, let these coming weeks be a time of rejoicing; let this month be the season of our dreams come true. Let our house be filled with promise and joy, with the rays of

Your radiance shining upon us. It is to You we turn, God; in You we trust.[3]

Or consider this poetic *kavvanah* from CLAL, the National Center for Learning and Leadership:

> Immersion in water softens our form,
> Making us malleable,
> Dissolving some of the rigidity of who we are.
> This allows us to decide who we wish to be when we come out of the
> water.
> The water changes us neither by washing away something
> Nor by letting something soak in to us,
> But simply by softening us
> So that we can choose
> To remold ourselves into a different image.[4]

For the immersion itself (women customarily immerse an even number of times; men an odd number), some people like to stay underwater for many seconds; others bob up and down quickly. See what works best for you. When you find the mind wandering, especially if it's judging or planning, bring it back to the body, which is providing you with ample reasons to pay attention.

After the first immersion, women recite the blessing:

בָּרוּךְ אַתָּה יְיָ אֱלֹהֵינוּ מֶלֶךְ הָעוֹלָם אֲשֶׁר קִדְּשָׁנוּ

בְּמִצְוֹתָיו וְצִוָּנוּ עַל הַטְּבִילָה

Baruch ata adonai eloheinu melech ha'olam, asher kid'shanu bv'mitzvotav, v-tzivanu al ha'tevilah.

Praised are You, Adonai, God of all creation, who sanctifies us with Your commandments and commanded us concerning immersion.[5]

Finally, as you leave the mikva, especially after you are showered, dressed, and back in the normal world, I suggest moving a bit slower than usual, if you can. See if the body feels differently, as if maybe there is something to this primitive act that we still don't fully understand. Taking on a mikva practice, whether for halachic or purely spiritual reasons, is a way to tap into some of the oldest magic in the Jewish tradition. It is a practice laden with kabbalistic symbolism and enriched by mindful attention. And though it sometimes requires a bit of effort, its deepest teachings seem to come from a source so simple as to be inexplicable.

Communal Mikva Practices

Essentially the mikva is a solitary place. Communication is impossible within its waters, and immersion is an act of becoming alone with your deeper self. Nonetheless, mikvas are frequently communal spaces as well. In both men's and women's mikvas, it's not unusual to see families or friends going together, chatting the entire time. For Americans, most of whom rarely see one another without clothes, the experience can be somewhat jarring. We're not used to seeing fathers and sons interact this way, or male friends sharing such physical intimacy without the protective machismo of the locker room. In many women's mikvas, the intimacy is even greater, as women check one another's bodies to be sure all barriers have been removed (nail polish, stray hairs, bandages), and people watch over the mikva itself to ensure that those using it immerse fully.

Of course, it's natural to feel shy in such contexts, but precisely due to the intimacy of the mikva, it has become a place for powerful communal rituals in recent years. In some communities, for example, groups of people go to the mikva together before Shabbat, singing *niggunim* and sharing the sorts of intentions and aspirations we reviewed earlier. There is an undeniable power to such confession. Simply being naked physically, in a supportive communal setting, allows us to be naked emotionally, as the breaking of one boundary eases the breaking of another. It's not "normal" to do this, but that's the point: to create a temporary zone of the non-normal, where rules that ordinarily keep us safe may be momentarily suspended. The metaphor of clothing is an apt one: without clothing, we cannot survive, and with it, we express ourselves, play roles, and send important messages. But if we never take our clothes off with another person, the finest garments can become like prison uniforms.

Naturally, creating a communal mikva ritual requires some preparation—it's not wise to approach another man or woman in the mikva and spontaneously ask if they would like to "share"! Here are some "best practices" that I've learned over years of leading and participating in group mikva rituals.

1. First, choose your setting with care: a natural mikva, such as a secluded lake or stream; or a formal mikva where you will not be disturbed; or even a "spiritual mikva," which may not conform to halachic requirements but that provides privacy or ease.

2. Once you've chosen your setting, create sacred space by refraining from chitchat, connecting with your co-participants, and listening to what they say. The singing of a song, or chanting of a *niggun*, can help create the mood and make newcomers feel more comfortable.

3. As you undress, notice the mind. How does it feel to be in this space, with these people? If this is not for you, can you specify why? If it is working for you, what about it is working? Typically, I learn a lot about myself before the practice is even underway. Also, there's a religiously important difference between feeling uncomfortable and *being aware of* feeling uncomfortable. If you can learn to cultivate an awareness large enough to contain even difficult states of mind, the practice is worth it for this reason alone.

4. Once everyone is standing in (or alongside) the mikva, proceed one at a time, with each participant having the opportunity to speak—either to share his or her intention, or say what he or she would like to let go of this week, or talk about whatever he or she is feeling, before immersing in a way that feels comfortable. Some people may want to tell a story (if there's time); other people may want to say nothing. That's fine; what's important is to let the mikva do the work. Of course, everything that is said in the mikva should be held in confidentiality.

5. As each person immerses, the remainder of the group can "hold the space" either in silence or with a *niggun*. Try to discourage ordinary speech during this extraordinary time; a noble silence, in

which conversation is limited to necessary words only, allows everyone to go inward.

6. And finally, when everyone has finished, you may want to conclude with another *niggun*, a shared blessing, or simply by expressing gratitude to the group for their openness, bravery, and honesty. Take a few breaths, if you've got the time, and close the ritual with attentiveness, not rushing off to get showered and changed, but being watchful for any changes of mind, heart, or body.

A shared mikva practice is an easy way to link this powerful, embodied spiritual practice to the forging of bonds of community, friendship, and fellowship. It's a bit weird at first, but let's not be overly afraid of the weird. That word often covers a lot of anxieties, fears, and assumptions, all of which merit exploration. Find the practices at the edge of your comfort zone, because there they will teach you more than you expect. Eventually, they may help gradually expand that space, allowing a wider and fuller experience of the world you thought you understood.

Beyond the Mikva

For women, the practice of the mikva is intimately connected with the natural cycles of the body, in particular the menstrual cycle. As we saw in the last chapter, the language used by the tradition to describe these processes, *tumah* and *taharah*, is susceptible to many interpretations, from ancient cultic notions of purity and contamination to contemporary ones of ending and renewal. In recent years, many women have spoken quite forcefully on this subject, reclaiming both the language of *taharah* and the practice of visiting the mikva once a month. For example, the movement from *tumah* to *taharah* is one, traditionally, of red to white, *gevurah* to *hesed*, constriction to opening—processes that parallel parts of the menstrual cycle itself. Or, perhaps more radically, many women have gone "beyond the mikva," creating new rituals to celebrate, rather than fear, the natural cycles of the body.

Of course, as a man, I am unable to share in this embodied experience. To be sure, there is plenty of Jewish male writing on menstruation, but text is not experience. And since no Jewish book on "God in your body" would be complete without the significance of menstruation, I have asked Holly Taya Shere, a gifted folklorist, ritual facilitator, and educator, to share practices she and her community have developed for exploring conscious menstruation, beyond the mikva. Some of these practices are new, some are ancient; some may seem challenging, others inviting. As a whole, though, they offer a range of ritual options that complement that of the mikva, and offer transformative ways for women to experience this most sacred of processes, and the meaning of the Talmudic prayer that *Elohai, neshama shenata bi, tehora*: "God, the soul you have planted within me is pure."[6]

Your Blood Is a Blessing: Exploring Conscious Menstruation by Holly Taya Shere

In ancient times, women's menstruation was revered as deeply powerful. Today, however, it is often regarded with dread, disgust, and denial. Experiencing shame or annoyance at the sacred life-giving cycles of our bodies disconnects women from our power and our spirit, and keeps us from embracing and celebrating our whole selves as sacred.

When I first explored new ways of relating with my menstrual cycle, I was surprised to experience profound changes in my physical, emotional, and spiritual health. Shifting the way I related to my menstruation changed my life. Since that time, I've witnessed the following menstrual-awareness practices bring profound change and healing to many women. I invite you to explore these practices, and create others, for one cycle or for many. Open to the possibility of sacred flow in your life!

ROSH HODESH: CONNECT WITH THE MOON
When women live surrounded by only natural light, with no electricity brightening the night, we cycle in accordance with the moon. In most indigenous cultures it is understood that women bleed with the new moon and ovulate with the full moon. The Jewish calendar is a lunar one, and Rosh Hodesh, the new moon celebration at the beginning of each month, is often honored, in Susan Berrin's words, "as a symbol of renewal, as a women's covenant, as a marking of time, and as a re-

minder of cyclical development and focus."[7] The Talmud records that "Whoever blesses the new moon in her time welcomes the Divine Presence,"[8] the feminine aspect of God.

Today, while it may not be possible for all of us to live in such accord with the moon, there are many ways to make the moon part of our monthly cycle. You might simply go outside at night and gaze at the moon, paying attention to her cycles, and knowing where they are when your own cycle begins. Or you might sing to her, study her energies, dance in her shadows. Use a moon calendar (*We'moon* is my favorite—www.wemoon.ws), coloring in the days of your moon blood and making notes about your experience so you can trace patterns across time. As you are mapping your cycle, be compassionate with yourself and let go of self-judgement. Today, some women in the process of reconnecting with the lunar cycle as their body-map bleed with the full moon for a year or two before eventually bleeding with the new moon. There is no right or wrong time for your moon blood to arrive. Trust the wisdom of your body.

You may also wish to gather in a circle of women to celebrate and mark Rosh Hodesh. Explore the renewal you are opening to in your own life, as the moon is renewed.

SHABBAT: KEEP A BLEEDING SABBATH

The importance of marking times of rest and renewal is emphasized throughout the Torah and Judaism. Teachings on honoring Shabbat appear in Genesis' description of creation, in the Ten Commandments, and in directives in Leviticus on keeping a Jubilee year, a Sabbath time for the earth. The practice of a "Bleeding Shabbat" can be potent and healing when practiced during a woman's bleeding time.

Take the first day of your moon time as a bleeding Sabbath. As soon as your moon blood begins, cancel whatever you can. Make time to give your bleeding body the space it needs. Whether you take the whole day or just two hours to yourself, be clear about allotting some amount of time and space to honor your bleeding body—and stick with what you define. Once your body is absolutely clear that you are not going to try to force it to do things it doesn't want to do, or interact with people when it is not ready, your cramps will likely dissipate. Every woman has different needs, and every woman's needs change from cycle to cycle. Some moons you may need four hours of space to yourself, and some moons you may need two and a half days. Give yourself as much time as you can in Sabbath space, and be open to exploring during the coming moons what works best for your body. Listen to what your body needs.

During your moon, engage in sacred reminders to honor your blood. Experiment. Be creative. Give yourself a moon time uniform—for example, dressing only in flowy maroon clothes. Eat reddish-purple foods—beets, blood oranges, and pomegranates. Drink red juices. Only read books or listen to music created by women. Use burgundy sheets. Transform your space into a womb sanctuary.

YOM KIPPUR KATAN: LET YOUR BLOOD FLOW

The traditional but little-known Jewish ritual of *Yom Kippur Katan*, an end-of-the-month practice of personal review and atonement, can be a potent premenstrual or menstrual practice. On a psychospiritual level, *Yom Kippur Katan* parallels the shedding of the uterine lining and loss of potential life that occurs on a physical level for a menstruating woman. On a physical level, *Yom Kippur Katan* can be supported by allowing blood to flow and allowing the physical and energetic body to shed, release, and transform.

I invite you to explore an embodied *Yom Kippur Katan*. Do not put anything inside your body to catch your blood during your menstruation, particularly on the first day of your flow. That means no tampons, no "Instead cups," and so on; switching to pads is an important step in honoring your body and your cycle. (Many women I know who had extremely difficult moon times, involving cramping, nausea, and digestive discomfort, experienced significant healing and release when they transitioned from tampons to pads.) During menstruation, you are shedding your uterine lining, letting go of whatever you have been holding onto from the past month, as well as releasing the potential life in that particular egg that made the journey to your womb. Letting go is a process that necessitates going with the flow. Stopping up your body with tampons not only impedes blood flow (and puts you at risk for toxic shock syndrome), it creates an energetic compression that is stressful and counterintuitive for a physical and energetic body that is in a mode to shed, release, and transform.

EMBRACE CONSCIOUS LANGUAGE AND THOUGHT

The word *Abracadabra* has its origins in two ancient Aramaic words meaning "I create as I speak." Language is powerful and can be a tool for creating our realities. Do you speak of your menstruation with dread and negativity? Do you complain to friends that your period is a drag? If so, a change in language and thinking can be key in opening to transformation.

Honor menstruation in your language and your thoughts. Regard your blood as a blessing. Some women choose to speak of menstruation as moon time, and their flow as moon blood, making explicit the connection of the menstrual cycle to the cycle of the moon. This naming serves as an important reminder that our bleeding bodies are sacred, in tune with nature cycles and mysteries, and should be honored. When friends share with me that they are bleeding, I respond with joy and reverence, and ask them how they are creating sacred space to honor their bleeding bodies this cycle. At the beginning of each moon time, I offer a blessing of gratitude for the ability to release, renew, and cycle with the moon, such as *Baruch ata adonai, m'chadesh et amcha* [or *isha*] *im ha levana*, A fountain of blessings are you, holy one, my God, who renews your people (or women) with the moon.

Many blessings on your menstrual-awareness journey!

13
Nature

The foregoing generations beheld God face to face; we, through their eyes. Why should not we also enjoy an original relation to the universe? Why should not we have a poetry and philosophy of insight and not of tradition, and a religion by revelation to us, and not the history of theirs? Embosomed for a season in na-ture, whose floods of life stream around and through us, and in-vite us by the powers they supply, to action proportioned to nature, why should we grope among the dry bones of the past?
Ralph Waldo Emerson[1]

It goes without saying that our bodies are influenced by our environ-ment. Mood shifts in context, and studies have shown that merely being in a natural place with trees, water, and open space triggers re-laxation within the body. This may be for mystical or for purely evolutionary-biological reasons—trees, water, and open space connote shelter, food, and drink, and organisms that respond positively to such stimuli are more likely to succeed than those that do not. But perhaps reasons are secondary. Perhaps doubt, which Abraham Joshua Heschel calls "an interdepartmental activity of the mind," might be subordinated to wonder and to the quite real shifts that take place in the body as a result of being within nature.

Just as the body undermines the reductions of science and the curlicues of esotericism, so, too, does it deny the objections of the cynic. One who gazes at a sunset and only sees the mechanical operation of the solar system is lacking something essentially human. It is natural, noble, and ennobling to be moved by the blooming of flowers. Of course, failing to notice cliché is naïveté—but a person who never transcends it is trapped.

The whole momentum to theologize, philosophize, or otherwise reduce that which we call "nature" is a subtle error: toward ideas about the thing, away from the thing itself, to paraphrase the poet Wallace Stevens. Speculations are interesting, but none can substitute for the actual changes that take place in the body as a result of being in nature—and the changes in the mind, heart, and soul that quickly follow.

For example, it has been observed for centuries that the Hebrew word for nature, *hateva*, is numerically equivalent to one of the words for God, *Elohim*.[2] Depending on your perspective, this may be mere numerological wit or a linguistic insight into the cosmos, but the sensibility is sublime. What would it mean to experience the natural world, the context of the body, as merely a mask of God? What is the significance of the fact that when we simply leave our homes and enter the wilderness, a change takes place within us?

The Bible reveals a curious pattern of revelation in the wilderness. Abraham was told to get walking (*lech lecha*) away from his father's house. Jacob dreamed of ladders to heaven on his night journey in the wilderness, and on another journey years later, he wrestled until dawn. Moses and the burning bush, the Children of Israel at Sinai, Elijah, Ezekiel, Miriam, Jonah—the deepest experiences of nearly every Jewish prophet or prophetess are connected, in some way, to the world apart from civilization. Let alone Jesus in the wilderness, the Buddha under the Bodhi tree, and Muhammad in the desert.

The Torah also prescribes a thrice-annual pilgrimage, on Passover, Shavuot, and Sukkot—the Hebrew word for these festivals is *regel*, which also means "leg." Imagine what such a pilgrimage must have been like—to take family and livestock on a week-long journey through pristine wilderness, finally reaching Jerusalem and uniting with thousands of other pilgrims.

These two notions—of entering wilderness as the precedent for revelation, and of pilgrimage as sacred journey—are not allegorical. They are about actual nature, and actual leave-taking. Of course, the

Bible does not have our notion of "nature"; that concept depends on its privation, and makes no sense in a time in which everyone experienced it all the time. In biblical times, what would today be the most rustic of vacations was the default tone of everyday life: peace and quiet, no electricity or running water, and creatures of all sorts, always nearer than we might prefer. Our texts tell us that wilderness is the realm of the sacred, and the journey is irreplaceable.

There is no substitute for actually going there yourself. *Lech lecha*—go. As with eating, walking, and all the other embodied practices in this book, we need to work in order to attain the state of mind that was routine for our ancestors, since we lack the baseline immersion in nature that they took for granted. But with some basic preparations and practice, you can observe physical changes in the body that take place when it is hiking, walking, or simply being in nature—and, as we've seen before, grow so attuned to your soul's fluctuations that you notice even the subtlest of movements.

Mindfulness in Nature

Mindfulness is utterly transparent. On the outside, your embodied spiritual nature practice may look like a simple walk in the woods or a hike in the desert. On the inside, what is happening is that the body is changing, and the soul is shifting—and you are aware of it all. In particular, focusing on a few key elements of your experience in nature can transform a simple day trip into an embodied spiritual practice:

Solitude. Choose a spot that is unlikely to be crowded. If you can, go alone. If you do not feel safe alone, then bring a trusted friend or loved one—and don't talk much. I find that on many hikes, I'm so happy to talk with my friends that I have to interrupt the conversation just to look at the scenery, let alone to notice changes in the body. These are fun trips, and there's nothing wrong with that, but the noise blots out the quieter sounds of spirit. When you are alone, pause to appreciate the sensations of being on your own, not filling the emptiness with more thought, sound, and fury—but slowing down enough for the emptiness to fill you instead. Use your physical disposition to influence your mental and emotional ones.

Transition. Set the intention that this trip will be a bit different from the ordinary. Promise not to fiddle with the settings on your camera. And transition into your hike with a ritual, to shift your consciousness from your everyday mind into a more receptive mode. Your transition ritual can be very simple—just ten mindful breaths, for example, with eyes closed, to wash off the "travel dust" and begin. Or you may prefer a more colorful practice, such as burning incense or saying a prayer. As we saw in the previous chapter, the symbols that mark transition may seem arbitrary; but the fact that they mark it is not. You may need to take this on faith; from the perspective of mundane mind, spiritual mind looks tedious, or silly, or good-but-not-right-now. That's the great trap, and it is answered only by remembering that the point of leaving a place is to leave, not to replicate the conditions of where you were. Begin your hike aware that you are entering sacred space, the cathedral of nature.

Attention. As you walk, feel your weight and the momentum that propels you—just begin to turn on your perceptual apparatus, heightening your sensitivity and opening up. Go for a while without judgment or expectation. Maybe the first few minutes will be boring or difficult. Maybe you'll worry about whether you locked your car. Once you've started, though, just notice, and literally let nature take its course. Does the mind shift as things quiet down? Have you noticed the birds or the trees more? Just turn your attention to what you're feeling, seeing, smelling, and hearing; drink it in with mindfulness.

Pace. I've lived much of my life in New York City, where people walk very quickly, and sometimes I hike along a mountain ridge as if I'm rushing for the subway. See if you can catch yourself rushing, and when you do, notice the mind. Chances are, simply cutting your pace in half will produce an immediate shift in perception. The flowers look brighter, the quiet is more noticeable; there's an almost textural difference that, with practice, you can learn to perceive. Take a few steps at this slower pace—see if you can feel your steps more, relax more, experience more. You can also try speeding up and seeing if you can maintain your relaxed resting in open awareness even as you begin to walk faster.

Pausing. Like dancing, hiking and walking in nature are as much about the stillness as the movement. Every so often, perhaps even suddenly, stop randomly and look around. Notice that you have been speeding past whole worlds: insects, flowers, microecosystems. Feel the breeze, if there is one; the sunlight, if there's sun. Feel your circulation, your breath. Don't only stop moving when you need to eat a granola bar; stop randomly, look, feel.

Gaze. Once you begin moving again, focus on your gaze. What would it be like to keep looking ahead at eye level while you hiked? Even if the ground is uneven, you probably don't need to watch your feet as much as you think. I find, when I keep my gaze ahead and only turn my head slowly, that the shift in body posture itself creates increased mindfulness, gratitude, and love. It doesn't even depend on a beautiful landscape; I might be walking through an ordinary stand of trees, but if I am moving slowly, and looking carefully, the veins of each leaf mirror the veins of my hands, and it becomes a bit easier to dissolve the spaces between.

Breathing. Breathing mindfully is another simple embodied way to "tune in" to the Presence you seek in the woods. Just taking a deep breath can remind your heart of smells in the air that you didn't know you had forgotten. One more complex practice comes from Native American culture, where messengers are reported to have run the equivalent of a marathon with only the water they could hold in their mouths, breathing through their noses, exclusively, for over twenty-five miles. See if you can breathe through your nose for twenty-five minutes—and notice what it does to the mind. As we saw earlier, the intellectual soul, *neshama*, is intimately bound up with breath, *neshima*, and when you alter your breath, you alter your consciousness. Chances are you'll also need to slow down, since you're not taking in as much oxygen, but, as a side benefit of this practice, you're more likely to burn fat (rather than muscle) when you breathe in this way. As before, the point is very simple: to be present, in the body, with the mind quiet enough to let in the world. Simple, but not easy.

The Path of Blessing

Being in nature is the ideal time to pray, chant, or otherwise connect with the sacred. Kabbalat Shabbat, the enormously popular service that greets and begins the Sabbath, was originally performed by the circle of the Ari in the fields surrounding Safed. A Talmudic legend tells of two rabbis who were walking through a forest, expounding on the mysteries of creation, when suddenly the trees themselves burst into song to join them (singing, incidentally, Psalm 148, sometimes known as "the psalm of the trees"). Praying in nature, though it may take some effort at first, eventually flows easily. What to say is secondary. You might choose your own words (perhaps beginning with how you feel, physically or emotionally), or choose a favorite psalm, prayer, or chant. (I find the *Ashrei* prayer almost always resonates with a beautiful natural setting.) Or you might consider one of the great Jewish nature prayers, such as this petition by Rabbi Nachman of Breslov:

> Master of the Universe,
> grant me the ability to be meditate alone;
> may I be able to leave every day for the fields
> among the trees and grasses and every growing thing,
> and there may I be worthy to meditate in seclusion
> and enter into conversation,
> my prayer between myself and my master,
> to speak there all that is in my heart.
> And all the herbs of the field,
> and all the grasses and the trees, and all the plants—
> all will awaken at my call.
> And rise up and lend their strength and vitality
> to the words of my confession and prayer,
> until my prayer and confession are utterly perfected
> by the weeds of the field
> which take all their power, and life-force, and spirit
> to the highest root—all bound up in my prayer.
> And in this way, I shall merit to open my heart
> to be abundant in prayer and petitions, and
> in holy conversation before You who are full of Mercy.

And before You I will pour out my words
until I can pour out my heart like water before God,
and lift my hands to You, for my soul
and the souls of all who are with me.[3]

Whether you use these words, those of formal liturgy or those of your own creation, this is the natural setting for prayer. Use it.

Rabbi Nachman also prescribed solitary meditation in nature to his followers:

When summer begins to approach, it is very good to meditate in the fields. This is a time when you can pray to God with longing and yearning. When every bush of the field begins to return to life and grow, they all yearn to be included in prayer and meditation ... It is best to seclude yourself and meditate in the meadows outside the city. Go to a grassy field, for the grass will awaken your heart.[4]

Rabbi Nachman's particular practice, *hitbodedut*, is an emotional, cathartic meditation-prayer practice that uses the solitude (yet not aloneness) in nature as a space for the solitary (but not alone) pouring out of the heart. The body relaxes in nature, and so the heart opens. Rabbi Nachman advises simply to start with whatever is on your mind and to speak these thoughts out loud. Surrounded by plants and animals, the words can flow more easily. Try for half an hour to speak to God directly—even if you can only say, "I wish I believed in you, God, but I can't." It's harder than it sounds, but being in nature is the place to start.

Other forms of meditation are enabled by nature as well. After all, the Buddha attained enlightenment sitting under a tree—not in an apartment building. In addition to basic sitting practices, you might try adapting walking meditation (discussed earlier) for the trail. It's interesting to walk at the very slow meditative pace in a natural setting, for example; the body instantly aligns itself with the slower rhythms of nature, and, especially if the walking meditation follows a period of faster pace, a great, attentive relaxation often arises. You'll likely notice details that you would otherwise miss, and relax into your body's remembering. Or, you might try taking a certain number of steps for each breath, grounding the attention in the body if it has wandered. There are dozens of permutations—play with them; shift your attention from your feet, to sounds, to the whole picture at once. Meditate in movement and in stillness. Paraphrasing poet Carl Sandburg, you're in nature—let it work.

In addition to meditation practices, there are two traditional blessings that can be recited in places of natural beauty. Both have the standard beginning—*Baruch ata adonai eloheinu melech ha'olam*. The first then concludes *she'kacha lo b'olamo*, who has such beauty in his world. The second concludes *oseh ma'aseh bereshit*, who does the work of creation. That there are two blessings is, itself, significant. The first is meant for when we see places or objects of beauty—streams, fields, and so on; the second is meant for objects of awe, such as mountains, craters, and sublime vistas. At least a thousand years before Kant, our rabbinic sages knew about the difference between the sublime and the beautiful, and found it to be religiously significant.

Sometimes the identical view is amenable to either blessing—the choice, in such a case, depends on which response it evokes. Do you feel a sense of awe, of smallness in the face of immensity? Or do you feel a sense of closeness and communion? You can explore each of these feelings as embodied phenomena. For me, the experience of *she'kacha lo b'olamo* is one of relaxing; of merging into the Divine. It is an intimacy with the immanent, the (Shechinah). The body feels grounded, yet open; it is as if I have been anointed. *Oseh ma'aseh bereshit*, in contrast, is an experience of speechlessness—"this takes my breath away"—even trembling. I am in the presence of a great power (*yesod*) that reveals the transcendent beauty (*tiferet*) of creation itself. The body feels *yirat shamayim*, the fear of heaven.

Finally, there are moments of being in the woods, or the desert, or the mountains, at which the natural sentiments of humanity are awakened by the body's return to its intended habitat. Dogmas vanish, and theological debates seem, if not resolved, then suspended by the immediacy of reverence. Whatever its source, the phenomenon is real, and so gratitude—without regard to the object of that gratitude—arises naturally. There is no recipe for this practice other than to clear the mind, breathe the air, and let the heart build a bridge to spirit. Thus are four worlds integrated, and a walk in the woods becomes *l'shem shamayim*, for the sake of heaven. As Emerson wrote:

> Standing on the bare ground—my head bathed by the blithe air and uplifted into infinite space—all mean egotism vanishes. I become a transparent eyeball; I am nothing; I see all; the currents of the Universal Being circulate through me; I am part or particle of God.[5]

❊   ❊   ❊   ❊

14
The Five Senses

The heart hears. Although technically we hear through our ears, the process must be completed with the heart.

Rabbi Nachman of Breslov[1]

The faculties of sound, smell, touch, taste, and sight are the portals between our bodies and the world. Through them we glimpse the physical world, partake of it, and are able to interact with it. Yet so seamless are the processes of perception that we often pass through these portals without even noticing that we are doing so. Of course, if we were always entranced by the physicality of seeing, we wouldn't be able to navigate our way across the street. However, the instinctive and immediate rush to process perception, rather than notice it, is worth interrupting for several reasons.

First, doing so inserts a pause into what is otherwise a continuum of *ratzon*, desire. Usually, upon encountering a sight, sound, or smell, we immediately form a subtle like or dislike of it, an almost imperceptible judgment that reinforces the identification with the *yetzer*, the selfish inclination. Slowing down enough to notice perception as it happens allows for a small *p'sik*, a little space in which these tightly wound knots may be loosened.

Second, pausing in this way is like taking a microvacation, available at any time. At any moment, noticing the sensation of touch—fingers against paper, skin against clothing—can instantly move the attention away from what you were worrying about to what is happening now. Of course, this doesn't work when the stress is too great, but often, miraculously, it does.

Finally, experiencing sense-perception as an embodied phenomenon loosens the conventional sense of a being behind the becoming, a doer behind the doing. As the Hasidim say, all is in the hands of heaven—or, *l'havdil*. In the words of Nietzsche, paraphrasing the Buddhist Visuddhimagga, or "Path of Purification," "there is no 'being' behind the doing, acting, becoming; the 'doer' has simply been added to the deed by the imagination—the doing is everything."[2]

Sound

We hear all the time—but how often do we listen? In English, when we want someone to pay attention, we say "look." In Hebrew, we say *sh'ma*, "listen." The *Shema*, the polysemous, ever-evolving watchword of the Jewish faith, is a demand to pay attention: Listen, you Godwrestler, That Which Is—YHVH, that which we set as our god—YHVH is One.

Listening is not often thought of as an embodied phenomenon, even though it is obviously exactly that. Not only is it something done with the body; it's something that happens *to* the body. Sound is vibration that is reproduced upon a medium in the ear. The materiality of sound is its foundation, and there is nothing like the physical world of *asiyah* to cut through the noise of the other ones. Normally, when we listen, we jump right to the cognitive level (what is being said) or the emotive one (how we feel about it), and thus immediately depart from What Is in favor of the reactive mind's responses to it. Listening meditation is a form of *tshuvah*, of return to the real. Here is the basic practice. As soon as you're finished with this paragraph, pause your reading and listen to the sounds around you. Don't label them, don't judge them as either pleasant or unpleasant—just let the physical sensations happen. When thoughts come up, let them drop—and return your attention to the sensation of hearing. Try it for thirty seconds. Now.

If you're a *beinoni*, an "in-betweener" like myself, those thirty seconds probably took a long time to pass—listening meditation can be boring. Then again, boredom is a neglected gateway to enlightenment. What did you hear? What was the effect on your body, heart, and mind? Did your mind spin and fidget, trying to find something to *do*, or *think*, instead letting the world intrude on its thoughts? With practice, you can learn to let go easier, and in my experience, a relaxation of the body follows almost inexorably. The mind gives up, and sounds begin to be allowed rather than judged. And tension that was being held in the body, which was waiting for what's next, drops. Other times, listening meditation can be a symphony. Composer John Cage's *6'33"*, often erroneously called "Six minutes and thirty-three seconds of silence," is really an effort to enable the hearing of ordinary sounds that usually escape our notice. In Cage's work, a pianist sits down at a piano, opens the keyboard, and sits still for six minutes and thirty-three seconds before closing the keyboard again. Whatever takes place in that time—air-conditioning noise, seats being reshuffled, hoots of protest—is the form of the musical composition. You can do this even without John Cage. On the subway, in the car, or in the waiting room, attend to listening consciously for five (or six and a half) minutes. The timbres and rhythms that appear naturally, without any deliberate composition, can form a work of great beauty and complexity. Of course, we are hearing the same sounds as always, but to paraphrase Rabbi Nachman, now the heart hears.

It's even possible for bare listening to be a kabbalistic mystical practice, by abstaining from the automatic conceptual thinking that attends the perception of most sounds. Normally, when you hear the sound of a car, for example, the mind quickly labels the sound to be "car," even though what's really heard is a series of tones that, on their own, do not carry any specific referent. With practice, instead of hearing "car," you can learn simply to have the physical, embodied perception of sound, devoid of judgment and label. Not unlike Abraham Abulafia's mysticism of deconstruction, this reducing of aural phenomena to their constituent parts can, paradoxically, bring about a greater sense of unity than occasions the normal perception of objects.

All of these aspects of listening meditation result from the relinquishment of the mind's dominion over the self, which allows space for that which is beyond the mind to grow. By allowing the body, in *asiyah*, to predominate, we allow the world of *atzilut* to be known. This is not an additional world layered on top of the other four; it is the true reality of all. Working on computers and sitting at desks in ventilated rooms, it can be very easy to spend an entire day fully in the head. Yet a few minutes of sitting quietly, listening to ambient sound, can be a reminder of what is really going on: a body, in an environment, acting on and being acted on by the manifest, material universe. This is how to marry spirit and matter together.

This transparent, pure meditation practice is a wonderful way to interrupt the demands of the *yetzer hara* and ground in the real. At times, though, there may be too much stress, or too much suffering, for gentle methods of mindfulness—there are spiritual practices for such times as well. This simple Mother Letters meditation is one such practice.

Recall from Chapter 7 that the *Sefer Yetzirah*, the ancient Book of Creation, depicts how God creates the universe through language. According to the *Sefer Yetzirah*, there are three primary "mother" letters: *aleph*, which has no sound; *shin*, which has a sound like white noise ("Shhh!"), and *mem*, which has a pure, harmonic sound ("Mmmm"). These letters are the root of creation for the *Sefer Yetzirah* and embody the energetic ebbs and flows of the universe. *Shin* is the sound of *eish*, the word for fire; it is the male principle and the element of fire. *Mem* is the sound of *mayim*, water; it is the female principle and the element of water. *Aleph* is the first letter of *avir*, air; it has no gender and is the element of air. These three together with earth (*adamah*, the same root as *adam*, the human being, the earth-creature) form life. For the *Sefer Yetzirah*, God didn't just breathe into the earth to create humanity; God spoke the three primary letters.

We can imitate God by using the three mother letters in meditation. What's more, the sounds of the letters *shin*, *mem*, and *aleph* are similar to the sounds of the letters *shin*, *mem*, and *ayin*—the letters of the word *shema*, listen. The practice, which I sometimes do before I recite the *Shema*, is useful when I'm really at the end of my rope and need a break, and it's not difficult. Close the eyes and take a few breaths to prepare. Take a deep breath in and then exhale completely, pronouncing "Shhh." Really exhale all the way, until there is no carbon dioxide left in the lungs. Repeat with "Mmmm" and "Ahhh." Repeat the whole sequence three times, with the eyes closed, drinking in the experience of the sounds—how they feel in the body, how they resonate with the breath leaving the body.

Stay with this *Shema* practice, even if the first couple of times through are difficult. Fake the sigh if you have to on the "Ahhh"; fake the delight on the "Mmmm." At a certain point, the mind will probably loosen its grip, your jaw will relax, and a shift will take place.

To deepen the practice, try it with your ears closed; push shut your pinnas—the little "flaps" on your ears—with your forefingers and see how the resonances shift (the Talmud relates that ears are designed for "self-sealing" in this way[3]). You might visualize fire, water, and air as you pronounce the *shin*, *mem*, and *aleph*. Or you might imagine masculinity, femininity, and the transcendence of gender binarism. Or you can visualize the physical forms of the letters, carving out their shapes within your mind's eye—perhaps like white fire on black fire, in the forms of the Torah's mystical letters. Each of these additional layers will deepen your experience, though the purpose is just to wake up to the divine reality of this moment, in and through your body.

There are many words in the Jewish tradition, and many books to read. But without the ability to listen, none of them will penetrate beneath the reflective surface of the self, and thus none will be of any use deeper than amusement. Fortunately, there is always the world to call you back—if you choose to listen.

Smell

The sense of smell is simultaneously the most primitive sense, according to neurologists, and the loftiest, according to the Kabbalah. In both conceptions, it is the deepest of the senses, capable of evoking memories and delighting the soul. More so than sight or sound, fragrances are embodied; for better or worse, we really do become one with what we smell, as molecules of it enter our very bodies. And the many English words for pleasant smells—aroma, fragrance, scent, essence—suggest a exquisite attunement to the nuances of odor.

In the Jewish tradition, scent is the most mystical of the senses. The Holy Ari once said that all of the senses were affected by the sin of Adam except for the sense of smell, which still retains its purity and its power. And the Baal Shem Tov, it is said, would sniff tobacco during Torah study, as well as during prayer, and perceive in its scent "the sweet fragrance of the garden of Eden."[4] The word *mashiach* (Messiah) literally means "anointed one," since kings were anointed with fragrant oil; it, too, is an embodied Jewish word. Even God is said to enjoy the *re'ach nichoach*, the pleasant smell of the sacrifices. And there is a delightful Hasidic teaching that says that in the world to come, there are actual fragrances of kindness, charity, faith, and truth.

In religious practice, scents often play a role. The spices at Havdalah are perhaps the best known Jewish example—as the sweetness of Shabbat passes, they provide the last, lingering nuance of the day. But there are many others as well: the sweet *etrog* on Sukkot, the Sabbath smells of *cholent* or *hammin*, and perhaps most importantly, though absent from our lives, the incense burned in the ancient Temple. Today, incense is probably associated most with the counterculture, or perhaps with other religions. But the use of incense (according to a very detailed recipe) was central to the sacrificial cult of the Temple, and to the Talmudic texts that preserve it to this day. The *ketoret*, referred to in the Torah many times[5] but more fully described in the Talmud,[6] was like a potpourri made of cinnamon, myrrh, saffron, and other spices—eleven ingredients in all—and was burned at the astonishing rate of five pounds per day. The individual ingredients of the *ketoret* are each pregnant with symbolism—not least the *chelbenah*, which on its own is a foul-smelling herb, and thus symbolizes the inclusion of that which we perceive to be evil within the good—and, united, were seen as uniting heaven and earth.

The Rabbis of the Talmud, perhaps seeking to fill the void left by the loss of the incense ritual, instituted several blessings for fragrant smells that, like the blessings discussed in Chapter 1, cultivate gratitude, mindfulness, and recognition of the divine source of joy. Interestingly, the Rabbis located the biblical source for this practice in the Psalmist's phrase that "all the soul shall praise God," explaining that fragrance reaches the parts of the soul that could not be touched otherwise.[7] Food and drink sustain the body, but fragrance is the connecting point between the physical and what lies beyond.

There are five distinct blessings over fragrances. They all begin with the standard *Baruch ata adonai, eloheinu melech ha'olam*:

בָּרוּךְ אַתָּה יְיָ אֱלֹהֵינוּ מֶלֶךְ הָעוֹלָם בּוֹרֵא מִינֵי בְשָׂמִים

... *borei minei v'samim.*
... who creates varieties of fragrance. (For mixed spices or incense, perfume, or scent of nonvegetable or uncertain origin.)

בָּרוּךְ אַתָּה יְיָ אֱלֹהֵינוּ מֶלֶךְ הָעוֹלָם בּוֹרֵא עֲצֵי בְשָׂמִים

... *borei atzei v'samim.*
... who creates fragrant trees. (For shrubs, trees, or their flowers.)

בָּרוּךְ אַתָּה יְיָ אֱלֹהֵינוּ מֶלֶךְ הָעוֹלָם בּוֹרֵא עִשְׂבֵי בְשָׂמִים

... *borei isvei v'samim.*
... who creates fragrant herbs. (For herbs, grasses, and wildflowers.)

בָּרוּךְ אַתָּה יְיָ אֱלֹהֵינוּ מֶלֶךְ הָעוֹלָם בּוֹרֵא שֶׁמֶן עָרֵב

... *borei shemen areiv.*
... who creates fragrant oil.

בָּרוּךְ אַתָּה יְיָ אֱלֹהֵינוּ מֶלֶךְ הָעוֹלָם הַנּוֹתֵן רֵיחַ טוֹב בַּפֵּרוֹת

... *ha'noten reiach tov ba'perot.*
... who gives a good aroma to fruits.

As with other blessings, these are best performed with intention and quietness of mind; indeed, they are only to be recited, halachically, when smelling something deliberately. Why not take on the practice of ensuring that you recite at least one of these blessings every day? Literally "stop and smell the roses" as a spiritual practice: pause, enjoy the scent, and slowly recite the words of the blessing. The practice will extend even beyond the few moments it takes; you'll probably find yourself on the lookout for beautiful smells, and oriented toward sensory perception in a way you hadn't been before.

You might also find yourself devoting greater attention toward creating a healthy, organic olfactory environment. We are all familiar

with immaculate kitchens whose cleanliness is undermined by un-
bearable, chemically saturated faux-lemon scents, and with offices
with stale air, no plants, and bad fluorescent lighting. Such environments are not conducive to holy work. Treat your senses as religious
organs. Use less harsh, less toxic cleansers; bring plants into every
room; use natural soaps and massage oils on your skin; consider, in
creating environments for ritual or social gatherings, how to create
sacred spaces for all five senses, perhaps "smudging" a room, or even
people, with incense. Give honor to the accoutrements of aroma—
think of the beautiful spice boxes in the Jewish tradition, or the wonderful incense holders in the Buddhist one. Just seeing the beauty
and *kavod* given to a *kli kodesh*, a sacred vessel or implement, can be
a potent reminder of the body-grounded holiness that it helps to create. Our physical surroundings influence our souls because we are
embodied beings. If God created the faculties of the senses, they
should be sanctified.

Touch

All touch is sensual touch. Where our bodies encounter the world of
textures, and the energies of other human beings, lives the spark of ecstasy, the comfort of familiarity—even the possibility of transformation. And so, in the Jewish tradition, "touch" is often a euphemism for
sexuality, for better or for worse. Maimonides, who as a rationalist was
concerned that too much bodily sensation not distract from intellectual pursuits, regarded touch as a source of shame. As is well known
today, many rabbis forbid men to touch women (and vice versa), sens-
ing even in casual contact the electric energy of eros.

Touch can be taboo, transgressive—and also deeply healing. It is so
powerful, and so dangerous when misused, that such prohibitions are
unsurprising, if disappointing. And yet, precisely because of its power,
touch is among the most important of embodied spiritual faculties, and
is ever-present in Jewish ritual life. Think of the feel of crispy matzah,
the cool kiddush cup, the kissing of the Torah and the mezuzah, and the
body of the holy lover. Touch is also involved with some of the most sacred objects in Judaism: the tzitzit, the fringes worn as a reminder of

God; the tefillin, that great literalization of the figurative that binds sacred text to the body; and the head coverings worn by Jewish men and women. All three of these holy objects are quite traditional, but as we will see, they can be transformative as well. More than mere special garments, they can be tools of intimate connection with God.

Wearing special clothes is a common practice whenever we enter special space, whether culturally or religiously defined. But tzitzit, tefillin, and head coverings are more than special garments; they are intended to be tools of intimate connection with God.

In theory, tzitzit are primarily visual; the Torah states that "You shall see it, and remember all of the *mitzvot* of YHVH, and you will do them."[8] Yet for me, they are tactile first and foremost. Sometimes I bristle underneath them, particularly on warm days. Other times, pressed against my chest, the *tallit katan*, colloquially referred to as tzitzit (in Ashkenazic pronunciation, *tzitzis*), acts as a sort of second skin. It's private, personal, even intimate. It is no surprise that the Talmudic Rabbis tell stories in which tzitzit are the last barrier between a straying sage and the sexual sin he was about to commit. The feel of the fabric against the body is an omnipresent reminder, perceived within the alluring sense itself. Even when the eye does not see the tzitzit, the body knows it is there.

The tactile sensation of tefillin is rather different. It is worn only during prayer time (except by some Hasidim, who wear it all day), and thus feels less like a second skin and more like a set of magical tools. There is nothing rational about the ancient magic of tefillin. Surely the Torah's injunction to "bind these words on your arms, and they will be like frontlets between your eyes"[9] could have been read metaphorically: that the Torah should guide our every action and be before us at all times. But it was not; and so, like the ancient shamans of many cultures who bound sacred texts to their bodies, the leather straps and casings reify, and embody, this fundamental precept. Today, there are those who claim that the tefillin trace lines of energy in the body.

And finally, the head coverings: from the *kippa* (yarmulke in Yiddish) to the black hat, the *snood* (a kind of close-fitting hood) to the *sheitel* (wig), Orthodox and other observant Jews are distinguished by their heads. Unlike tallit and tefillin, there is no commandment in the Torah for men to cover their heads, and the traditional practice for women to do so stems from debatable interpretations of modesty (even within Orthodox circles, the practice was only sporadically followed until the last few decades). Nonetheless, the *kippa* is surely the most well-known of Jewish body practices. It is a recognizable marker of a Jew even to those who know nothing about Judaism. This can be for better and for worse, as many people associate the *kippa* with values that the person wearing it may not hold at all, and within the Jewish community, the size, material, and color of the *kippa* all convey political and ideological messages. For all that, however, the embodied facticity of the *kippa* remains: the sense of connectedness, of association with an ancient tradition, and of memory. Some say that the *kippa* is a reminder that "God is above you." For me, because it signifies my own willingness, it is more a reminder that God is within.

All three of these sacred touch practices are imbued with notes of love. Wrapping the tefillin around the finger, words of betrothal are recited; men kiss the *kippa* and tzitzit—because love and touch go together. The English word for tefillin, "phylacteries," is derived from the Greek *philacteron*, meaning guard, or defender; and that is what the tefillin is, whether in an ancient, magical context or a contemporary, psychological one. Sometimes the pantheism of "God is everywhere" can seem impersonal, a God that is as transparent as oxygen. But when experienced with the body—rather than merely thought with the mind—eros, companionship, and love are ubiquitous aspects of religious life. To speak of God as the Friend, or the *ribbono shel olam* (master of the universe), or as the helper, savior, and shield, is not to engage in bad philosophy. It is to enter a different discourse altogether, one that includes the body and the heart, and expresses the yearnings of each. Perhaps this is why Kabbalah has struck such a chord of late—not because of the magic red strings (another embodied practice, of course) and Neoplatonic emanations, but because it speaks in the language of myth, which is the deepest language of humanity.

Placing emblems of the Beloved upon our bodies *is* intimate; it is energetic and even, in the general sense, erotic. Approach these practices as adornments, as if they are the jewelry bought for you by your lover, which in a sense they are. Take time to feel the tactile sensations of the tzitzit, tefillin, or *kippa*; relate to them primarily as experiences, secondarily as myth or commandment. Feel them on your skin, erasing the distance between heaven and earth.

Taste

There are more than ten thousand taste buds in your mouth. Deeply experiencing some of their sensory input was the subject of much of Chapter 1, which dealt with eating meditation. Rather than repeat those practices, what I'd like to emphasize here is the ubiquity of Jewish occasions to do them.

Of course, Jews have a complicated relationship with eating: it's at once a symbol of divine providence and a source of endless regulation. Believe it or not, over two-thirds of the *sugyot* (topical sections) in the Talmud deal, in some way, with food. Many of us grow up with Jewish mothers and grandmothers who stuff our bellies full of high-fat food ("it's good for you!"), and for whom having "enough" to eat is the primary marker of living well. And yet there's still all that guilt, shame, and expectation that we eat lots of kugel and not show it in our bodies. Ashkenazic culture may have given the world the bagel and shmear, but we're still working on how to enjoy it.

Holidays, both Jewish and non-Jewish, are almost always focused around food. Thanksgiving turkeys, Chanukah latkes, barbecues on the Fourth of July, matzah ball soup on Passover, hamentashen on Purim, apples and honey on Rosh Hashanah—we celebrate the passage of time with our mouths. Sometimes it's just about celebration. But often the taste is the gateway to myth—as when we eat bitter herbs on Passover to remember the bitterness of slavery. In such instances, "eating meditation" is an indigenous Jewish practice.

There are occasions, too, when the myth can block the experience itself. For example, the sweetness of challah on Shabbat can sometimes get lost in halachic measurements, salt to remember the Temple, and two loaves to commemorate the manna (or the union of male and female, according to Kabbalah). This movement, away from the thing itself and toward a web of legal, mythic, or symbolic significance, can often block our experience of reality itself. It's possible to fulfill all the halachic requirements of *hamotzi* without taking any notice of the world that God has created—the body, the bread, the miracle of eating.

Here is where pausing and eating mindfully can reunite the transcendent and immanent, the Holy One and the Divine Presence. In its ideal form, Jewish practice is a nondual embrace of both the material and the spiritual, the One and the many. This is the path of seeing the downward-pointing triangle of the Jewish star (i.e., this world, nature, the body) and the upward-pointing triangle (i.e., heaven, God, the spirit) as being two sides of the same reality.

Both triangles are essential. Some people worry about enjoying the bread (or art, or beauty) too much, lest we lose sight of its central significance, which is legal: the reasons why we do something, rather than the actual doing of it. (I'm reminded of the medieval church authorities who tried to ban liturgical music because its beauty was distracting people from the texts being sung.) Others rebel against any act of signification, and drain the body of its sanctity. But the simplest, and most obvious, realities of our experience are also the ways beyond myths of God to realities of God.

Eating a *kezayit* (olive-size piece) of matzah takes a while. Perhaps the philosopher would rather read a text, and the hedonist would rather just eat. Yet if both sides are honored, then the history of Passover comes alive in the actual taste of the unleavened bread. The physical experience of the Passover seder (at which one rebellious Jewish rabbi invited his disciples to experience matzah as the divine body) is ineluctable. It's where the "here and now" of the contemplative meets the here and now of the epicurean, leaving dogmatists with their dusty books and stories. And so, too, with latkes on Chanukah, cheese on Shavuot, nuts on Tu B'Shevat, hamentashen on Purim, symbolic foods on Rosh Hashanah, and the whole host of other Jewish food traditions. The Jewish tradition provides all the ingredients for mindful, embodied spiritual practice. But it's up to you to taste the dish.

Sight

Perhaps the most subtle of all the sense-meditation practices is that of seeing. This is not because it is difficult to see—it's because it is so easy. Our eyes automatically register light and color, and the brain's processing is so speedy as to be utterly invisible to us. If you are looking at a book, you see "book," not white, black, light, and shadow. Not even a book; probably you just see words. And not even words; rather, you immediately absorb ideas, leaving physicality behind.

This is much more than seeing. It is seeing, recognizing, processing, comprehending. But seeing is itself a sensual pleasure. In deeply concentrated mind states, when the mind moves slowly enough that it can interrupt even basic cognitive processes, it is possible to experience pure seeing without the cognitive apparatus of categorization. This, perhaps, is similar to what Rabbi Abraham Abulafia describes as the world without language: perception without categorization, substance without quite so much form. A blade of grass is not grass, but "green"—and not even green, but rather, a dozen gradations of light and dark hues, like the movements of an analog clock that defy the compartmentalization of the digital.

It takes practice to refine concentration this way, but it's not impossible. It's quite common, in fact, when tired or ill, for us to simply gaze out into space, perfectly satisfied with the most mundane shapes and forms. At such times, the thinking mind is weakened, and thus far more easily satiated than normally. But you don't have to wait until you're sick. Start with any centering meditation practice, such as focusing on the breath as described in Chapter 3. After at least fifteen minutes, being sure to keep the body in stillness, let the eyes open, and let the gaze rest wherever it falls. See if you can notice the mind grabbing and labeling—car, rock, table, tree—and just step back a bit to the naked seeing of color and light itself. It's a bit like staring, except your attention and focus are more refined, not less. Try to keep your gaze steady for a period of time, not forcing too hard, but seeing with your body, instead of with your mind, letting the physical act of seeing take precedence over the mental acts of recognition.

I find that "seeing meditation" conveys the now-familiar benefits of embodied spiritual practice: the mind slows, perception opens, and the ordinary wonders of the divine manifestation become a bit more tangible. What, really, is the difference between hearing "everything is holy" and actually feeling it? Nothing about the world—nothing changes with enlightenment. But everything changes about the readiness of the mind to receive It.

As with smell and touch, there are many occasions in Jewish ritual life at which conscious seeing is invited, and at which "seeing clearly" can deepen your Jewish experience. The lighting of candles at the beginning of Shabbat and holidays is one such time, particularly if you follow the custom of closing the eyes until the blessing is recited. This custom has a halachic basis—that you shouldn't enjoy the light of the candles before the blessing is completed—and a legendary one: because the angels, or even the Sabbath Queen herself, surround the candles as they are lit, and we shield our eyes out of respect. Either way, the moment when the eyes are open is one of revelation. The rushing is over, there's nothing else to do—and here you are, basking in the simple beauty of candlelight. At such a moment, maybe you can feel that delightful satisfaction of the truly rich person—the one who is happy with his or her share of the world. Just seeing—just that simple pleasure.

Try adding seeing meditation to your candle-lighting and see what happens. Or try it at Havdalah, the service that ends the Sabbath and contains a blessing over the light of the candle itself: *borei me'orei ha'eish* ... who creates the light of fire. It's customary to hold the fingernails up to the Havdalah candle, to see this light reflected in our bodies. Try to "see clearly" then.

And at other times: the light of the Chanukah candles, the array of the Passover seder plate, the white shrouds of Yom Kippur, the bonfires of Lag B'Omer—all of these are occasions on which we are invited, almost begged, to open our eyes. Like photographers who carefully balance light and shadow, color and composition, these are times to step away from the screens of concept (with their notes of desire and distaste), and back to the reality of sight itself. Sometimes this eye-opening can be transcendent, reminding us of timeless truths or the Infinite itself. Other times, it can be even greater: an opening to the Immanent, to the physicality of sight and its object, to the exquisite sensuality of the real.

15
Embodied Emotions

My heart and my flesh shout with joy unto the Living God.

Rav Kook[1]

Nothing exists apart from God. All of Being, including that which we consider the self, is a vast, infinitely complex manifestation of the One. This is easy to say, but difficult truly to know. To attain this form of knowledge (in Hebrew, *da'at*) requires a training of the mind not to fall into the false conceptions and attachments of the self. In Kabbalah, this bundle of selfish inclinations is known as the *yetzer hara*, the cause of estrangement from our Source. In Theravada Buddhism, it is known as *tanha*, the clinging desire that is the cause of suffering.

Through contemplation, ecstasy, art, prayer, and a thousand other paths, it is possible to glimpse the truth of life beyond the selfish ego. The resultant "peak experiences," if we are open to receive them, often occasion great rapture and joy, and an overpowering love radiating from the unity of Being.

But what about the rest of the time? In theory, since God is everywhere, we are fully connected with God even when we experience great distress, sadness, anger, or pain. But in practice it does not feel that way. God seems absent when emotions cloud the heart; we prefer for God to come only in flavors that suit our taste. So what to do? Should we simply push negative emotions away, through medication, distraction, or religion? Should we save our spirituality for the pleasant parts, when bad things never happen to good people?

No. To transcend the *yetzer hara* is to extend the light of the Infinite into all of experience, including (and especially) those aspects the *yetzer* does not like. And one of the most effective ways to do this, as developed in similar ways by two very different traditions, Kabbalah and Theravada Buddhism, is to feel emotions in the body.

Feeling Emotions in the Body

Usually, emotions are understood as mental states, not physical ones, and we approach them in terms of stories: *why* we are joyful, sad, angry. But if you observe emotions carefully, you'll see that they always have a bodily component as well. Delight feels light; sadness feels heavy. Anger has one energy; contentment another. If you think about it, these embodied states are actually more real than the stories. If you look for the story of your emotion in present experience, it is never there—it's always in the past or the future. But now, while the emotion *is* happening, you are having an experience. What is it? A constriction in the throat, or a heaviness in the chest. Possibly, in the mind, a certain flavor of mood, not unlike a flavor of food.

Every emotion can be felt in the body, and relating to emotions in this way enables a greater "receiving" (the literal meaning of "Kabbalah") of experience, in all its variation, and arrests the spiral into negative emotions without repressing or denying what's going on. It is a way out of a lose-lose situation; on the one hand, repressing an emotion, or on the other, venting it in ways that may be destructive to self or others. Being honest with emotions obviates the need for such strategies. Just see clearly—which means neither falling into the story of an emotion nor pretending it isn't there. Here is how it works.

First, create an internal quiet so that the emotion can be felt. Whatever it is—yearning, joy, sadness, boredom, anger, contentment— really let it happen, trusting *hinei el yeshuati, eftach v'lo efchad*; the here and now is the God of my salvation, I will trust and not fear.

Next, instead of moving the mind immediately to the object of the emotion (whatever it is—a person, or a place, or a time, or achievement), turn your attention to the body and see what you discover. There might be a constriction in the throat, or a heaviness in the chest—or maybe an excited heartbeat, or a sensation of energy in the arms or legs. Scan through the body, and see what's there.

Stay with that feeling. See if you can experience the physical sensation without automatically releasing the tension, or relaxing the face, or changing the body in any way. As usual, as thoughts come up—in particular, the thoughts of why you are feeling a certain way— gently let them go. In psychotherapy, it is very important to explore these thoughts. But this is not psychotherapy. Just stay with the feeling, watch it for several minutes, as if the physical sensation in your body is a television show, or a play. What does it look like, feel like?

Finally, watch the feeling for a while, and see if it changes, or if it stays. Chances are, by doing nothing other than watching the body, the emotion will shift in its character—if you don't force it. The first of many insights that come from this practice is that emotions arise and pass within the body. We all know intellectually that all things must pass. Kohelet (Ecclesiastes) says it, the Buddha says it, even George Harrison says it. But it is quite another thing to know it from direct experience. Likewise, to know experientially that emotions are stored within the body can shift the entire way in which we see our physical and spiritual selves. It's one thing to be taught that the body feels, knows, and remembers. But when one actually experiences—by observing emotions, by receiving healing touch, or in any number of other ways, only a handful of which are examined here—how the body knows things of which the mind is not aware, the unity of body and mind becomes less a theoretical proposition than a deeply felt reality.

Second, feeling emotions in the body helps clarify what's really going on at a particular moment. When you're "in" the *yetzer hara*, viewing the entire world from its limited perspective, it's difficult to get out. But the body is not in any perspective, and so embodied emotions are clarifying. For example, the statement "I am sad" usually encompasses much more than the experience of sadness itself— including the reasons for sadness, the justifications for why those reasons are sound, and the sadness or anger about feeling sad. These thoughts are not pearls of insight, and they're not helping to alleviate suffering. On the contrary, they're what cause suffering. Feeling emotions in the body drops the stories, explanations, justifications, and the wishes that things were different from how they are. The emotion is plenty; it doesn't need the stories and thoughts. Feel it in your body, at this present moment, and stay with it.

Third, feeling emotions in the body leads to all kinds of discoveries, since we are often experiencing emotions we don't notice. For example, say you're planning, or in some other way thinking for the future. Ask, "What is my body feeling now?" You'll probably find more stress and less balance in the body than you expect. Taking thirty seconds in the midst of planning to see what's happening in the body, what emotions are unfolding, and what's going on outside your mind can help you regain the balance. Or, to take another example, sometimes I'm not really sure how I'm feeling, except that I know I'm feeling lousy. But then I'll meditate for a few minutes, scanning through the body to locate any places of tension or pressure—and, to my surprise, find all the evidence of a particular emotion located in my arms, or chest, or face. Thus the body becomes a diagnostic tool, showing what the mind can't yet see.

A fourth insight is that all of these emotions can be accepted, a bit like unwanted but unavoidable houseguests. Again, the point of spiritual practice is not to increase our pharmacopeia of spiritual narcotics so that we always feel sweetness and light, but to enable more "receiving," gradually to widen the sphere of acceptable faces of the Divine. Both the places of enlightenment (what the foreign prophet Balaam called *mishkenotecha yisrael*, the dwelling places of Israel) and the tents of grasping desire (the *ohalecha ya'akov*) are "good" in a fundamental way. Sadness, anger, and uncertainty are not intrinsically evil; they are simply flavors of reality—neither to be embraced nor to be avoided.

After doing this practice time and time again, eventually one learns that emotions are sometimes nothing *more* than states in the body. In *A Christmas Carol,* Scrooge says to the nightmarish ghost of Christmas past, "You are a piece of undigested meat." In the book, Scrooge turns out to be wrong, but in life, he's often right. At times I've gone through days of puzzling despair, not knowing why I'm feeling sad or angry, and unable to do anything about it—before just breaking out of the rut by taking a good, long run or changing my diet. And then the mind-state vanishes, along with all the stories my mind had concocted to convince me why I was feeling the way I was. Where are the stories now, which once felt so truthful? Learn to feel emotions as states of the body; often they're nothing more.

Feeling emotions in the body doesn't always work if the emotions are too strong and mindfulness too weak. But it does work sometimes, and at the end of the day, it is more honest than papering them over, or repressing them, or rushing to explain why we feel what we feel, and whether or not we're entitled to feel that way. "YHVH is a God of Truth," says Jeremiah[2] —what Is, is what is True. Thus experiencing emotions for what they are is a path to experiencing God in your body. That it also removes the anguish of suffering is either grace or good fortune... whichever you prefer.

Kabbalah's Map of the Heart-Body

Earlier we explored some of the kabbalistic maps of the soul, including that of the *sefirot*. On their own, these maps are interesting; in practice, they can be transformative. And one way to put them into practice is what I half-jokingly call "kabbalahsana," which blends the map of the *sefirot* with the attention to mind-states that we have just learned.

The method is a variation on that in the previous section. The next time you experience a powerful emotion, see if you can find its place on the matrix of the *sefirot*, as presented earlier. At first, this will be a challenge—theosophical Kabbalah is not for beginners. But as you learn to differentiate between *hesed* and *hod*, *tiferet* and *yesod*, you can observe, in your own life, how these various energies are always interacting with one another, on the levels of body, heart, mind, and spirit.

Next, as with the general practice, see if you can feel the *sefirah* in the body. Without being overdeterminative (e.g., this is *tiferet*, so I must feel something in my heart center), inquire into where, in the body, the emotion is felt. Remember, there's no such thing as "what the Kabbalah says"—different Kabbalists have different understandings of how the *sefirot* manifest. Explore these maps with an open mind, seeing how they correspond to your own experience.

Then proceed as above. Take careful note of the sensations in the body as they come and go. Let thoughts and stories drop, just coming to know the "energy" of the *sefirah*—or combination of *sefirot*—in question.

To make this practice work for you, you'll need to become familiar enough with the map of the *sefirot* that they become second nature. This is one of the purposes of the theosophical Kabbalah: to form a conceptual, symbolic matrix through which experience is understood as a play of divine energies. Eventually you'll outgrow the map; ten *sefirot* on four worlds will not be sufficient to describe the full range of your emotional, spiritual, physical, and intellectual realities. And so you'll learn to feel each emotion as a tone of one *sefirah* within another—*gevurah* in *tiferet*, *yesod* in *hod*, and so forth. For example, suppose you are driving yourself to stay with a diet so that you can be kind to your body—this might be *hesed* in *netzach*. When you actually make the choice not to eat an unhealthy food, that may be *hesed* in *yesod*, or perhaps *gevurah* in *yesod*, depending on the act's feeling-tone and context. The point is not to parse endlessly the combinations, or to pore over the charts, but rather to use the Kabbalah to fine-tune the emotional-embodied attention. Personally, I've found these maps very helpful; emotional states I'd thought were one thing were really, on closer inspection, something else entirely. My aversions and desires have been clarified, understood, and worked with more skillfully. And the richness of my emotional, and physical, life has been enhanced.

One way to enter into this rather daunting practice is to work with it during the Omer, the seven-week period between the holidays of Passover and Shavuot. Traditionally, each of the forty-nine days is a unique combination of the lower seven *sefirot* (these seven are generally seen as the seat of the emotions; the top three are those of the mind and spirit), and you can find "Omer calendars" online to guide you. Rather than simply seeing what emotion is in the body, you can, over the course of the Omer, contemplate all forty-nine combinations, exploring the subtleties of each. Over time, you'll learn to "read" *sefirot* the way master musicians read musical notation, and experience them as they play their instruments. You'll even learn to improvise, and dance.

As you can see, "kabbalahsana" is a very subtle practice. Purely on an embodied level, since "the left leg in the right arm" makes no sense literally, a more symbolic understanding of the body is required. For example, *gevurah* in *tiferet*, which refers, roughly, to the proportion of restraint needed for compassion, boundary, and harmony, might be felt as a protective layer around the heart—not quite a closing of the heart, but a guard in front of it. This resonates, for me, with a physical experience of knowing when to hold back: the body tenses a bit, the chest tightens up—it really is *gevurah* in *tiferet*, on the embodied level. Likewise with a desire for sexual expression (*hesed* in *yesod*), or a flexible, giving willingness (*hesed* in *hod*), or dozens of other combinations.

Such a complex, symbolic system is not for everyone, and you may prefer the more conventional method of the previous section. The symbols often seem to obscure more than they reveal. Yet as one studies Kabbalah more, the opposite movement takes place. The Infinite becomes infinitely close, because every veil or concealment is really an attribute or a lack in disguise. Then the truest map is both the most complicated, since it reveals the infinite topography of presence, and the simplest, since its territory is nothing other than this.

❈   ❈   ❈   ❈

16

Sickness and Health

Be extremely protective of your lives.

Deuteronomy 4:15

A Torah scholar should not live in a city that has no physician.

Sanhedrin 17b

The Jewish doctor is one of the few stereotypes that Jews are happy to accept. It is a familiar image, but one rooted in hundreds of years of Jewish medical tradition. Many important rabbis were also doctors and healers, Maimonides most famously. There are hoards of Jewish texts on healing, anatomy, and health; the writings of Rabbi Nachman of Breslov alone (who suffered from ill health for most of his life) would fill a volume. And throughout Jewish history, the value of preserving human life, and thus human health, has been held dear. Never within the mainstream of the Jewish tradition, including the Jewish mystical tradition, has there been a fear of medicine, or a belief that healing should be left in the hands of heaven. Healing one's own body and others is not God's work; it is godly work. And recovery is a process of becoming more available to holiness.

Of course, practice often lags behind theory. For all the Jewish rhetoric on health, the sickly, undernourished yeshiva student is still with us today—not to mention pervasive problems of smoking and obesity, particularly in the religious world. And to be sure, many Jews, like everyone else, believe that God is involved in healing the sick, and have had recourse to religion, magic, and superstition in the fight against disease. Even today in Israel, it is possible to visit Kabbalists for folk remedies for conditions ranging from backaches to infertility.

It is also true that there is a wonderfully rich tradition of Jewish folk healing, which, like all such traditions, contains a mixture of wisdom and folly. The Talmud alone contains an encyclopedia of folk remedies, such as "Eighty-three illnesses are caused by the gall, and all of them are neutralized by eating a breakfast consisting of bread with salt and drinking a jugful of water,"[1] and "dates are healthful in the morning, at noon, and in the evening. They are not good in the afternoon, and they do away with three things: evil thoughts, stress of the bowels, and abdominal troubles."[2] Some of the Talmud's advice holds up to modern medicine, such as "clean hands are necessary when covering and protecting the eyes."[3] And some of it, like "too much alcohol consumption can cause a child to be excessively hairy,"[4] does not.

Or consider the benefits the Talmud lists regarding breakfast, centuries before it became known as "the most important meal of the day":

> Thirteen things are said about the "morning bread." It is an antidote against heat and cold, winds and demons. It instills wisdom into the simple, causes you to triumph in a lawsuit, enables you to study and teach the Torah, to have your words heeded, and retain what you learned. He who has bread in the morning does not perspire, lives with his wife, and does not lust after other women; and it kills worms in one's intestines. Some say it also banishes envy and induces love.[5]

Obviously, Jewish folk medicine is an ancient, detailed system whose remedies often defy rational analysis. Perhaps more importantly, though, the fact that these various statements and promises are in the Talmud shows that care of the body was important to the Rabbis. Whatever we may make of this literature's specific advice, its general principles—that health is important, and that it cannot be divorced from religious concerns—still can be applied today. So, our discussion here will focus not on the specific elements of Jewish folk healing but rather on contemplative practices of health and illness, and on how even when the body is compromised—indeed, precisely then—it is possible to know deeply the truths of our Being.

Spiritual Practice in Sickness and in Health

The most obvious practice for sickness and health is: stay healthy! Judaism maintains an overwhelmingly "pro-life" perspective—not in its contemporary meaning, but in the sense of pro-health, pro-living, pro-happiness. In contrast to religions that prize martyrdom above all else, there are only three occasions on which a Jew must choose death rather than transgression (when forced to commit murder, idolatry, or incest). There are mitzvot designated for saving human life (*hatzalat nefashot*) and visiting the sick (*bikur cholim*). And in daily life, *shmirat habriyut*—maintaining health—is a divine service.

How these ideas translate into practice varies. Some rabbis laud the supposed health benefits of *kashrut*, others mandate more up-to-date healthy diets, sometimes including vegetarian ones. Some prohibit smoking and drug use; others allow it. In some Jewish traditions, bodies we would today consider overweight were the ideal; in some contemporary sources, thin is in. But the overall perspective is the same throughout: that life is a precious gift.

Rabbi Yosef Yitzchak of Lubavitch tells a story of his grandmother, who fell ill as a young girl and was ordered to eat immediately upon waking up. But the pious girl did not want to eat before prayer, and so she would pray first and only afterwards eat her breakfast. When her father-in-law, the Tzemach Tzedek (the third Lubavitcher rebbe), heard of this, he said to her: "A Jew must be healthy and strong. Concerning the precepts of the Torah it is written, 'live in them.'[6] This means one is to infuse life into the *mitzvot*; and in order to infuse life into the *mitzvot*, one must be healthy and joyful." He concluded: "Better to eat in order to pray, than to pray in order to eat."[7]

As contemplatives, however, the practice of health is more than simply staying healthy. Rather, we are invited also to notice shifts in health as part of the transitory nature of all of life. In fact, mild sickness can be a great time to practice: to observe what happens to the mind, and act as a witness of the changes in body and mind that occur when health is altered. This is true on all four levels of the soul. On the level of the body, you can see how much easier it is to observe the motions of the body when they are impeded; how tastes change; how your heart shifts (more open, more closed, more patient, or less); how your body moves. Use the altered sensations of the body as an occasion for mindful attention, not rushing into the stories and preferences that things be otherwise, but taking this opportunity to become more awake.

In the world of the heart, it is possible to cultivate gratitude in times of health as much as in times of sickness. Vietnamese Buddhist teacher Thich Nhat Hanh observes that "when we have a toothache, we know that not having a toothache is a wonderful thing. But when we do not have a toothache, we are still not happy. A non-toothache is very pleasant ... When we practice mindfulness, we come to cherish these things and we learn how to protect them."[8] This is the essence of *hakarat hatov*: noticing the body when it works, as well as when it doesn't. Consider pausing, maybe once an hour, and noticing some part of the body you hadn't paid attention to: a tooth, or a toe, or wherever. Notice how it is doing its job, innocent of your sources of stress, and, all things considered, how well the machine is running. You might even add the Jewish blessing recited when you have survived a threat to your life: the *Gomel*, or "survival blessing." Traditionally, you "bench *Gomel*" after having survived danger, such as serious illness or long-distance travel. But following Thich Nhat Hanh, you might recite your own version of the *Gomel* blessing for the smaller things too. The traditional words are simple enough: the standard introduction (*Baruch ata adonai eloheinu melech ha'olam*) followed by *hagomel l'hayavim tovot, she'g'malani kol tov*—who graciously bestows favor on the undeserving, even as bestowed upon me.[9] Cultivate gratitude for your nontoothache, or nonslip in the tub, and see what happens to the heart.

In the realm of mind and spirit, there are a range of practices for sickness. First, try meditating when you're a little sick. Because of the altered mind-state that results from illness, the processes of consciousness are, as it were, more visible. Not only do you get to notice the mind, but you also get to notice that you notice. Throughout all the vicissitudes of mental disruption, the knowing of the disruption remains—and the distinction is a critical insight. The mirrorlike mind observes, even when the brain is addled by disease. See if this practice of *briyah* works for you the next time you are moderately ill, if you can spend time in a place that simply notices and observes, rather than immediately reacts. You might even learn a different relationship to illness.

None of this is to say that illness or injury is some kind of perverse gift from God. Those of us who have helped loved ones recover from illness, or persevere in the midst of it, know that to speak of such trials as a "gift" can be as demeaning as to speak of them as just desserts. Illness and injury happen—that is all. The question is how we are to heal, and whether our whole selves can be present for the process. Does the affliction of the body unravel the connections of the soul? Or is it possible to be present with pain, not with facile assurances that this is all for the best, and not with alienation or despair, but showing up with our whole selves, even in the midst of travail?

Of course, many Jewish teachers will say that we should ask "why me," since, who knows, it might be a punishment or a warning, or an invitation to repent. At one time, the idea that God allocates disease on the basis of merit must have provided a sense of comfort and control in a time of chaos; otherwise, the idea wouldn't have caught on.[10] Today, though, most of us see things rather differently. Rather than searching for divinity in the alleged reasons for suffering, we might find God in the presence abiding within it.

The Deeper Meaning of Health

For most traditional Jewish thinkers, bodily health is purely instrumental. Maimonides, for example, wrote two complete treatises on health and prescribed all kinds of precautions and behaviors—but only so that the intellect can function. In the *Mishneh Torah*, he writes:

> Maintaining a healthy and strong body is the will of God—for one cannot have knowledge of the Creator if one is hungry or ill. Therefore one must avoid that which harms the body and strive to acquire habits that which helps it become healthy.[11]

In other words, health is important, but only because contemplation is impossible without it. And, when the body gets in the way of contemplation, Maimonides reins it in; for example, limiting permitted sexual activity to procreation only, and advising dietary restrictions to diminish the body's appetites. The point is to have, in the words of the Roman poet Juvenal, "a sound mind in a sound body,"[12] but only because the latter is necessary for the former. Likewise Samson Raphael Hirsch, the great forerunner of modern Orthodoxy, who said:

> You may not in any way weaken your health or shorten your life. Only if the body is healthy is it an efficient instrument for the spirit's activity.... Therefore you should avoid everything which might possibly injure your health.... And the law asks you to be even more circumspect in avoiding danger to life and limb than in the avoidance of other transgressions.[13]

Here again, health is valued—in marked contrast to those who would punish or disregard the body—but only to be "an efficient instrument for the spirit's activity," rather like the commonplace analogy that compares the body to a horse and the soul to its rider. These are, to be sure, sound arguments against the wasteful, overconsumptive, and sedentary lifestyles that are so common today—and also against the ascetic, world-denying impulse found in some religious traditions. But they are essentially superficial; the body, here, is no different from any other tool that is necessary to practice spirituality effectively. Like a horse, it is fed, reined in, and used as needed.

There is, however, a deeper meaning of health. Recall from the first chapter that biblical and early rabbinic tradition lacks the familiar dualism of spirit and flesh. There, the body is not an instrument for the self—it *is* the self. Consciousness, love, and poetry—these are not separate from the materiality of the brain and body. They are beautiful, *and* they are neurological events; they are holy, and embodied.

We've lost this notion due to two thousand years of dualist culture. Recall, as we saw in Chapter 1, that there were two "new testaments" in the first centuries of the common era: one (the "second covenant" of Christianity) holding physical commandments to be less important than spiritual intentions; the other (the "second" book of law, or *Mishnah*) detailing the physical, embodied laws of the Jewish religion. At first, the Rabbis read the commandments literally, not figuratively as did the Christians, which is why traditional Jews today literally bind a sacred text on their arms and heads and literally affix it to their doorposts. Eventually, though, the dualists won. Now the dualism of body/*chomer* (matter) and spirit/*tzurah* (form) is commonplace in Jewish texts, and many Jewish teachers state that the spirit is the true self, trapped within the prison of the body.

But what would it be like if we were not so dualistic, if we really believed, as the Talmud says, that God plants the soul *in* the body, and that the health of the body *is* the health of the soul? In fact, the truth sets us free, because the nonduality of the embodied self leads to an enlightenment far deeper than the dualistic flight from the body. Holding onto a separation between the body and the soul, it's easy to imagine a soul independent from the rest of the world, like a puppetmaster pulling the strings of our body: an autonomous, separate "soul," apart from the body, and the seat of our actual, separate essence.

But this whole picture is simply not true. What we call "the soul" is actually a net of causes and conditions determined by genetic information, environment, culture, society, and the myriad "accidents of living" we encounter. Consciousness, a trick played by a well-functioning brain, is not some immaterial puppetmaster pulling strings; it's a result of decades of data, and millennia of genetic evolution. Of course, there are so many of these factors that none of us can keep track. No one can predict how a boy will grow into a man, and thus no one but that man is responsible for his conduct and destiny. But ultimately, if we really look at the causes of every act and decision, we will see that none of them spring from nowhere. Everything has its conditions, including your reading, my writing, and the sounds around you right now. In fact, since everything is fully dependent upon those conditions, you might ask: who really is reading, who really is writing, and what really is going on?

Some people worry that, without immortal, immaterial souls, we are merely machines, with no accountability and no humanity. But neither consequence is true. Actually seeing oneself as a "machine," that is, as a body governed by the laws of the universe, is not a diminishment; it is a release from the delusion that who you are is this small self, separate from the rest of the universe, a soul trapped in a body. And accountability remains; as the nondualist sage Nisargadatta said, "As long as you imagine yourself to be in control, you should imagine yourself to be responsible."[14] Precisely the scientific materialism so derided by many religious people is the key to enlightenment itself. You are not a soul unfortunately trapped in a body. You are star stuff (in Carl Sagan's words), and your mind is a temporary repository of the dreams of the universe.

See for yourself. The next time you're sick or fasting, observe what changes. Perhaps the knowing, the witnessing of what goes on in the world remains, but everything else transforms—even your personality, if the change in the body is significant enough. Where is this fixed "you" now? We say sometimes, when someone is ill, "he's not himself." Well, who is he? Is his "self" just having trouble communicating, or is he really not himself, because "himself" is a shifting construction of brain chemistry? "You" are ever-changing, a verb more than a noun. Our minds are learned by culture and defined by convention, our souls temporary ripples on a lake, mistaking the contours of the waves for the form of the shapeless water.

Two grave errors of dualism can be cured by a simple flu. First is the belief that you are your mind, or that your soul is separate from the body. This ignorance of your true self causes egocentrism, suffering, and a false sense of separation from everything else in the universe. Second is the concurrent belief that, since your essential nature is nonmaterial, the material world is, at best, an amusement, or at worst, a burden to be thrown off. This ignorance causes the error of supposing that God is not present in the material world, leading either to asceticism on the one hand, or to hedonism on the other. A little dose of reality—that, with a different balance in blood sugars or a change in neurochemistry, the supposedly separate "you" changes completely—can remove both obstacles to realization.

Return again to the model of the six-pointed star, a symbol of the integral life. To live only materially, denying the movements of the soul, is an impoverished life. But to live as if the soul, disembodied, is all that matters in life, is likewise a form of impoverishment, an embrace of one portion of human experience, and a denial or denigration of the rest. Kabbalah, like the symbol of the Star of David, is centrally about balance—bringing into balance the ever-shifting forces of creation. Thus it, too, is an invitation to live in an integral way: bodily and spiritually, experiencing the joys and sorrows of human life *and* their transcendence, uniting heaven and earth. The messianic age is that time at which the sacred marriage will be consummated: the meeting of sky-god and earth-goddess, masculine and feminine, spirit and matter, line and circle, the Holy One and the Presence, temporality and eternity, soul and body. And the "secret of Unity" of which these same Kabbalists speak is that they are already one—since time itself is only half of the infinite. Unity may be experienced now, but not by leaving anything behind.

❀   ❀   ❀   ❀

17
Life Cycle

*Five years old: For Torah study. Ten: For Mishnah. Thirteen:
For Commandments. Fifteen: For Talmud. Eighteen: For
Marriage. Twenty: For pursuit [of livelihood]. Thirty: For
strength. Forty: For understanding. Fifty: For counsel. Sixty:
For eldering. Seventy: For gray hair. Eighty: For strength.
Ninety: For a bent back. One hundred: As if dead, passed, and
erased from the world.*

Mishnah Avot 5:21

Notwithstanding our spiritual and intellectual striving, human lives
are defined by physicality: birth, passage into adulthood, partnering,
and death. Some of the rituals that mark these passages of time, like
circumcision, are ancient; others, like the bar mitzvah, hardly exist in
the Bible. Yet they are among the most widely observed of Jewish
practices today. What is sometimes missing, however, is a reminder of
these rituals' sources in changes that happen to the body. In this chapter, we will look at ways to remember, reground, and reexperience
these stations on the Jewish life cycle as embodied phenomena.

Birth and Childhood
Birth is a miracle, taken for granted only by those who have never witnessed it. Particularly in premodern times, when childbirth was much
more uncertain than it is today, many layers of folk practices developed around the stunning transition between nonlife and life.
Amulets, protective spells, special diets, the unique women's prayers

201

known as *techines* (petitions)—all were seen to affect the well-being of the unborn child, whose physical constitution was shaped by acts and intentions of love. The wisdom of midwives was held equal to that of magicians.

In premodern Judaism, as in most traditional cultures, child-bearing was "women's space"; men were rarely even in the room, and were bound by laws of purity and modesty from being too involved in it. True, the Torah did institute offerings for purification and rededication following childbirth,[1] but most Jewish male sages were ambivalent about the birthing process, the pain of which was seen to be related to the sin in the Garden of Eden,[2] and instituted few rituals for the actual moments of birth. Today, however, as women's spaces are being reclaimed and renewed, this neglect has been turned into an opportunity: there are a number of new rituals and *kavvanot* (intentions) for all stages of pregnancy and childbirth, even for miscarriages and abortions.[3]

The uncertainty and miracle of childbirth is crucial, I think, to understanding *brit milah* (circumcision), probably the best known and most controversial of embodied Jewish observances. The ritual itself, commanded by God to Abraham[4] and redolent of a religiosity more primal than rational, was for centuries the quintessence of Jewish embodied ritual both for its proponents and for its strongest detractors. The apostle Paul, for example, used circumcision to differentiate "old" Judaism from the new Christianity. "Real circumcision is a matter of the heart—it is spiritual and not literal," as Paul says in Romans 2:29, drawing on the euphemism of Deuteronomy 30:6: "And the Lord your God shall circumcise your heart, and the heart of your seed, to love the Lord your God with all your heart, and with all your soul, that you may live ..." What God desires, Paul said, is not the marking of the flesh, but the opening of the heart. Most people, I think, still agree with him today.

Paul may have been the first critic of circumcision, but he was hardly the last. Today, many object to a ritual performed without consent, and with obviously no immediate spiritual benefit to the newborn.[5] How can a baby have a meaningful experience from something he cannot understand and can only know, if at all, as trauma?

Moreover, as even proponents of circumcision (such as Maimonides) acknowledged, the removal of the foreskin diminishes sexual pleasure. Even if the benefits outweigh the costs, even if the mark in the flesh leads to qualities of spirit—indeed, even if the body is the site of the soul—shouldn't the child decide? These are complicated ethical questions, and we will not attempt to resolve them here. But there are certain ways in which a body-centered perspective can help us appreciate the *brit*'s importance.

First, circumcision is a primal, brutal act that runs against every parental instinct—and that is the point. According to tradition, the *brit* is one of the few mitzvot a person performs with no hope of personal reward—and traditionally, fathers are supposed to perform it on their sons. This is not rattle-your-jewelry-on-Rosh-Hashanah religion; it is messy, primal, and inscribed upon the body. It's not that circumcision is healthier, or more sanitary, or more chaste; it's that the *brit*, the covenant, sanctifies the flesh itself.

Second, the *brit*, which carries no immediate subjective benefit, partakes of no "free choice," and, even later in life, is of dubious "spiritual" efficacy, is precisely the site at which embodied spirituality transcends the dangers of narcissism or utility that might otherwise attend it. There is no nonembodied purpose to this ritual. It is a sign inscribed in flesh, and the shift of consciousness it invites is not a spiritual feeling but a transcendence of the *notion* of spiritual feeling as the only sphere of importance. You are not your mind, this carnal act insists; the body, even when it does not stir the heart, is a place of central importance.

Third, the *brit* is a sexualized, gendered phenomenon. It is, of course, only performed on men. But notice, too, how, in precisely the place where it might be alienated from divinity, the body is marked as holy. As Rabbi Ohad Ezrachi once told me, it's significant that men make a covenant with God on their penises; the place of sexuality is the place of sanctity. Moreover, total masculinity and total femininity are, in the Kabbalah, undesirable attributes, out of balance, unstable. The *brit* is thus understood as inscribing femininity, in a way, on the organ of maleness. According to the Zohar, the exposure of the corona ("crown") of the penis mirrors the revelation of the *atara* ("crown") of the Divine, a name for the Shechinah, the Divine feminine.[6] It is, in a way, opening the male body for God.

Seeing the *brit* in these ways can transform it from an uncomfortable, primitive ritual to a practice that is valuable precisely because it is uncomfortable and primitive. It's not meant to be easy. It's not meant to be "spiritual" in the conventional sense. Rather, it's messy, embodied, and tied to sex and gender. Consider, the next time you are at a *brit* ceremony, that the discomfort is really part of the point. Be present for the making of a Jewish body.

Of course, this initiation ritual is only performed on men—what is sometimes called "female circumcision" in other cultures is a form of mutilation more akin to castration. To address this imbalance, the *simchat bat* (joy of a daughter) ceremony has gained acceptance among all stripes of the Jewish community (an earlier Sephardic custom, the *zeved habat*, has also gained some wider observance).[7] There is no fixed form for the *simchat bat*. Some observe it in conjunction with the naming of the baby in synagogue (it was a longstanding custom for a man to receive an *aliyah* when his wife gave birth to a girl). Others, deliberately to distinguish it from the receiving of an *aliyah*, and perhaps to make it a bit more like a *brit*, observe the *simchat bat* at home. Some choose to focus on readings of sacred text, or explanations of the name they chose for their child; others use water, wine, even henna to provide a material component to the ritual.

One final, much less widespread childhood custom is the *upshirin*, which in many Hasidic communities marks a boy's first haircut, and which has been extended beyond those communities to both young boys and girls. Hair is seen, kabbalistically, as extensions of *hesed*, radiating energy in all directions, flowing and bouncing. Like the long-haired youth of the 1960s, it's wild, untamed. And yet, there is no Kabbalah without ethics, which requires a taming of the wild. As in Antoine Saint-Exupéry's *The Little Prince*, to exist in relationship is to be tamed—and despite the opposing pull of the unbounded, the wild, long-haired abandon of energy and dance and freedom, the deeper tug for most human beings is that toward love, community ... taming. Like the *brit* and *simchat bat*, this ritual marks the acculturation and civilization of the body, and the transition from baby to child. And all of them are focused on the body, so much so that we might not even notice.

Adulthood: Coming of Age, Partnering, and Aging

The contemporary bar or bat mitzvah, in which a child chants haftarah, throws a party, and receives gifts, is a relatively recent innovation. As late as the early modern period, the significant adolescent rite of passage was not bar mitzvah but marriage: the Talmud recommends marriage for boys by age eighteen,[8] and that time, not the legal "coming of age," was the significant turning point in young people's lives. Even so, the Talmud recognized that puberty was the time when a boy became a man and a girl became a woman for the purposes of observing the commandments, swearing vows, and adhering to the laws of modesty. The Talmudic Rabbis even tried to propose criteria for officially having entered puberty—two pubic hairs—though ultimately they decided on fixed ages rather than biological traits.[9]

Naturally, the physical changes that occasion the bar and bat mitzvah are in little evidence in most contemporary celebrations. Perhaps a boy's voice cracks a bit during his speech, or a girl wears her first "real" dress at the party, but we usually regard these features as incidental to the central theme of accepting the responsibilities of being a Jewish adult. At the same time, due to changes in sexual mores, many *b'nai mitzvah* are once again about the entry of children into sexual maturity, only this entry is marked not by formal ritual but by furtive trysts at lavish parties. This divorce of the religious from the physical diminishes the value of each: the physical becomes degraded, and the religious, irrelevant.

There are many people today, though, who celebrate and honor the physical changes of adolescence by expanding the bar or bat mitzvah observance. This might include rituals borrowed from other cultures, such as the sweat lodge, or embodied rituals of our own like the mikva, both of which make a powerful pre-bar-mitzvah weekend ceremony. Or it might mean the study of Jewish sexual ethics—texts that most Jewish teenagers don't know exist, if my teaching experience is any indication—or models of Jewish womanhood or manhood. It may include new rituals, such as that described by Rabbi Phyllis Berman for a girl's first period.[10] Or it may simply mean a refocusing of intention, from the pat themes of "becoming a Jewish adult" to what it really means to become a man or woman. Times have changed from the days when marriage marked the entry into adolescence. Thirteen-year-olds today are regarded as kids. But perhaps one reason that so much Jewish education ends at the bar mitzvah is that we treat them that way.

As with the bar mitzvah, it's easy to forget that marriage and other partnering rituals are also about sanctifying the physical. However, it has become increasingly common for couples of widely ranging patterns of observance to, amid the pomp and circumstance, suddenly disappear into the *yichud* (unification) room, where, in earlier days, the marriage was consummated on the spot. Even in Orthodox circles, few couples actually have sex in the *yichud* room anymore; halachic *yichud* can take place simply by being in a closed room with a member of the opposite sex, and so the room is often just a place to rest and take a break from the party for a few minutes. But imagine the intensity of that moment for traditional couples, who may have scarcely touched one another over the preceding months, or who may have observed the strictures of *hilchot negiah,* which in the ultra-Orthodox interpretation bar any physical contact with the opposite sex: the revelation of the body of the beloved, and the holiness with which sex can be imbued. Incorporating the *yichud* room into a partnering ceremony, from traditional to nontraditional, is an excellent way to remember the embodied center of the wedding.

There are other body-centered practices at a wedding as well. Fasting the day of the wedding and wearing the customary *kittel* (the simple white robe that is worn by men on Yom Kippur, at the wedding, and eventually as a death shroud) evoke the similarities between the wedding day and Yom Kippur, both of which are seen as enacting death and rebirth. Immersing in the mikva before a wedding can mark the life change in a powerful, embodied beginning way, especially with the new liturgies and resources that have been developed for this purpose.[11] And so much depends upon intention; simply attuning the mind to the corporeal delights of the food, the dancing, and the drinking helps ground the spiritual momentousness of the day in the bodily truths that occasion it.

"The glory of youths is their strength; the majesty of old men is their gray hair," says Proverbs 20:29. Yet there is little formal ritual marking the many changes that take place in adulthood. Perhaps this is because of Judaism's focus on creating new life, or perhaps because lives are longer now than they used to be. Fortunately, in a time marked by increasing mechanization and technologization, the power of ritual to mark physical changes is undergoing a resurgence. There are Jewish liturgies and resources for marking new jobs, first gray hairs, menopause, and separations from loved ones—and I invite you to consider how you might create such ritual yourself.[12] When there is a transformation in the body, when there is a moment in your life cycle of which you suddenly become aware, consider how to connect this physical shift to the myths and narratives of the traditions that speak to you. Consider how to express the shift with something physical, such as water, fire, or objects from nature. And don't be afraid of messing up.

Death

In the end, as in the beginning, there is the body, "For dust you are, and to dust you will return."[13] We all have bodies, we can all see them, and we all see that they pass away. For the ancient Greeks, and their heirs in Western religion, this was the fundamental problem that gave birth to the notion of the disembodied soul. If all of the molecules in my body have changed in the years that I have been alive, and if they will all, one day, disappear, what is my essence, that which remains the same throughout the changes in my material form?

In contrast to philosophies of the immortal soul, Jewish death rituals are ancient, and brutally honest. We do not bury our loved ones in impermeable caskets of fiberglass and steel; they are placed in simple boxes so that they become one with the earth. We do not dress, embalm, or perfume their bodies; we wash and guard them, and bury them in simple shrouds. Even flowers are rarely found at traditional Jewish funerals, because this is not a time of comfort, fragrance, beauty, or renewal. In short, Jewish death rituals recognize even what our liturgy sometimes avoids: that the body has died, the life-soul has departed, and that this is really happening.

Of course, over time, Judaism acquired as many beliefs about the soul, reincarnation, heaven, and hell as our sister religions. We "evolved" from the biblical statement that "the dead do not praise God"[14] to mystical visions of saints singing praises in heaven. Throughout the many layers of spiritualizing rhetoric, however, the death rituals themselves remain focused on the concrete, the material world in which Being manifests. We have already seen some examples of how this works for the deceased. In the case of mourners, these practices have to do with neglecting the care of the body: for a week after a funeral, mirrors are covered, shaving and haircuts are prohibited, and the body, which is usually cared for so attentively, is ignored. (Diet is, unfortunately, disrupted as well; during the week of *shiva* I sat for my father, I subsisted on bagels and was ill by the end.) It's as if the tradition recognizes that care of the body is care of the self, and that both can distract from the reality of death.

Other religions have wonderful customs of moving immediately to celebration, but the Jewish practice is not to do so. The veil of grief lifts only slowly, during the week-long period of *shiva*, the month-long period of *shloshim*, and finally the eleven-month period of *avelut*, during which Kaddish is recited. Death is real, not an illusion, because, to the extent that anything is real, the body is. Naturally, it is unsettling to think about dead bodies—"becoming one with the earth" is itself a conveniently vague euphemism—but the ineluctable facticity of the body's demise ought not be papered over with conveniently chosen palliatives.

The life cycle, by definition, is a process that happens to the living body. From its beginning to its end, the body's various transformations are honored, in the Jewish tradition, by rituals old and new that link the passages of time to timeless myths and truths. Some might say that all this ritual is outmoded, even harmful, inasmuch as it stimulates irrational, emotional attachments to the passages of life. Perhaps we should focus our eyes only on the unchanging, or that which can be comprehended by logic. But ritual binds families and communities together, and as Rabbis Arthur Waskow and Phyllis Berman note, the process of affirming the body leads to a process of affirming community. In their words, "As we come to love ourselves, including the wondrous workings of our bodies, the love flows naturally to our daughters and sons, our friends and lovers, our mothers and fathers, our community, and those whom we still consider strangers."[15] Only by embracing the body can the *Ein Sof*, the Infinite, truly be extended to all of life, in manifestation as well as essence, community as well as contemplation. We are the Infinite having a human experience, in all its depths and colors and forms. Let's not deprive God of the ride.

* * * *

18
Just Being

Delight is a secret. And the secret is this: to grow quiet and lis-
ten; to stop thinking, stop moving, almost to stop breathing; to
create an inner stillness in which, like mice in a deserted house,
capacities and awarenesses too wayward and too fugitive for
everyday use may delicately emerge.

Alan McGlashan[1]

The mind thinks of the future; the heart mourns the past. But the
body always *is*. Rooted in its present experience, it frees the self from
the mind. It calls attention back to what is actually happening, with
sensitivity as subtle as one is able to cultivate. As attention sharpens in
its acuity, the body gradually reveals that concepts ordinarily assumed
to be real are illusory: "walking" is a composite of a thousand gradations of movement; "joy" is but a summary; "consciousness" is an illusion produced by a well-functioning machine, like the images at the
cinema that seem to be so whole.

Thus the body awakens one not only to the facticity of present experience, but also to its unity. As we closely raise, inspect, and drop the
phenomena of the body, each reveals itself to be a concept only, a useful label without separate reality, existing only according to the level
of abstract seeing. What, then, is real, in the sensation of a breeze gently caressing your face? If "the body" and all its constituent parts are
real only as labels, what *is*?

Beginning as they do from the premise of divinity, the sages of
Kabbalah often speak in a language moderns cannot understand.

They start with what we would deem the conclusion, if the proofs were satisfactory: that God exists, and is infinite. From there they proceed down the chain of being, through the emanations of the One to the many, and then back again. Thus they ask, if God is infinite, then what is your body, your heart, and your mind, but God itself? What are joy and terror, open fields and pits of darkness, other than the skin of the Infinite?

We meet—rabbis beginning from the transcendent, and contemplatives from the immanent—in Being itself. The label of "God" makes no factual difference, for God is not a figure within the ground of the universe; the universe is a figure within the ground of God. What is, is; Being, not separate selves; truth, not superstition. We cannot help but divide perception into pieces: we see a tree, not God; feel our fingers, not God; experience pain and bliss, not God. Yet in a sense, there is only one thing in the universe.

Simply to be, to experience Being as Being, is the practice of Shabbat, perhaps the cornerstone of Jewish religious life. We have waited until the end to encounter the Shabbat, since it can be at once very distant and very near. Shabbat is the sum of all the practices we have seen so far: the experience *of* Being as Being. This is nearer than any "spiritual" sensation—those are sensations of something, no more and no less proximate to the divine than anything else—but also so transparent as to be invisible.

"Just Being" is a subtractive aspect of ordinary consciousness, a gradual loosening of the grip of concepts. In the body, it is becoming mindful of experiences too subtle to note ordinarily. Pressure on the back, sounds being heard, the expansion and contraction of the chest. And then: just pressure, just sound, just expansion and contraction. Slowly the mind quiets, and the body rests in repose—in Sabbath, which we are told is a taste of the world to come, a world none other than this one, yet seen from God's point of view.

Shabbat is observed with the body, of course, for it is the body that manifests the will to create and destroy. And most of its practices are, like meditation, subtractive rather than additive in nature. Often, this devolves into a series of Don'ts: don't make a fire, don't play music, don't drive or write. But the deeper meaning of Don't is Be. On

Shabbat, life transpires for its intrinsic quality alone; it ceases to be an instrument to get us to the next place, where perhaps our preferences might be better accommodated. Being simply *is*.

When the body is allowed to rest in this way, it detaches from the *yetzer*, the will to arrange the conditions of the world to enable our maximum happiness. Only then does true happiness appear. As Byron Katie says, what we really want is to want what we have. Or, in the words of the *Pirke Avot (Ethics of the Ancestors)*: "Who is rich? He who is happy with his share."[2] Not doing, not changing, not thinking or talking or arguing—just Being—this is the essence of Shabbat. The rest of the week we go about the business of pursuing justice and peace—and of course, the desires of the ego as well. But one day a week ... not.

There are holidays, too, that are observed in this way. Sukkot, nicknamed by the sages "The Holiday," whose joy and practice derive simply from placing the body in a temporary home and resting under the shade of the tabernacle, is a good example. Just Being—without planning, creating, chanting, or doing—allows the boundaries of self slowly to become transparent. And without purposefulness, the self loses its definition. Not regressing, but transcending the delusions of need. Ending, for once, the competition.

Nonduality includes both doing and nondoing, but it is best known through the latter. At some later time, there can be the return of the monk to the marketplace; the descent of Moses from Sinai; a return to the material, where the Infinite puts on masks of distinction. But Shabbat ensures that our return is not a regression, that it maintains an almost transparent knowing—that all this is real, that none of this is real. Ironically, it is the most physical, the most separate-seeming part of the material world, that is the greatest vehicle for remembering. Spiritual states may come and go, but the body endures for a lifetime.

We cannot get beyond the body except through the body, *in* the body itself. Otherwise there is still something to be denied, or utilized, as if "we" are merely inhabiting our bodies, trapped souls waiting for release into paradise. The pious will argue that some desires are loftier than others; hedonists will reply in kind. But all the while, Being will be unfolding, just out of range of periphery, in the shape and form of the ordinary. It is, in a way, a solitary path, for there is, in the truest possible way, no one else here. But then again, you aren't either.

There is only Me, God says. You are not alone, because this ego, this "you," is not what is ultimately real. To whom are these bodily sensations happening, if consciousness is but a phenomenon of the brain? Who is really here? And how do "you" know anything? In the end, the solitude of the nondual path is only as temporary as the intimacies of the alternative, because when the true Self is known, suddenly there is love within the fabric of Being itself. Not beyond, not denying, not leaving behind the substantial; but in it, *as* it, inviting you to join heaven and earth. And promising, in a silent and intimate vow: Be faithful to Me, and I will show you love.

*   *   *   *

Appendix
Four Worlds—A Kabbalistic
Map of Our
Experiential Universe

The notion that the universe is comprised of four "worlds," or levels of reality, is an ancient one in the Kabbalah and reflects the understanding that existence is multilayered and in a state of dynamic flux. Originally, the four worlds were described from "God's point of view," as levels of manifestation and differentiation, from will to plan to formation to project, or as angelic realms. In later Kabbalah and Hasidism, they came to be described more from the human point of view, as reflecting the experience of spirit, mind, heart, and body. The four worlds are also associated with the "lower" four of the five souls, which derive from the midrash in *Bereshit Rabba*h 14:9, and are explicated in the *Raya Mehemna* portion of the Zohar. The fifth level of the soul, *yechidah*, is less a separate level of the soul than a state in which all manifestation is erased in essential unity. Following the Hasidic paradigm, the four worlds are here presented as they are known experientially, from the human point of view.

	ATZILUT אֲצִילוּת The World of Emanation	BRIYAH בְּרִיאָה The World of Creation	YETZIRA יְצִירָה The World of Formation	ASIYAH עֲשִׂיָּה The World of Action
Soul:	*Chayah*/life-soul	*Neshamah*/ breath-soul	*Ruach*/wind-water soul of the heart	*Nefesh*, the "animal soul," life-force, or *anima*
Self:	Trans-rational	Faculties of mind (reasoning, doubting, wisdom, understanding)	"Soul" colloquially, faculties of heart (compassion, fear, and desire)	The physical, moving, tasting, pulsing, sexual body
In the body:	"Crown" (i.e., no-body)	Brain, breath	Heart center, lungs, circulation/oxygenation	The "body of the body," especially legs and midsection
Human expression:	*Devekut* (merging embrace of the One)	Science, contemplation, reasoning	Art, poetry, awe, love	Eating, sleeping, sports, sex, bodily functions
World expression:	Timeless, Divine, "the Now"	Physical world, laws of nature, matter and energy, four basic forces, science	Emotional world, eros, love and passion, feelings, the sublime and the beautiful	The material world as it appears to us, dualistic, subject/object difference
Separation:	none	Hyper-rationalism, separation from heart and body, "living in the head"	Sex and violence, hatred, craving-desire	"Flatland" materialism, alienated carnality, greed
Prayer:	The *Amidah*, meditation	The *Shema*, the acknowledgement of unity	The Psalms, cultivating the heart	*Birchot hashachar*
Element:	Fire	Air	Water	Earth
Torah:	*Sod*/secret	*Drash*, discursive midrash/tales, as well as philosophy and theory.	*Remez*, allusion, poetry	*Pshat*, the surface level, and halacha: What should we *do*?

Notes

Introduction

1. Although the doctrine of the four worlds dates back to the thirteenth century, it is largely absent from the main text of the Zohar, the masterpiece of Kabbalah, and came into its current form only relatively recently. Nevertheless, it is a useful and relatively straightforward structure, and so we will use it here. For a contemporary exposition of it, see Rabbi Zalman Schachter-Shalomi, *Gate to the Heart*.
2. Swami Vivekananda, commentary on Yoga Aphorisms of Patanjali, ch. II, #18.
3. *Kitzur Shulchan Aruch* 31:1.
4. See *Vayikra Rabba* 18:1.
5. *Likutei Moharan* II, 1:2.
6. Jorge N. Ferrer, "Embodied Spirituality, Now and Then," *Tikkun*, May/June 2006, 45.

Chapter 1

1. Isaiah 55:2.
2. William S. Burroughs, *Naked Lunch,* p. xxxvii.
3. *Darchei Tzedek* p. 18. Translated by Yitzhak Buxbaum in *Jewish Spiritual Practices*, p. 226.
4. *Pesachim* 118a.
5. Michel Foucault, "Friendship as a Way of Life," in *Foucault Live*, p. 310.
6. Quoted in *Mazkeret Shem HaGedolim* (M. H. Kleinman, ed.), p. 79. Translated by Buxbaum in *Jewish Spiritual Practices*, p. 231.
7. *Berachot* 55.
8. Rabbi Bahya ibn Pakuda, *The Duties of the Heart*, Gate of Discernment, chapter 5, translated into Hebrew by R. Yehuda ibn Tibbon, in Haberman, ed., p. 196.
9. Wei Wu Wei, *Ask the Awakened*, p. 1.
10. The blessing, in slightly different form, is discussed in *Berachot* 40b.
11. Baal Shem Tov, *Tzavaat HaRivash*, p. 14.

12. Rumi, Mathnawi I:3165, translated by Coleman Barks in *Delicious Laughter*, p. 95 (adapted).

Chapter 2

1. Rabbi Yitzhak Abuhav, *Menorat ha-Maor*, sec. 103, p. 208. Translated by Buxbaum in *Jewish Spiritual Practices,* p. 166.
2. See, e.g., Esther 3:2–4. Rodger Kamenetz's book, *The Jew in the Lotus*, has an absorbing story of how this played out when a delegation of Jews met with the Dalai Lama and debated whether or not to bow or make the *Namaste* sign with their hands.
3. See *Berachot* 12b, discussed in Chapter 8: Exercising.
4. *Bava Kama* 16a. The text may also mean "at the end of seven years."
5. Rabbi Shlomo of Karlin, *Shema Shlomo* II (Y. M. HaLevi, ed.) p. 44. Translated by Buxbaum in *Jewish Spiritual Practices*, p. 151.
6. Baal Shem Tov, *Tzavaat HaRivash* 7b.
7. *Berachot* 31.
8. Quoted in *Mazkeret Shem HaGedolim*, p. 157. Translated by Buxbaum in *Jewish Spiritual Practices*, p. 168.
9. Rabbi Nachman of Breslov, *Likutei Etzot*, prayer #41.
10. Rabbi T. H. Kaidenver, *Kav ha-Yashar Ha-Shalem*, ch. 63. Translated by Buxbaum in *Jewish Spiritual Practices*, p. 168.
11. *Likkutei Yekarim*. Translated by Arthur Green and Barry Holtz in *Your Word Is Fire,* p. 84.
12. *Berachot* 60b.

Chapter 3

1. Rabbi Nachman of Breslov, *Likutei Moharan* I, 8:1.
2. *Or HaGanuz HaTzaddikim*, p. 45. Translated by Buxbaum in *Jewish Spiritual Practices,* p. 109.
3. Rabbi Nachman of Breslov, *Likutei Moharan* I, 133.
4. Satipatthana Sutra, §A.1. Translated by Thanissaro Bhikkhu, online at www.accesstoinsight.org.
5. Ibid., §E.

Chapter 4

1. Genesis 5:24.
2. "Make peace upon us" is a bit awkward in English, but it's more faithful to the original, as is the gendered language. Many add *v'al kol yoshvei tevel*, "and all who live on the earth," at the end.
3. Hafiz, "You Are God in Drag," in *The Gift: Poems by Hafiz*, p. 252.

4. *Chayah,* the fourth level of the soul, is that transrational capacity that gives us an intimation of unity, *yechidah.* Although *yechidah* is sometimes referred to as a fifth soul, it is really the state of union of all the lower four with the universe as it is in its essence.

Chapter 5

1. Carl G. Jung, *Analytical Psychology: Its Theory and Practice,* p. 23.
2. Baal Shem Tov, *Tzavaat HaRivash*, p. 4
3. Rabbi Bahya ibn Pakuda, *The Duties of the Heart*, Gate of Discernment, chapter 5, translated into Hebrew by R. Yehuda ibn Tibbon, in Haberman, ed., p. 196.
4. Rabbi Kalonymus Kalman Epstein, *Maor V'Shemesh* on *Bereshit Rabba* 19:7.
5. *Berachot* 60b.
6. See Shulchan Aruch §4.

Chapter 6

1. Rabbi Baruch of Kosov, *Amud Haavoda*, p. 29b.
2. *Bava Metzia* 84a.
3. Mishnah *Ketubot* 5:6.
4. *Ketubot* 8a.
5. *Yoma* 54a.
6. *Bereshit Rabba* 19:3, 6.
7. See, e.g., Zohar I:15b (describing how male and female reflect cosmic creation); I:49a ("The breath of life was enclosed in the earth, which became pregnant with it."); I:49b–50b (describing how sexual love arouses divine love and protection).
8. See Zohar III:283b.
9. See the *Takanat Hashavin* by Rabbi Zadok HaCohen of Lublin for a fascinating attempt to reconcile the Zohar's attitude with the Torah's silence.
10. See *Niddah* 13a–b. For their part, while the Kabbalists are quite aware of female orgasm, and regard the "female waters" as embodiments of the divine flow, they do not, to my knowledge, speak of female masturbation.
11. Song of Songs 4:3.
12. Ibid., 4:16.
13. Ibid., 5:10–15.
14. Quoted in Rabbi Elijah de Vidas, *Reishit Hochmah,* Shaar Ha-Ahava, ch. 4, #32.
15. *Shulchan Aruch*, §280.
16. Rabbi Naphtali Hertz, *Yifrach biYamav Tzaddik,* p. 48b. Translated by Buxbaum in *Jewish Spiritual Practices*, p. 598.

Chapter 7

1. George Herbert, "Man," in *The Works of George Herbert*, p. 91.
2. Malbim, *HeCharash VeHamasger*, ch. 8. Quoted in Diane Bloomfield, *Torah Yoga*, p. 3.
3. Ralph Waldo Emerson, *Selected Writings of Ralph Waldo Emerson*, p. 204.
4. *Avot de Rabbi Natan* 31:3.
5. Midrash HaGadol on Exodus 25:3.
6. *Makkot* 23b.
7. Rabbi Nachman of Breslov, *Likutei Moharan* I, 5:2.
8. Job 38:36.
9. *Berachot* 61a.
10. Tamar Frankiel and Judy Greenfield, *Minding the Temple of the Soul*, pp. 62–63.
11. *Berachot* 61b.
12. *Bereshit Rabba* 67:3.
13. Rabbi Nachman of Breslov, *Likutei Moharan* I, 160.
14. Ibid., I, 57:6.
15. Ibid., II, 6.
16. Ibid., I, 51:1.
17. Ibid., I, 267.
18. Moshe Cordovero, *Pardes Rimmonim* 4:4, 17d–18a. Translated by Daniel Matt in *The Essential Kabbalah,* p. 38.
19. Of the many attempts to explain the *sefirot* that have appeared in recent years, some of the best include Arthur Green, *A Guide to the Zohar*, pp. 28–38, and Gershom Scholem, *Kabbalah*, pp. 98–117. My own attempt to do so may be found online at www.learnkabbalah.com. Accessible primary sources include Rabbi Moses Cordovero (see previous note); Bahir 96–115; Rabbi Joseph Gikatilla, *Sha'arei Orah (Gates of Light)*; and Cordovero, *Tomer Devorah (The Palm Tree of Deborah)*.
20. See, e.g., Tikkunei Zohar 17a. Many have observed parallels between the *sefirot* and the chakras, which also are energy centers located along vertical columns of the body. The similarities remain intriguing, though scholars have yet to find a historical connection.
21. Zohar III:246b notes that God's "hands" are described three ways in the book of Exodus; as *gedolah* (great; 14:31—*hesed*), *chazakah* (strong; 6:1—*gevurah*), and *ramah* (exalted; 14:8—*tiferet*).

Chapter 8

1. Rav Kook, *Orot*, #33, in *Orot*, p. 189.
2. Rabbi Nachman of Breslov, *Likutei Moharan* II, 6.
3. Rav Kook, *Orot*, #34, in *Orot*, p. 189.

4. Rav Kook, *Orot HaKodesh*, vol. I, pp. 66–7.

5. Rav Kook, *Orot*, #33, in *Orot*, p. 189.

6. Rav Kook, *Olat Reayah*, p. 11.

Chapter 9

1. Hafiz, "Wow," in *The Gift: Poems by Hafiz*, p. 259.

2. Exodus 15:20–21.

3. I Samuel 18:6.

4. Jeremiah 31:13.

5. Ecclesiastes 3:1, 4.

6. I Samuel 10:5–6.

7. II Samuel 6:14–15.

8. *Sukkah* 51:b.

9. *Sukkah* 53a.

10. Rabbi Nachman of Breslov, *Sefer Hamidot,* entry "Simcha," pt. 1, #8.

11. Rabbi Noson of Nemirov, *Yemei Moharnat 3*.

12. Rabbi Yehudah Loew ben Bezalel, *Be'er HaGolah,* Be'er 4, p. 75a.

13. Psalm 63:2.

14. Rabbi Moshe Chaim Luzzatto, *The Path of the Just*, ch. 7.

15. Reported by Dvora Lapson, quoted in the *Encyclopedia Judaica* entry "Dance" (Jerusalem: Keter Publishing House Ltd., 1971, p. 1267).

16. *Pesachim* 109a, Chapter 10.

Chapter 10

1. Carolyn Walker Bynum, *Holy Feast, Holy Fast*, p. 295.

2. Rabbi Nachman of Breslov, *Likkutei Moharan*, 57:6.

Chapter 11

1. Rabbi Elijah de Vidas, *Reishit Hochmah,* Shaar Ha-Ahava, ch. 11, #23.

2. Rabbi Bahya ibn Pakuda, supplication appended to *The Duties of the Heart*, translated into Hebrew by R. Yehuda ibn Tibbon, in Haberman, ed., p. 917.

3. *Makkot* 20a–21a.

4. Genesis 9:6.

5. *Vayikra Rabba* 34.

6. *Shulchan Aruch* §2 ("One must wash his face in honor of the Creator, as it is said (Gen 9:6): 'For God made man in God's image.'").

7. See *Berachot* 53b for a discussion of *mayim acharonim*, "after-waters." Interestingly, both spiritual and health reasons are provided for this custom: one washes both to purify the hands and to rinse off any salt that may have clung to them, which otherwise might get in the eyes.

8. Rabbi Meir ben Rabbi Yehuda Leib, *Or Tzaddikim* (1889), p. 16a, 4:5–8. Translated by Buxbaum in *Jewish Spiritual Practices*, p. 80.

Chapter 12

1. k.d. lang, "Wash Me Clean," from *Ingenue*, Rhino Records NR 26840.
2. Bahir 84, cited in Aryeh Kaplan, *Waters of Eden*, p. 72.
3. Nina Beth Cardin, *Tears of Sorrow, Seeds of Hope*, pp. 32–33. This *kavvanah* was written specifically for a woman hoping to bear a child, but its wording could be read more generally as well.
4. Taken from the "Sample Ceremonies" page on www.mayyimhayyim.org. This *kavvanah* can also be used before washing the hands.
5. As only women are commanded to use the mikva, men customarily do not recite a blessing here. Though some have proposed liturgy for men, I find, given the many commandments traditionally reserved for men, that this a good opportunity for men to experience being in a nonprivileged gender role for a change.
6. *Berachot* 60b.
7. Susan Berrin, *Celebrating the New Moon*, p. xxi.
8. *Sanhedrin* 52a.

Chapter 13

1. Emerson, *Selected Writings of Ralph Waldo Emerson*, p. 181.
2. Rabbi Schneur Zalman of Liadi, *Tanya*, ch. 6.
3. Rabbi Nachman of Breslov, *Likutei Tefilot* II: 11.
4. Rabbi Nachman of Breslov, *Sichot HaRan* #98, in *Rabbi Nachman's Wisdom*, p. 227.
5. Emerson, *Selected Writings of Ralph Waldo Emerson*, p. 184.

Chapter 14

1. Rabbi Nachman of Breslov, *Likutei Moharan* II, 91:1.
2. Friedrich Nietzsche, *The Birth of Tragedy and the Genealogy of Morals*, pp. 178–179.
3. *Ketubot* 5b.
4. Buxbaum, *Jewish Spiritual Practices*, p. 324.
5. See, e.g., Exodus 30:34–35; Leviticus 16:12–13.
6. See *Keritot* 6a.
7. *Berachot* 43b.
8. Numbers 15:39.
9. Deuteronomy 6:8, 11:18.

Chapter 15

1. Rav Kook, *Orot* #61, in *Orot*, p. 208.
2. Jeremiah 10:10.

Chapter 16

1. *Bava Metzia* 107b.
2. *Ketubot* 10b.
3. *Shabbat* 108b.
4. *Shabbat* 80b.
5. *Bava Metzia* 107b. See also *Bava Metzia* 92b ("Have an early breakfast in the summer because of the heat, and in the winter because of the cold.").
6. Leviticus 18:5.
7. Recounted in *HaYom Yom*, Shevat 10, at www.chabadtalk.com/forum /printhread.php?t=198.
8. Thich Nhat Hanh, *Peace Is Every Step*, p. 38.
9. See Shulchan Aruch §219.
10. See Exodus 23:25 ("Worship the lord your God, and God's blessing will be on your food and water. I will take away sickness from among you.").
11. Maimonides, *Mishneh Torah*, Hilchot Deot, 3:3, 4:23.
12. Juvenal, *Satires*, §10.356.
13. Rabbi Samson Raphael Hirsch, *Horeb*, (translated by I. Grunfeld), ch. 62, sec. 428.
14. Nisargadatta, *I Am That*, p. 151.

Chapter 17

1. Leviticus 12:6–7.
2. See *Eruvin* 100b.
3. See Rabbi Debra Orenstein, ed., *Lifecycles: Jewish Women on Life Passages and Personal Milestones*, and Nina Beth Cardin, *Tears of Sorrow, Tears of Joy*. There are also many online resources for such rituals, including those on rit-ualwell.org, myjewishlearning.com, and Rabbi Goldie Milgrom's site, reb-goldie.com.
4. Genesis 17:11.
5. See Glick, *Marked in Your Flesh*, for a discussion of the contemporary de-bates. Rabbis Arthur Waskow and Phyllis Berman grapple with these issues in an embodied spiritual context in *A Time for Every Purpose Under Heaven: The Jewish Life-Spiral as a Spiritual Path*, pp. 7–23.
6. See Zohar II:36a. Elliot Wolfson has greatly elaborated on this theme in his books, most recently *Language, Eros, Being* (New York: Fordham University Press, 2004). Continuing with the gender-bending of circumcision, the

circumcision blood, usually a feminine symbol, is imbued by the Zohar with masculine symbolism. See Zohar III:13b–14a.

7. See Waskow and Berman, *A Time for Every Purpose Under Heaven*, pp. 23–28.
8. Mishnah *Avot* 5:21.
9. See *Niddah* 45b–46a, *Kiddushin* 81b, *Yoma* 82a.
10. Waskow and Berman, *A Time for Every Purpose Under Heaven*, pp. 81–89. The book also describes, on pp. 61–80, a variety of possible ways to teach healthy sexual ethics as a part of bar and bat mitzvah observances.
11. See, e.g., ww.mayyimhayyim.org, the website of Mayyim Hayyim, Boston's community mikva and educational center.
12. See, e.g., Orenstein, *Lifecycles*; Cardin, *Tears of Sorrow, Tears of Joy*; and the online resources above.
13. Genesis 3:19.
14. Psalm 115:17.
15. Waskow and Berman, *A Time for Every Purpose Under Heaven*, p. 89.

Chapter 18

1. Alan McGlashan, *The Savage and Beautiful Country*, p. 134.
2 Mishnah *Avot* 4:1.

Glossary

Abulafia, Abraham (1240–1291). The most important figure in prophetic Kabbalah. Developed a system of meditative exercises based upon the Hebrew alphabet and the ten *sefirot*, as well as a mystical theology based on Maimonides and esoteric thought.

Amidah. Literally, "standing prayer," the *Amidah* is the centerpiece of the thrice-daily liturgy. Also called the *Shmoneh Esrei*, The Eighteen, because it usually has eighteen blessings; or *Hatefilah*, The Prayer.

Ari. Acronym for Elohi Rabbi Yitzhak. The godly Rabbi Yitzhak Luria (1534–1572), renowned Kabbalist active in Safed. One of the primary figures in Lurianic Kabbalah, which advanced new elaborations on the cosmic myth of the breaking and repairing of the world. Ari also means "lion."

asiyah. "Lowest" of the four worlds; the world of action, corresponding to the body, physicality, duality, and appearance.

atzilut. "Highest" of the four worlds; the world of emanation, corresponding to the soul, spirituality, nonduality, and the *Ein Sof*.

avodah. Practice, work, worship, service of God.

Baal Shem Tov (1698–1760). The founder of Hasidism; charismatic and miracle-working rabbi who advocated a "popular mysticism" based on devotional love of God and the pursuit of *devekut*.

Bahya ibn Pakuda. Medieval preacher and judge (eleventh century) who wrote the emotional and philosophical masterpiece *Duties of the Heart*, which argued that internal obligations such as philosophy, devotion, and faith were as important as external ones.

Barchu. Literally "kneeling prayer." The call to prayer that begins the formal morning and evening service.

beinoni. Literally "in-betweener." One who is neither wholly good nor wholly evil, but somewhere in between.

beit midrash. House of learning; can refer to a yeshiva, or the actual room, study hall, or library in which learning takes place.

bracha. Usually translated as "blessing," but related to the word for "knees," and more properly denoting an expression of gratitude and recognition for the divine source or commandment for a given action, substance, or moment. (See Chapter 1 for traditional format.)

briyah. Second highest of the four worlds; the world of creation, corresponding to the mind, intellect, laws of nature, and philosophy.

chayah. "Life-soul," the highest of the four individual souls, and the gateway to *yechidah*, unity.

devekut. "Cleaving" to God; the state of mystical adhesion to the Divine, and a primary goal of Hasidic practice.

Ein Sof. The Infinite; name given to the Divine Infinite in kabbalistic thought. Early Kabbalists conceived of the *Ein Sof* as the absolute perfection in which there is no distinction or plurality. While "God" may be thought of in relational or conceptual terms, the *Ein Sof* transcends these categories. Since the infinite really is infinite—it does not end at the front of your brain, or anywhere else—it is all there is.

halacha. "The way"; Jewish law. Traditionally, halacha is made up of the written law, as recorded in the Pentateuch, and the oral law, which includes the Talmud and later responsa as well as established customs, and has been codified in such works as the *Mishneh Torah* by Maimonides and the *Shulchan Aruch* compiled by Joseph Caro.

Hasidism. Literally "pietism" or "lovingkindness-ism," but usually used to denote the ecstatic, popular revival movement begun in eastern Europe in the late eighteenth century that valued emotional faith and devotionalistic prayer over text study and traditional authority.

hitbodedut. Literally "secluding," but often used to refer to a mode of prayer-meditation developed by Rabbi Nachman of Breslov in which an individual retreats into nature to talk and cry to God.

hitbonnenut. Contemplation; one of the core meditation practices in Kabbalah and Hasidism.

Kabbalah. The body of Jewish esoteric and mystical thought. Literally "receiving," either in the sense of a received teaching dealing with mystical or esoteric matters or in the sense of receiving direct experience of ultimate reality. Technically, Kabbalah refers to Jewish esoteric teachings that evolved primarily in the Medieval period regarding the hidden life of God and the secrets of God's relationship to creation.

kashrut. The Jewish dietary laws; "keeping kosher."

kavvanah/kavvanot. Intention/intentions set for a particular act. Can also have a technical kabbalistic meaning, referring to that act's theurgical significance.

kedusha. Holiness.

Kook, Rabbi Abraham Isaac (1864–1935). Mystic and original rabbi and thinker; first chief rabbi of modern Israel. Among other things, Rav Kook believed that both physical and spiritual redemption were necessary, and he thus supported both secular Zionism and religious revival.

Luria, Rabbi Yitzhak. See Ari.

Maimonides, Moses (1135–1204). Greatest of the Jewish rationalist philosophers, as well as a compiler of Jewish law, rabbi, doctor, and sage. Also called the Rambam, an acronym for Rabbi Moshe Ben Maimon. Influenced by Medieval Aristotelianism, the Rambam created what is today the authoritative Jewish creed, and he is among the most important figures in halacha and Jewish philosophy.

midrash. A mode of biblical exegesis that often involves legends, tales, moral principles, or halachic teachings loosely based upon the original text. The term, when capitalized, also refers to the corpus of *midrashim* written over the centuries, most importantly the *Rabba* ("great") series compiled in the eighth century.

mikva. A natural gathering of water used as a ritual bath for immersion and purification.

mitzvah. Commandment. A mitzvah may be an ethical precept or a prescribed ritual action. In Jewish law commandments are either positive (*mitzvah aseh*) or negative (*mitzvah lo ta'aseh*). According to tradition, there are 613 commandments in the Torah, corresponding to the 248 limbs of the human body and the 365 days of the year.

Nachman of Breslov, Rabbi (1772–1810). Emotional and highly original Hasidic rebbe who emphasized the paradoxical nature of faith and the need for devotionalistic worship and meditation. Often ill himself, Rabbi Nachman was also very concerned about maintaining the body's health.

nefesh. "Vital-soul," the flesh-and-blood vitality of the human body, the foundational layer of the soul.

neshamah. "Breath-soul," the second highest of the four individual souls, corresponding to intellect, air, and the world of *briyah*.

niggun. Wordless melody popular in Hasidism.

pasuk. Verse of the Bible.

ratzo v'shuv. "Running and returning," the oscillation, typical of the spiritual path, between moments of union and distance, enlightenment and confusion. The phrase is taken from Ezekiel's vision of heavenly beings.

ruach. "Wind-soul," the third highest of the four individual souls, corresponding to emotion, water, and the world of *yetzirah.*

samadhi. Sanskrit term for a concentrated mind-state in which the mind is extremely still and, sometimes, consciousness of the experiencing subject becomes one with the experienced object.

sefirot. Emanations or manifestations of God that explain how a transcendent, inaccessible Godhead (*Ein Sof*) can relate to the world. The ten *sefirot* are: (1) *keter*, the Supreme Crown; (2) *hochmah*, wisdom; (3) *binah*, intelligence; (4) *hesed*, lovingkindness; (5) *gevurah*, strength; (6) *tiferet*, beauty; (7) *netzach*, endurance; (8) *hod*, majesty; (9) *yesod*, foundation; and (10) *malchut*, kingdom, Presence.

Shabbat. The Sabbath, day of rest, observed every week from before sunset on Friday until nightfall on Saturday. According to tradition, the Sabbath is celebrated to honor God's day of rest after creation. No work should take place on the Sabbath; rabbinic legislation stipulates thirty-nine categories of activity that are forbidden.

Shema. Literally "listen"; the primary statement of Jewish monotheism (or, in some interpretations, monism): God is One.

Shmoneh Esrei. See *Amidah.*

shuckling. Rhythmically bowing back and forth during prayer.

Shulchan Aruch. The "Set Table"; codification of Jewish law composed by Rabbi Joseph Caro in the sixteenth century. Considered authoritative by all Orthodox Jews.

Talmud. Vast record of the discussion and administration of Jewish law by scholars in various academies from ca. 200 to ca. 500. Comprises the Mishnah (law) together with Gemara (commentary and supplement to the Mishnah text), as well as legendary and other material.

tefillin. Phylacteries; sacred texts from the Torah bound to the body by means of special leather straps and cases.

theurgy. Causing a change in the Godhead or supernal realms by means of human action.

tikkun. Mending, completing, repairing. Can refer to *tikkun olam*, the kabbalistic notion that the performance of mitzvot (or its contemporary equivalent regarding acts of social justice) repairs the brokenness of the world, or to any number of *tikkunim*, special services or practices that "complete" certain times or occasions.

tshuvah. Return, repentance; coming back to one's true self, or, in traditional language, religious observance.

tzitzit. Fringes; the four fringes now usually attached to a special garment worn under the clothes. Also attached to the tallit, which is worn over the clothes during prayer.

yechidah. Union; the true nature of the soul, beyond its four layers: unified with God.

yeshiva. A Jewish academy for Torah study.

yetzer. "Inclination," sometimes *yetzer hara*, evil inclination; the delusive mind that seeks selfish gain as a means to happiness.

yetzirah. "Formation," the third of the four worlds, corresponding to the world of the emotions and the creative energies. The *Sefer Yetzirah*, or Book of Creation, is an ancient kabbalistic text describing how God created the universe through language.

yoga. Literally "joining"; refers to spiritual practices, primarily in Hinduism, that included physical movement, moral principles, and instruction by a guru. Lately used to refer specifically to certain physical practices emphasizing flexibility, breath, and posture that were originally designed as forms of meditation but today are used as exercise as well.

Zohar. The masterpiece of the Kabbalah, the Zohar takes the form of a mystical commentary on the Torah. According to tradition, it was composed in the second century by Simeon ben Yohai. However, the work as we have it was first published in the thirteenth century by Moses de Leon in Spain and contains language that is certainly medieval in origin.

Bibliography

Works Cited

BIBLICAL SOURCES

Genesis 3:19, 5:24, 9:6, 17:10-11
Exodus 6:1, 14:8, 14:31, 15:20–21, 23:25, 30:34–35, 34:28
Leviticus 12:6–7, 13, 14, 15, 16:12-13, 18:5, 21:16–23
Numbers 15:39, 30:14
Deuteronomy 4:15, 6:8, 8:10, 11:18, 30:6
Judges 20:26
I Samuel 7:5, 10:5–6, 14:24, 18:6, 28:20
II Samuel 1:12, 6:14–15, 12:16–23
Isaiah 55:2
Jeremiah 10:10, 31:13, 36:9
Joel 1:14
Jonah 3:5–10
Psalms 35:10, 63:2, 115:17, 145:16, 148, 149:3, 150
Proverbs 3:6, 13:25, 20:29
Job 19:26, 38:36
Song of Songs 4:3, 4:16, 5:10–15
Ecclesiastes 3:1–4
Esther 3:2–4, 4:6
Daniel 10:2

RABBINIC SOURCES

Berachot 12b, 28b, 31a–b, 40b, 43b, 53b, 55a–b, 60b, 61a–b
Shabbat 50b, 80b, 108b, 109a, 114a
Eruvin 28a, 48b, 100b
Pesachim 109a, 118a
Yoma 54a, 82a

Sukkah 5a, 8a, 51b, 52b, 53a, 109a
Yevamot 8:7, 103a
Mishnah *Ketubot* 5:6
Ketubot 5b, 8a, 10b, 48a
Nedarim 20a–b, 32b
Yerushalmi Nedarim 9:1
Sotah 4a
Kiddushin 2b, 81b
Bava Kama 16a
Bava Metzia 84a, 92b, 107b
Sanhedrin 17b, 52a
Makkot 20a–21a, 23b
Mishnah *Avot* 4:1, 5:21
Keritot 6a
Niddah 13a–b, 45b–46a
Bereshit Rabba 6, 12, 14:9, 19:3, 67:3
Vayikra Rabba 18:1, 34
Avot de Rabbi Natan 31:3

KABBALISTIC, HASIDIC, AND OTHER TRADITIONAL SOURCES

Baal Shem Tov, Rabbi Israel. *Tzavaat HaRivash*. Available in English translation by Jacob Immanuel Schochet. Brooklyn, NY: Kehot Publication Society, 1998.

Bahir 84, 96–115

Bezalel, Rabbi Yehuda Loew ben. *Be'er HaGolah*.

Cordovero, Rabbi Moses. *Tomer Devorah*. Available in English translation by Moshe Miller as *The Palm Tree of Deborah*. Southfield, MI: Targum, 1994.

Epstein, Rabbi Kalonymus Kalman, *Maor V'Shemesh* on *Bereshit Rabba* 19:7.

Ganzfried, Rabbi Solomon. *Kitzur Shulchan Aruch*. Available in English translation by Rabbi Avrohom Davis. New York: Metsudah, 1987.

Gikatilla, Rabbi Joseph. *Sha'arei Orah*. Available in English translation by Avi Weinstein as *Gates of Light*. Walnut Creek, CA: Altamira, 1998.

ibn Pakuda, Rabbi Bahya, *Duties of the Heart*. Translated into Hebrew by Rabbi Yehuda ibn Tibbon, with English translation by Daniel Haberman. Jerusalem: Feldheim, 1996.

Judith 8:6

Kook, Rabbi Abraham Isaac HaCohen. *Olat Reayah*. *Tel-Aviv: Mossad Harav Kook, 1963.*

————. *Orot.* Translated by Bezalel Naor. Northvale, NJ: Jason Aronson, 1993.

————. *Orot Hakodesh.* Translated by Ben Zion Bokser. New York: Paulist Press, 1978.

Luzzatto, Rabbi Moshe Chaim. *The Path of the Just.* Translated by Yaakov Feldman. Northvale, NJ: Jason Aronson, 1996.

Maimonides (Rabbi Moshe ben Maimon). *Mishneh Torah.*

Nachman, Rabbi, of Breslov. *Likutei Etzot.*

————. *Likutei Moharan.* Available in English translation by Simcha Bergman. New York: Breslov Research Institute, 1986.

————. *Likutei Tefilot.* Edited by Rabbi Noson of Nemirov. Available in English translation by Avraham Greenbaum as *The Fiftieth Gate: Likutei Tefilot.* New York: Breslov Research Institute, 1993.

————. *Rabbi Nachman's Wisdom.* Translated by Aryeh Kaplan. New York: Breslov Research Institute, 1984.

————. *Sefer Hamidot.*

Noson, Rabbi, of Nemirov. *Yemei Moharnat.*

Schneur Zalman, Rabbi, of Liady. *Tanya.*

Romans 2:29

Sefer Yetzirah

Shulchan Aruch §§2, 4, 219, 280

Tikkunei Zohar 17a

de Vidas, Rabbi Elijah. *Reishit Hochmah.*

Zohar I:15b, I:49a–50b; II:36a, III:13b-14a, III:283b, III:246b

Zohar. Available in English as *The Zohar: Pritzker Edition.* Edited and translated by Daniel C. Matt. 3 vols. Stanford, CA: Stanford University Press, 2005.

OTHER PRIMARY SOURCES

Analayo, *Satipatthana: The Direct Path to Realization.* Birmingham, UK: Windhorse, 2004.

Broughton, James. *Packing Up for Paradise: Selected Poems 1946–1996.* Edited by Jim Cory. Santa Rosa, CA: Black Sparrow Press, 1997.

Burroughs, William S. *Naked Lunch.* New York: Grove Press, 1966.

Buxbaum, Yitzhak, ed. *Jewish Spiritual Practices.* Northvale, NJ: Jason Aronson, 1990.

Douglas, Mary. *Purity and Danger: An Analysis of Concepts of Pollution and Taboo.* Boston: Ark Paperbacks, 1984.

Emerson, Ralph Waldo. "Nature." In *Selected Writings of Ralph Waldo Emerson.* Edited by William H. Gilman, pp. 181–224. New York: Signet Classic, 2003.

Green, Arthur, and Barry Holtz. *Your Word Is Fire: The Hasidic Masters on Contemplative Prayer.* Woodstock, VT: Jewish Lights Publishing, 1993.

Hafiz. *The Gift: Poems of Hafiz.* Translated by Daniel Ladinsky. New York: Penguin, 1999.

Herbert, George. *The Works of George Herbert.* Edited by F. E. Hutchinson. Oxford: Clarendon Press, 1941.

Hirsch, Samson Raphael. *Horeb: A Philosophy of Jewish Laws and Observances,* Translated by I. Grunfeld. 2 vols. London: Soncino Press, 1962.

Matt, Daniel, ed. *The Essential Kabbalah: The Heart of Jewish Mysticism.* San Francisco: HarperSanFrancisco, 1995.

Nietzsche, Friedrich. *The Birth of Tragedy and the Genealogy of Morals.* Translated by Francis Golffing. Garden City, NY: Doubleday, 1956.

Nisargadatta. *I Am That: Talks with Sri Nisargadatta.* Translated by Maurice Frydman. Durham, NC: Acorn Press, 1990.

Rumi. *Delicious Laughter: Rambunctious Teaching Stories from the Mathnawi of Jelaluddin Rumi.* Translated by Coleman Barks. Athens: Maypop Books, 1990.

Saint-Exupéry, Antoine de. *The Little Prince.* Translated by Katherine Woods. San Francisco: Harcourt Brace Jovanovich, 1993.

Schachter-Shalomi, Rabbi Zalman. *Gate to the Heart: An Evolving Process.* Philadelphia:ALEPH—Alliance for Jewish Renewal, 1993.

Thich Nhat Hanh. *Peace Is Every Step: The Path of Mindfulness in Everyday Life.* Edited by Arnold Kotler. New York: Bantam Books, 1992.

SECONDARY SOURCES

Berrin, Susan. *Celebrating the New Moon.* Northvale, NJ: Jason Aronson, 1996.

Bloomfield, Diane. *Torah Yoga: Experiencing Jewish Wisdom Through Classic Postures.* San Francisco: Jossey-Bass, 2004.

Bynum, Caroline Walker. *Holy Feast, Holy Fast: The Religious Significance of Food to Medieval Women.* Berkeley: University of California Press, 1987.

Cardin, Nina Beth. *Tears of Sorrow, Seeds of Hope: A Jewish Spiritual Companion for Infertility and Pregnancy Loss.* Woodstock, VT: Jewish Lights Publishing, 1999.

Diamond, Eliezer B. *Holy Men and Hunger Artists: Fasting and Asceticism in Rabbinic Culture.* New York: Oxford University Press, 2004.

Eilberg-Schwartz, Howard. *People of the Body: Jews and Judaism from an Embodied Perspective.* Albany: State University of New York Press, 1992.

Foucault, Michel. *Foucault Live: Interviews, 1961–1984.* Edited by Sylvère Lotringer. Translated by Lysa Hochroth and John Johnston. New York: Semiotext(e), 1996.

Frankiel, Tamar, and Judy Greenfield. *Minding the Temple of the Soul: Balancing Body, Mind, and Spirit Through Traditional Jewish Prayer, Movement, and Meditation*. Woodstock, VT: Jewish Lights Publishing, 1997.

Jung, Carl G. *Analytical Psychology: Its Theory and Practice*. New York: Pantheon, 1968.

Kamenetz, Rodger. *The Jew in the Lotus: A Poet's Rediscovery of Jewish Identity in Buddhist India*. San Francisco: HarperSanFrancisco, 1994.

McGlashan, Alan. *The Savage and Beautiful Country*. London: Chatto & Windus, 1966.

Orenstein, Debra, ed. *Lifecycles: Jewish Women on Life Passages and Personal Milestones*. Woodstock, VT: Jewish Lights Publishing, 1998.

Waskow, Arthur, and Phyllis Berman. *A Time for Every Purpose Under Heaven: The Jewish Life-Spiral as a Spiritual Path*. New York: Farrar, Straus & Giroux, 2002.

Wei Wu Wei. *Ask the Awakened: The Negative Way*. Boulder, CO: Sentient Publications, 2002.

For Further Reading

Any book such as this one is an attempt to follow Hillel's example and teach Torah "standing on one foot," in a summarized and accessible way. But Hillel's answer concluded with an injunction: "Go and learn!" The best way to do so is to deepen your practices of meditation, Jewish spirituality, and embodied spiritual practice at the many centers around the world that offer intensive retreats in them. In the United States, these include Elat Chayyim: The Center for Jewish Spirituality, the Insight Meditation Society, Spirit Rock Meditation Center, Kripalu Center for Yoga and Health, Chochmat HaLev, and the Garrison Institute—as well as many other places with which I do not yet have firsthand acquaintance. There is no substitute for intensive, silent meditation retreat. But when you're not on retreat, the books listed here are good places to "go and learn" as well. Some are academic in nature, others quite traditional, and still others innovative in their efforts to renew Jewish and Buddhist spiritualities. My listing a book here does not mean that I personally agree with everything it says, or think that it's right for every reader. If you find one voice too radical, find another that is more conservative; if you find one too academic, find another that is more experiential. In learning, as in living, the journey is the destination.

Mindfulness, Meditation, Kabbalah, and Spirituality

Analayo. *Satipatthana: The Direct Path to Realization.* Birmingham, UK: Windhorse, 2004.

Boorstein, Sylvia. *That's Funny, You Don't Look Buddhist: On Being a Faithful Jew and a Passionate Buddhist.* San Francisco: HarperSanFrancisco, 1997.

Chodron, Pema. *When Things Fall Apart: Heart Advice for Difficult Times.* Boston: Shambhala Classics, 2000.

Cooper, David. *God Is a Verb: Kabbalah and the Practice of Mystical Judaism.* New York: Putnam, 1997.

————. *Three Gates to Meditation Practice: A Personal Journey into Sufism, Buddhism, and Judaism.* Woodstock, VT: Skylight Paths, 2000.

Glick, Yoel. *Living the Life of Jewish Meditation: A Comprehensive Guide to Practice and Experience.* Woodstock, VT: Jewish Lights Publishing, 2014.

Goldstein, Joseph. *The Experience of Insight.* Boston: Shambhala, 1987.

Goldwag, Arthur. *The Beliefnet Guide to Kabbalah.* New York: Three Leaves, 2005.

Green, Arthur. *Ehyeh: A Kabbalah for Tomorrow.* Woodstock, VT: Jewish Lights Publishing, 2003.

————. *A Guide to the Zohar.* Stanford, CA: Stanford University Press, 2004.

Heschel, Abraham Joshua. *Man Is Not Alone.* New York: Farrar, Straus & Giroux, 1951.

————. *The Sabbath.* New York: Farrar, Straus & Giroux, 1951.

Kaplan, Aryeh. *Meditation and Kabbalah.* York Beach, ME: S. Weiser, 1985.

————. *Sefer Yetzirah: The Book of Creation.* York Beach, ME: S. Weiser, 1993.

Keenan, John, ed. *Beside Still Waters: Jews, Christians, and the Way of the Buddha.* Somerville, MA: Wisdom Publications, 2003.

Kook, Rabbi Abraham Isaac. *Lights of Holiness.* Translated by Ben Zion Bokser. New York: Paulist Press, 1978

Kornfield, Jack. *After the Ecstasy, the Laundry: How the Heart Grows Wise on the Spiritual Path.* New York: Bantam, 2000.

————. *Meditation for Beginners* [Audio CD]. Sounds True, 2004.

Kramer, Chaim, and Avraham Sutton. *Anatomy of the Soul.* New York: Breslov Research Institute, 1998.

Kushner, Lawrence. *Honey from the Rock.* Woodstock, VT: Jewish Lights Publishing, 2000.

Ladinsky, Daniel, ed. *Love Poems from God.* New York: Penguin Compass, 2002.

Maharshi, Ramana. *Talks with Ramana Maharshi.* Carlsbad, CA: Inner Dimensions, 2000.

Matt, Daniel C. *Zohar: Annotated & Explained.* Foreword by Andrew Harvey. Woodstock, VT: Jewish Lights Publishing, 2012.

Michaelson, Jay. "Learnkabbalah.com." www.learnkabbalah.com.

Ostow, Mortimer. *Ultimate Intimacy: The Psychodynamics of Jewish Mysticism.* London: Karnac Books, 1995.

Pinson, Dovber. *Meditation and Judaism: Exploring the Jewish Meditative Paths.* Lanham, MD: Rowman & Littlefield Publishers, 2004.

Rose, Or N. *God in All Moments: Mystical and Practical Spiritual Wisdom from Hasidic Masters.* Woodstock, VT: Jewish Lights Publishing, 2004.

Rosenberg, David. *Dreams of Being Eaten Alive: The Literary Core of the Kabbalah.* New York: Harmony Books, 2000.

Schachter-Shalomi, Rabbi Zalman. *Jewish with Feeling: A Guide to Meaningful Jewish Practice.* New York: Riverhead Books, 2005.

Schneersohn, Rabbi Menachem Mendel. *On the Essence of Chassidus.* Brooklyn, NY: Kehot, 1986.

Scholem, Gershom. *Kabbalah.* 1978; repr. New York: Plume, 1987.

———. *Major Trends in Jewish Mysticism.* New York: Schocken Books, 1974.

———. *On the Mystical Shape of the Godhead: Basic Concepts in the Kabbalah.* New York: Schocken Books, 1991.

Slater, Jonathan P. *Mindful Jewish Living: Compassionate Practice.* New York: Aviv Press, 2004.

Thich Nhat Hanh. *Peace Is Every Step: The Path of Mindfulness in Everyday Life.* Edited by Arnold Kotler. New York: Bantam Books, 1992.

Tolle, Eckhart. *The Power of Now: A Guide to Spiritual Enlightenment.* Novato, CA: New World Library, 2004.

Wilber, Ken. *One Taste: The Journals of Ken Wilber.* Boston: Shambhala, 2000.

———. *A Theory of Everything: An Integral Vision for Business, Politics, Science, and Spirituality.* Boston: Shambhala, 2000.

THE BODY IN JUDAISM

Boyarin, Daniel. *Carnal Israel: Reading Sex in Talmudic Culture.* Berkeley: University of California Press, 1995.

———. *A Radical Jew: Paul and the Politics of Identity.* Berkeley: University of California Press, 1994.

Buxbaum, Yitzhak. *Jewish Spiritual Practices.* Northvale, NJ: Jason Aronson, 1990.

Eilberg-Schwartz, Howard. *People of the Body: Jews and Judaism from an Embodied Perspective.* Albany, State University of New York Press, 1992.

Finkel, Avraham Yaakov. *In My Flesh I See God: A Treasury of Rabbinic Insights about the Human Anatomy.* Northvale, NJ: Jason Aronson, 1995.

Gilman, Sander. *The Jew's Body.* New York: Routledge, 1991.

Specific Topics in Embodied Spirituality

Adelman, Penina. *Miriam's Well: Rituals for Jewish Women Around the Year.* Fresh Meadows, NY: Biblio Press, 1986.

Barkan, Leonard. *Nature's Work of Art: The Human Body as Image of the World.* New Haven, CT: Yale University Press, 1975.

Biale, David. *Eros and the Jews: From Biblical Israel to Contemporary America.* New York: Basic Books, 1992.

Biers-Ariel, Matt. *Spirit in Nature: Teaching Judaism and Ecology on the Trail.* Springfield, NJ: Behrman House, 2000.

Bynum, Caroline Walker. *Holy Feast, Holy Fast: The Religious Significance of Food to Medieval Women.* Berkeley: University of California Press, 1987.

Diamond, Eliezer B. *Holy Men and Hunger Artists: Fasting and Asceticism in Rabbinic Culture.* New York: Oxford University Press, 2004.

Eilberg-Schwartz, Howard. *God's Phallus and Other Problems for Men and Monotheism.* Boston: Beacon Press, 1994

Feuerstein, Georg. *Sacred Sexuality: The Erotic Spirit in the World's Great Religions.* Rochester, VT: Inner Traditions, 1992.

Frankiel, Tamar, and Judy Greenfield. *Minding the Temple of the Soul: Balancing Body, Mind, and Spirit Through Traditional Jewish Prayer, Movement, and Meditation.* Woodstock, VT: Jewish Lights Publishing, 1997.

Glick, Leonard B. *Marked in Your Flesh: Circumcision from Ancient Judea to Modern America.* New York: Oxford University Press, 2005.

Green, Arthur, and Barry Holtz. *Your Word Is Fire: The Hasidic Masters on Contemplative Prayer.* Woodstock, VT: Jewish Lights Publishing, 1993.

Greenberg, Blu. *On Women and Judaism: A View from Tradition.* Philadelphia: Jewish Publication Society of America, 1981.

Hecker, Joel. *Mystical Bodies, Mystical Meals: Eating and Embodiment in Medieval Kabbalah.* Detroit, MI: Wayne State University Press, 2005.

Idel, Moshe. *Kabbalah and Eros.* New Haven, CT: Yale University Press, 2005.

———. *The Mystical Experience in Abraham Abulafia.* Albany: State University of New York Press, 1988.

Isaacs, Ronald H. *Every Person's Guide to Jewish Sexuality.* Northvale, NJ: Jason Aronson, 2000.

Jacobs, Louis. *Hasidic Prayer.* Oxford: Littman Library, 1993.

Jung, L. Shannon. *Food for Life: The Spirituality and Ethics of Eating.* Minneapolis, MN: Augsburg Fortress Publishers, 2004.

Kaplan, Aryeh. *Waters of Eden: An Exploration of the Concept of Mikvah.* New York: National Conference of Synagogue Youth of the Union of Orthodox Jewish Congregations, 1976.

"Mayim Rabim." www.mayimrabim.com.

"Mayyim Hayyim." www.mayyimhayyim.org.

Michaelson, Jay, ed. *Az Yashir Moshe: A Book of Songs and Blessings.* Hoboken, NJ: KTAV, 2006.

Roth, Gabrielle. *Sweat Your Prayers: The Five Rhythms of the Soul; Movement as Spiritual Practice.* New York: Tarcher, 1998.

Rubin, Janice. *The Mikvah Project.* www.mikvahproject.com.

Speads, Carola H. *Ways to Better Breathing.* Rochester, VT: Healing Arts Press, 1992.

Slonim, Rivkah, ed. *Total Immersion: A Mikvah Anthology.* Northvale, NJ: Jason Aronson, 1996.

Waskow, Arthur, and Phyllis Berman. *A Time for Every Purpose Under Heaven: The Jewish Life-Spiral as a Spiritual Path.* New York: Farrar, Straus & Giroux, 2002.

Wasserfall, Rahel, ed. *Women and Water: Menstruation in Jewish Law and Life.* Hanover, NH: Brandeis University Press, 1999.

Credits

"Asher Yatzar" © 2005 Rachel Barenblat, reprinted by permission of Rachel Barenblat and *Zeek: A Jewish Journal of Thought and Culture* (www.zeek.net).

"Water, Light, and Colors" (p. 38: author's translation of Moses Cordovero) from THE ESSENTIAL KABBALAH by DANIEL C. MATT Copyright © 1995 by Daniel C. Matt. Reprinted by permission of Harper Collins Publishers.

Diagram of the *sefirot* © 2006 Bara Sapir (www.barasapir.com), appears by permission of the artist.

Excerpt from *Tears of Sorrow, Seeds of Hope: A Jewish Spiritual Companion for Infertility and Pregnancy Loss* © 1999 by Nina Beth Cardin (Woodstock, VT: Jewish Lights Publishing). $19.95 +3.95 s/h. Order by mail or call 800-962-4544 or online at www.jewishlights.com. Permission granted by Jewish Lights Publishing, P.O. Box 237, Woodstock, VT 05091.

"Your Blood Is a Blessing" © 2005 Holly Taya Shere, appears by permission of the author.

Acknowledgments

First books always yield a lot of acknowledgments, and this one is no exception. I am grateful first of all to my teachers, from a variety of disciplines and traditions, who have shown me so many ways to experience light, and whose own light, I hope, shines in these pages: Rabbi David Cooper, Shoshana Cooper, Sharon Salzberg, Guy Armstrong, Rabbi Jeff Roth, Rabbi Michael Paley, Sylvia Boorstein, Dave Allen, William McMenamin, Joseph Kramer, Michael Cohen, Rabbi Ohad Ezrachi, Avraham Leader, and the many wise mystics in Jerusalem, New York, and around the world with whom I have had the privilege of learning, dreaming, and improvising. Thanks, too, to my brilliant teachers in the academic world, including Rachel Elior, Moshe Idel, and Daniel Boyarin. For years I've thought that when my first book was published, I would thank my high school English teacher, Sylvia Sarrett, for encouraging me to write and to think in terms of horizons, not boundaries. Done. Thanks especially to Ari Weller, my gifted co-teacher and fellow traveler, as well as to Rabbi Jill Hammer, Shoshana Jedwab, Rabbi David Ingber, Eliezer Sobel, Rabbi Shir Yaakov Feinstein-Feit, David Schildkret, Rabbi Dovber Pinson, Diane Bloomfield, and Holly Taya Shere—all of whose wisdom appears, in one form or other, in this book. Thanks to Alana Newhouse, Yitzhak Buxbaum, Chris Fields, Bara Sapir, Sam Brody, Avi Shmidman, Aliza Dzik, Alys Yablon Wylen, and everyone at Jewish Lights who helped bring this project to fruition, and to my family, my friends, and my communities at Zeek, Nehirim, Beerot, Elat Chayyim, Easton Mountain, Burning Man, and a dozen other places of wisdom for all of their support.

Topical Index

Index of Practices

AVAILABLE FROM BETTER BOOKSTORES.
TRY YOUR BOOKSTORE FIRST.

Bible Study / Midrash

Passing Life's Tests: Spiritual Reflections on the Trial of Abraham, the Binding of Isaac *By Rabbi Bradley Shavit Artson, DHL*
Invites us to use this powerful tale as a tool for our own soul wrestling, to confront our existential sacrifices and enable us to face—and surmount—life's tests.
6 x 9, 176 pp, Quality PB, 978-1-58023-631-7 **$18.99**

The Messiah and the Jews: Three Thousand Years of Tradition, Belief and Hope *By Rabbi Elaine Rose Glickman; Foreword by Rabbi Neil Gillman, PhD; Preface by Rabbi Judith Z. Abrams, PhD*
Explores and explains an astonishing range of primary and secondary sources, infusing them with new meaning for the modern reader.
6 x 9, 192 pp, Quality PB, 978-1-58023-690-4 **$16.99**

Speaking Torah: Spiritual Teachings from around the Maggid's Table—in Two Volumes *By Arthur Green, with Ebn Leader, Ariel Evan Mayse and Or N. Rose*
The most powerful Hasidic teachings made accessible—from some of the world's preeminent authorities on Jewish thought and spirituality.
Volume 1—6 x 9, 512 pp, Hardcover, 978-1-58023-668-3 **$34.99**
Volume 2—6 x 9, 448 pp, Hardcover, 978-1-58023-694-2 **$34.99**

Masking and Unmasking Ourselves: Interpreting Biblical Texts on Clothing & Identity *By Dr. Norman J. Cohen*
Presents ten Bible stories that involve clothing in an essential way, as a means of learning about the text, its characters and their interactions.
6 x 9, 224 pp, HC, 978-1-58023-461-0 **$24.99**

The Genesis of Leadership: What the Bible Teaches Us about Vision, Values and Leading Change *By Rabbi Nathan Laufer; Foreword by Senator Joseph I. Lieberman*
6 x 9, 288 pp, Quality PB, 978-1-58023-352-1 **$18.99**

Hineini in Our Lives: Learning How to Respond to Others through 14 Biblical Texts and Personal Stories *By Rabbi Norman J. Cohen, PhD*
6 x 9, 240 pp, Quality PB, 978-1-58023-274-6 **$18.99**

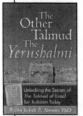

The Modern Men's Torah Commentary: New Insights from Jewish Men on the 54 Weekly Torah Portions *Edited by Rabbi Jeffrey K. Salkin*
6 x 9, 368 pp, HC, 978-1-58023-395-8 **$24.99**
Moses and the Journey to Leadership: Timeless Lessons of Effective Management from the Bible and Today's Leaders *By Rabbi Norman J. Cohen, PhD*
6 x 9, 240 pp, Quality PB, 978-1-58023-351-4 **$18.99**; HC, 978-1-58023-227-2 **$21.99**
The Other Talmud—The Yerushalmi: Unlocking the Secrets of *The Talmud of Israel* for Judaism Today *By Rabbi Judith Z. Abrams, PhD*
6 x 9, 256 pp, HC, 978-1-58023-463-4 **$24.99**

Sage Tales: Wisdom and Wonder from the Rabbis of the Talmud
By Rabbi Burton L. Visotzky
6 x 9, 256 pp, Quality PB, 978-1-58023-791-8 **$19.99**; HC, 978-1-58023-456-6 **$24.99**
The Torah Revolution: Fourteen Truths That Changed the World
By Rabbi Reuven Hammer, PhD 6 x 9, 240 pp, HC, 978-1-58023-457-3 **$24.99**
The Wisdom of Judaism: An Introduction to the Values of the Talmud
By Rabbi Dov Peretz Elkins 6 x 9, 192 pp, Quality PB, 978-1-58023-327-9 **$16.99**

Or phone, fax, mail or email to: **JEWISH LIGHTS** Publishing
Sunset Farm Offices, Route 4 • P.O. Box 237 • Woodstock, Vermont 05091
Tel: (802) 457-4000 • Fax: (802) 457-4004 • www.jewishlights.com
Credit card orders: **(800) 962-4544** (8:30AM–5:30PM EST Monday–Friday)
Generous discounts on quantity orders. SATISFACTION GUARANTEED. Prices subject to change.

Theology / Philosophy

Believing and Its Tensions: A Personal Conversation about God, Torah, Suffering and Death in Jewish Thought
By Rabbi Neil Gillman, PhD
Explores the changing nature of belief and the complexities of reconciling the intellectual, emotional and moral questions of Gillman's own searching mind and soul.
5½ x 8½, 144 pp, HC, 978-1-58023-669-0 **$19.99**

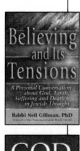

God of Becoming and Relationship: The Dynamic Nature of Process Theology *By Rabbi Bradley Shavit Artson, DHL*
Explains how Process Theology breaks us free from the strictures of ancient Greek and medieval European philosophy, allowing us to see all creation as related patterns of energy through which we connect to everything.
6 x 9, 208 pp, HC, 978-1-58023-713-0 **$24.99**

The Other Talmud—The *Yerushalmi:* Unlocking the Secrets of *The Talmud of Israel* for Judaism Today   *By Rabbi Judith Z. Abrams, PhD*
A fascinating—and stimulating—look at "the other Talmud" and the possibilities for Jewish life reflected there.   6 x 9, 256 pp, HC, 978-1-58023-463-4 **$24.99**

The Way of Man: According to Hasidic Teaching
By Martin Buber; New Translation and Introduction by Rabbi Bernard H. Mehlman and Dr. Gabriel E. Padawer; Foreword by Paul Mendes-Flohr
An accessible and engaging new translation of Buber's classic work—*available as an eBook only.*   eBook, 978-1-58023-601-0 Digital List Price **$14.99**

The Death of Death: Resurrection and Immortality in Jewish Thought
By Rabbi Neil Gillman, PhD 6 x 9, 336 pp, Quality PB, 978-1-58023-081-0 **$19.99**

Doing Jewish Theology: God, Torah & Israel in Modern Judaism *By Rabbi Neil Gillman, PhD*
6 x 9, 304 pp, Quality PB, 978-1-58023-439-9 **$18.99**; HC, 978-1-58023-322-4 **$24.99**

From Defender to Critic: The Search for a New Jewish Self
By Dr. David Hartman 6 x 9, 336 pp, HC, 978-1-58023-515-0 **$35.00**

The God Who Hates Lies: Confronting & Rethinking Jewish Tradition
By Dr. David Hartman with Charlie Buckholtz 6 x 9, 208 pp, Quality PB, 978-1-58023-790-1 **$19.99**

A Heart of Many Rooms: Celebrating the Many Voices within Judaism
By Dr. David Hartman 6 x 9, 352 pp, Quality PB, 978-1-58023-156-5 **$19.95**

Jewish Theology in Our Time: A New Generation Explores the Foundations and Future of Jewish Belief *Edited by Rabbi Elliot J. Cosgrove, PhD; Foreword by Rabbi David J. Wolpe; Preface by Rabbi Carole B. Balin, PhD* 6 x 9, 240 pp, Quality PB, 978-1-58023-630-0 **$19.99**; HC, 978-1-58023-413-9 **$24.99**

Maimonides—Essential Teachings on Jewish Faith & Ethics: The Book of Knowledge & the Thirteen Principles of Faith—Annotated & Explained
Translation and Annotation by Rabbi Marc D. Angel, PhD
5½ x 8½, 224 pp, Quality PB Original, 978-1-59473-311-6 **$18.99***

Maimonides, Spinoza and Us: Toward an Intellectually Vibrant Judaism
By Rabbi Marc D. Angel, PhD 6 x 9, 224 pp, HC, 978-1-58023-411-5 **$24.99**

Our Religious Brains: What Cognitive Science Reveals about Belief, Morality, Community and Our Relationship with God
By Rabbi Ralph D. Mecklenburger; Foreword by Dr. Howard Kelfer; Preface by Dr. Neil Gillman
6 x 9, 224 pp, HC, 978-1-58023-508-2 **$24.99**

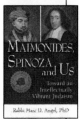

Your Word Is Fire: The Hasidic Masters on Contemplative Prayer
Edited and translated by Rabbi Arthur Green, PhD, and Barry W. Holtz
6 x 9, 160 pp, Quality PB, 978-1-879045-25-5 **$16.99**

I Am Jewish
Personal Reflections Inspired by the Last Words of Daniel Pearl
Almost 150 Jews—both famous and not—from all walks of life, from all around the world, write about many aspects of their Judaism.
Edited by Judea and Ruth Pearl 6 x 9, 304 pp, Deluxe PB w/ flaps, 978-1-58023-259-3 **$19.99**
Download a free copy of the *I Am Jewish Teacher's Guide* at www.jewishlights.com.

*A book from SkyLight Paths, Jewish Lights' sister imprint

Meditation

The Magic of Hebrew Chant: Healing the Spirit, Transforming the Mind, Deepening Love
By Rabbi Shefa Gold; Foreword by Sylvia Boorstein
Introduces this transformative spiritual practice as a way to unlock the power of sacred texts and make prayer and meditation the delight of your life. Includes musical notations. 6 x 9, 352 pp, Quality PB, 978-1-58023-671-3 **$24.99**

The Magic of Hebrew Chant Companion—The Big Book of Musical Notations and Incantations
8½ x 11, 154 pp, PB, 978-1-58023-722-2 **$19.99**

Jewish Meditation Practices for Everyday Life: Awakening Your Heart, Connecting with God
By Rabbi Jeff Roth
Offers a fresh take on meditation that draws on life experience and living life with greater clarity as opposed to the traditional method of rigorous study.
6 x 9, 224 pp, Quality PB, 978-1-58023-397-2 **$18.99**

Discovering Jewish Meditation, 2nd Edition
Instruction & Guidance for Learning an Ancient Spiritual Practice
By Nan Fink Gefen, PhD 6 x 9, 208 pp, Quality PB, 978-1-58023-462-7 **$16.99**

The Handbook of Jewish Meditation Practices
A Guide for Enriching the Sabbath and Other Days of Your Life
By Rabbi David A. Cooper 6 x 9, 208 pp, Quality PB, 978-1-58023-102-2 **$16.95**

Meditation from the Heart of Judaism
Today's Teachers Share Their Practices, Techniques, and Faith
Edited by Avram Davis 6 x 9, 256 pp, Quality PB, 978-1-58023-049-0 **$18.99**

Ritual / Sacred Practices

God in Your Body: Kabbalah, Mindfulness and Embodied Spiritual Practice
By Jay Michaelson
The first comprehensive treatment of the body in Jewish spiritual practice and an essential guide to the sacred. 6 x 9, 272 pp, Quality PB, 978-1-58023-304-0 **$18.99**

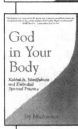

The Book of Jewish Sacred Practices: CLAL's Guide to Everyday & Holiday Rituals & Blessings *Edited by Rabbi Irwin Kula and Vanessa L. Ochs, PhD*
6 x 9, 368 pp, Quality PB, 978-1-58023-152-7 **$18.95**

The Jewish Dream Book: The Key to Opening the Inner Meaning of Your Dreams
By Vanessa L. Ochs, PhD, with Elizabeth Ochs; Illus. by Kristina Swarner
8 x 8, 128 pp, Full-color illus., Deluxe PB w/ flaps, 978-1-58023-132-9 **$16.95**

Jewish Ritual: A Brief Introduction for Christians
By Rabbi Kerry M. Olitzky and Rabbi Daniel Judson
5½ x 8½, 144 pp, Quality PB, 978-1-58023-210-4 **$14.99**

The Rituals & Practices of a Jewish Life: A Handbook for Personal Spiritual Renewal *Edited by Rabbi Kerry M. Olitzky and Rabbi Daniel Judson*
6 x 9, 272 pp, Illus., Quality PB, 978-1-58023-169-5 **$18.95**

The Sacred Art of Lovingkindness: Preparing to Practice
By Rabbi Rami Shapiro 5½ x 8½, 176 pp, Quality PB, 978-1-59473-151-8 **$16.99***

Mystery & Detective Fiction

Criminal Kabbalah: An Intriguing Anthology of Jewish Mystery & Detective Fiction *Edited by Lawrence W. Raphael; Foreword by Laurie R. King*
All-new stories from twelve of today's masters of mystery and detective fiction—sure to delight mystery buffs of all faith traditions.
6 x 9, 256 pp, Quality PB, 978-1-58023-109-1 **$16.95**

Mystery Midrash: An Anthology of Jewish Mystery & Detective Fiction
Edited by Lawrence W. Raphael; Preface by Joel Siegel
6 x 9, 304 pp, Quality PB, 978-1-58023-055-1 **$16.95**

*A book from SkyLight Paths, Jewish Lights' sister imprint

Inspiration

Into the Fullness of the Void: A Spiritual Autobiography *By Dov Elbaum*
The spiritual autobiography of one of Israel's leading cultural figures that provides insights and guidance for all of us.   6 x 9, 304 pp, Quality PB Original, 978-1-58023-715-4 **$18.99**

Saying No and Letting Go: Jewish Wisdom on Making Room for What Matters Most
By Rabbi Edwin Goldberg, DHL; Foreword by Rabbi Naomi Levy
Taps into timeless Jewish wisdom that teaches how to "hold on tightly" to the things that matter most while learning to "let go lightly" of the demands and worries that do not ultimately matter.   6 x 9, 192 pp, Quality PB, 978-1-58023-670-6 **$16.99**

The Bridge to Forgiveness: Stories and Prayers for Finding God and Restoring Wholeness *By Rabbi Karyn D. Kedar*   6 x 9, 176 pp, Quality PB, 978-1-58023-451-1 **$16.99**

The Empty Chair: Finding Hope and Joy—Timeless Wisdom from a Hasidic Master, Rebbe Nachman of Breslov *Adapted by Moshe Mykoff and the Breslov Research Institute*
4 x 6, 128 pp, Deluxe PB w/ flaps, 978-1-879045-67-5 **$9.99**

A Formula for Proper Living: Practical Lessons from Life and Torah
By Rabbi Abraham J. Twerski, MD   6 x 9, 144 pp, HC, 978-1-58023-402-3 **$19.99**

The Gentle Weapon: Prayers for Everyday and Not-So-Everyday Moments—
Timeless Wisdom from the Teachings of the Hasidic Master, Rebbe Nachman of Breslov
Adapted by Moshe Mykoff and S. C. Mizrahi, together with the Breslov Research Institute
4 x 6, 144 pp, Deluxe PB w/ flaps, 978-1-58023-022-3 **$9.99**

The God Upgrade: Finding Your 21st-Century Spirituality in Judaism's 5,000-Year-Old Tradition *By Rabbi Jamie Korngold; Foreword by Rabbi Harold M. Schulweis*
6 x 9, 176 pp, Quality PB, 978-1-58023-443-6 **$15.99**

God Whispers: Stories of the Soul, Lessons of the Heart *By Rabbi Karyn D. Kedar*
6 x 9, 176 pp, Quality PB, 978-1-58023-088-9 **$16.99**

God's To-Do List: 103 Ways to Be an Angel and Do God's Work on Earth
By Dr. Ron Wolfson 6 x 9, 144 pp, Quality PB, 978-1-58023-301-9 **$16.99**

Happiness and the Human Spirit: The Spirituality of Becoming the Best You Can Be
By Rabbi Abraham J. Twerski, MD
6 x 9, 176 pp, Quality PB, 978-1-58023-404-7 **$16.99**; HC, 978-1-58023-343-9 **$19.99**

Life's Daily Blessings: Inspiring Reflections on Gratitude and Joy for Every Day, Based on Jewish Wisdom *By Rabbi Kerry M. Olitzky* 4½ x 6½, 368 pp, Quality PB, 978-1-58023-396-5 **$16.99**

The Magic of Hebrew Chant: Healing the Spirit, Transforming the Mind, Deepening Love *By Rabbi Shefa Gold; Foreword by Sylvia Boorstein*
6 x 9, 352 pp, Quality PB, 978-1-58023-671-3 **$24.99**

Restful Reflections: Nighttime Inspiration to Calm the Soul, Based on Jewish Wisdom
By Rabbi Kerry M. Olitzky and Rabbi Lori Forman-Jacobi 4½ x 6½, 448 pp, Quality PB, 978-1-58023-091-9 **$16.99**

Sacred Intentions: Morning Inspiration to Strengthen the Spirit, Based on Jewish Wisdom
By Rabbi Kerry M. Olitzky and Rabbi Lori Forman-Jacobi 4½ x 6½, 448 pp, Quality PB, 978-1-58023-061-2 **$16.99**

The Seven Questions You're Asked in Heaven: Reviewing and Renewing Your Life on Earth *By Dr. Ron Wolfson* 6 x 9, 176 pp, Quality PB, 978-1-58023-407-8 **$16.99**

Kabbalah / Mysticism

Ehyeh: A Kabbalah for Tomorrow
By Rabbi Arthur Green, PhD 6 x 9, 224 pp, Quality PB, 978-1-58023-213-5 **$18.99**

The Gift of Kabbalah: Discovering the Secrets of Heaven, Renewing Your Life on Earth
By Tamar Frankiel, PhD 6 x 9, 256 pp, Quality PB, 978-1-58023-141-1 **$18.99**

Jewish Mysticism and the Spiritual Life: Classical Texts, Contemporary Reflections *Edited by Dr. Lawrence Fine, Dr. Eitan Fishbane and Rabbi Or N. Rose*
6 x 9, 256 pp, HC, 978-1-58023-434-4 **$24.99**; Quality PB, 978-1-58023-719-2 **$18.99**

Seek My Face: A Jewish Mystical Theology *By Rabbi Arthur Green, PhD*
6 x 9, 304 pp, Quality PB, 978-1-58023-130-5 **$19.95**

Zohar: Annotated & Explained *Translation & Annotation by Dr. Daniel C. Matt; Foreword by Andrew Harvey* 5½ x 8½, 176 pp, Quality PB, 978-1-893361-51-5 **$16.99**
(A book from SkyLight Paths, Jewish Lights' sister imprint)

See also *The Way Into Jewish Mystical Tradition* in The Way Into... Series.

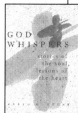

Spirituality / Prayer

Davening: A Guide to Meaningful Jewish Prayer
By Rabbi Zalman Schachter-Shalomi with Joel Segel; Foreword by Rabbi Lawrence Kushner
A fresh approach to prayer for all who wish to appreciate the power of prayer's poetry, song and ritual, and to join the age-old conversation that Jews have had with God. 6 x 9, 240 pp, Quality PB, 978-1-58023-627-0 **$18.99**

Jewish Men Pray: Words of Yearning, Praise, Petition, Gratitude and Wonder from Traditional and Contemporary Sources
Edited by Rabbi Kerry M. Olitzky and Stuart M. Matlins; Foreword by Rabbi Bradley Shavit Artson, DHL
A celebration of Jewish men's voices in prayer—to strengthen, heal, comfort, and inspire—from the ancient world up to our own day.
5 x 7¼, 400 pp, HC, 978-1-58023-628-7 **$19.99**

Making Prayer Real: Leading Jewish Spiritual Voices on Why Prayer Is Difficult and What to Do about It By Rabbi Mike Comins 6 x 9, 320 pp, Quality PB, 978-1-58023-417-7 **$18.99**

Witnesses to the One: The Spiritual History of the Sh'ma
By Rabbi Joseph B. Meszler; Foreword by Rabbi Elyse Goldstein
6 x 9, 176 pp, Quality PB, 978-1-58023-400-9 **$16.99**; HC, 978-1-58023-309-5 **$19.99**

My People's Prayer Book Series: Traditional Prayers, Modern Commentaries   Edited by Rabbi Lawrence A. Hoffman, PhD
Provides diverse and exciting commentary to the traditional liturgy. Will help you find new wisdom in Jewish prayer, and bring liturgy into your life. Each book includes Hebrew text, modern translations and commentaries from all perspectives of the Jewish world.

Vol. 1—The Sh'ma and Its Blessings
7 x 10, 168 pp, HC, 978-1-879045-79-8 **$29.99**
Vol. 2—The Amidah 7 x 10, 240 pp, HC, 978-1-879045-80-4 **$29.99**
Vol. 3—P'sukei D'zimrah (Morning Psalms)
7 x 10, 240 pp, HC, 978-1-879045-81-1 **$29.99**
Vol. 4—Seder K'riat Hatorah (The Torah Service)
7 x 10, 264 pp, HC, 978-1-879045-82-8 **$29.99**
Vol. 5—Birkhot Hashachar (Morning Blessings)
7 x 10, 240 pp, HC, 978-1-879045-83-5 **$24.95**
Vol. 6—Tachanun and Concluding Prayers
7 x 10, 240 pp, HC, 978-1-879045-84-2 **$24.95**
Vol. 7—Shabbat at Home 7 x 10, 240 pp, HC, 978-1-879045-85-9 **$29.99**
Vol. 8—Kabbalat Shabbat (Welcoming Shabbat in the Synagogue)
7 x 10, 240 pp, HC, 978-1-58023-121-3 **$24.99**
Vol. 9—Welcoming the Night: Minchah and Ma'ariv (Afternoon and Evening Prayer) 7 x 10, 272 pp, HC, 978-1-58023-262-3 **$24.99**
Vol. 10—Shabbat Morning: Shacharit and Musaf (Morning and Additional Services) 7 x 10, 240 pp, HC, 978-1-58023-240-1 **$29.99**

Spirituality / Lawrence Kushner

I'm God; You're Not: Observations on Organized Religion & Other Disguises of the Ego
6 x 9, 256 pp, Quality PB, 978-1-58023-513-6 **$18.99**; HC, 978-1-58023-441-2 **$21.99**

The Book of Letters: A Mystical Hebrew Alphabet
Popular HC Edition, 6 x 9, 80 pp, 2-color text, 978-1-879045-00-2 **$24.95**
Collector's Limited Edition, 9 x 12, 80 pp, gold-foil-embossed pages, w/ limited-edition silkscreened print, 978-1-879045-04-0 **$349.00**

The Book of Miracles: A Young Person's Guide to Jewish Spiritual Awareness
6 x 9, 96 pp, 2-color illus., HC, 978-1-879045-78-1 **$16.95** For ages 9–13

God Was in This Place & I, i Did Not Know: Finding Self, Spirituality and Ultimate Meaning 6 x 9, 192 pp, Quality PB, 978-1-879045-33-0 **$16.95**

Honey from the Rock: An Introduction to Jewish Mysticism
6 x 9, 176 pp, Quality PB, 978-1-58023-073-5 **$18.99**

Invisible Lines of Connection: Sacred Stories of the Ordinary
5½ x 8½, 160 pp, Quality PB, 978-1-879045-98-9 **$16.99**

The Way Into Jewish Mystical Tradition
6 x 9, 224 pp, Quality PB, 978-1-58023-200-5 **$18.99**; HC, 978-1-58023-029-2 **$21.95**

Spirituality

Amazing Chesed: Living a Grace-Filled Judaism
By Rabbi Rami Shapiro Drawing from ancient and contemporary, traditional and non-traditional Jewish wisdom, reclaims the idea of grace in Judaism.
6 x 9, 176 pp, Quality PB, 978-1-58023-624-9 **$16.99**

Jewish with Feeling: A Guide to Meaningful Jewish Practice
By Rabbi Zalman Schachter-Shalomi with Joel Segel
Takes off from basic questions like "Why be Jewish?" and whether the word God still speaks to us today and lays out a vision for a whole-person Judaism.
5½ x 8½, 288 pp, Quality PB, 978-1-58023-691-1 **$19.99**

Perennial Wisdom for the Spiritually Independent: Sacred Teachings—
Annotated & Explained   *Annotation by Rami Shapiro; Foreword by Richard Rohr*
Weaves sacred texts and teachings from the world's major religions into a coherent exploration of the five core questions at the heart of every religion's search.
5½ x 8½, 336 pp, Quality PB Original, 978-1-59473-515-8 **$16.99**

Aleph-Bet Yoga: Embodying the Hebrew Letters for Physical and Spiritual Well-Being
By Steven A. Rapp; Foreword by Tamar Frankiel, PhD, and Judy Greenfeld; Preface by Hart Lazer
7 x 10, 128 pp, b/w photos, Quality PB, Lay-flat binding, 978-1-58023-162-6 **$16.95**

A Book of Life: Embracing Judaism as a Spiritual Practice
By Rabbi Michael Strassfeld 6 x 9, 544 pp, Quality PB, 978-1-58023-247-0 **$24.99**

Bringing the Psalms to Life: How to Understand and Use the Book of Psalms
By Rabbi Daniel F. Polish, PhD 6 x 9, 208 pp, Quality PB, 978-1-58023-157-2 **$18.99**

Does the Soul Survive? A Jewish Journey to Belief in Afterlife, Past Lives & Living with Purpose   *By Rabbi Elie Kaplan Spitz; Foreword by Brian L. Weiss, MD*
6 x 9, 288 pp, Quality PB, 978-1-58023-165-7 **$18.99**

Entering the Temple of Dreams: Jewish Prayers, Movements and Meditations for the End of the Day   *By Tamar Frankiel, PhD, and Judy Greenfeld*
7 x 10, 192 pp, illus., Quality PB, 978-1-58023-079-7 **$16.95**

First Steps to a New Jewish Spirit: Reb Zalman's Guide to Recapturing the Intimacy & Ecstasy in Your Relationship with God   *By Rabbi Zalman M. Schachter-Shalomi with Donald Gropman* 6 x 9, 144 pp, Quality PB, 978-1-58023-182-4 **$16.95**

Foundations of Sephardic Spirituality: The Inner Life of Jews of the Ottoman Empire
By Rabbi Marc D. Angel, PhD 6 x 9, 224 pp, Quality PB, 978-1-58023-341-5 **$18.99**

God & the Big Bang: Discovering Harmony between Science & Spirituality
By Dr. Daniel C. Matt 6 x 9, 216 pp, Quality PB, 978-1-879045-89-7 **$18.99**

God in Our Relationships: Spirituality between People from the Teachings of Martin Buber   *By Rabbi Dennis S. Ross* 5¼ x 8¼, 160 pp, Quality PB, 978-1-58023-147-3 **$16.95**

The Jewish Lights Spirituality Handbook: A Guide to Understanding, Exploring & Living a Spiritual Life   *Edited by Stuart M. Matlins*
6 x 9, 456 pp, Quality PB, 978-1-58023-093-3 **$19.99**

Judaism, Physics and God: Searching for Sacred Metaphors in a Post-Einstein World
By Rabbi David W. Nelson 6 x 9, 352 pp, Quality PB, inc. reader's discussion guide,
978-1-58023-306-4 **$18.99**; HC, 352 pp, 978-1-58023-252-4 **$24.99**

Meaning & Mitzvah: Daily Practices for Reclaiming Judaism through Prayer, God, Torah, Hebrew, Mitzvot and Peoplehood   *By Rabbi Goldie Milgram*
7 x 9, 336 pp, Quality PB, 978-1-58023-256-2 **$19.99**

Repentance: The Meaning and Practice of Teshuvah
By Dr. Louis E. Newman; Foreword by Rabbi Harold M. Schulweis; Preface by Rabbi Karyn D. Kedar
6 x 9, 256 pp, HC, 978-1-58023-426-9 **$24.99** Quality PB, 978-1-58023-718-5 **$18.99**

The Sabbath Soul: Mystical Reflections on the Transformative Power of Holy Time
Selection, Translation and Commentary by Eitan Fishbane, PhD
6 x 9, 208 pp, Quality PB, 978-1-58023-459-7 **$18.99**

Tanya, the Masterpiece of Hasidic Wisdom: Selections Annotated & Explained
Translation & Annotation by Rabbi Rami Shapiro; Foreword by Rabbi Zalman M. Schachter-Shalomi
5½ x 8½, 240 pp, Quality PB, 978-1-59473-275-1 **$16.99**

These Are the Words, 2nd Edition: A Vocabulary of Jewish Spiritual Life
By Rabbi Arthur Green, PhD 6 x 9, 320 pp, Quality PB, 978-1-58023-494-8 **$19.99**

JEWISH LIGHTS BOOKS ARE AVAILABLE FROM BETTER BOOKSTORES. TRY YOUR BOOKSTORE FIRST.

About Jewish Lights

People of all faiths and backgrounds yearn for books that attract, engage, educate, and spiritually inspire.

Our principal goal is to stimulate thought and help all people learn about who the Jewish People are, where they come from, and what the future can be made to hold. While people of our diverse Jewish heritage are the primary audience, our books speak to people in the Christian world as well and will broaden their understanding of Judaism and the roots of their own faith.

We bring to you authors who are at the forefront of spiritual thought and experience. While each has something different to say, they all say it in a voice that you can hear.

Our books are designed to welcome you and then to engage, stimulate, and inspire. We judge our success not only by whether or not our books are beautiful and commercially successful, but by whether or not they make a difference in your life.

For your information and convenience, at the back of this book we have provided a list of other Jewish Lights books you might find interesting and useful. They cover all the categories of your life:

Bar/Bat Mitzvah	Life Cycle
Bible Study / Midrash	Meditation
Children's Books	Men's Interest
Congregation Resources	Parenting
Current Events / History	Prayer / Ritual / Sacred Practice
Ecology / Environment	Social Justice
Fiction: Mystery, Science Fiction	Spirituality
Grief / Healing	Theology / Philosophy
Holidays / Holy Days	Travel
Inspiration	Twelve Steps
Kabbalah / Mysticism / Enneagram	Women's Interest

Stuart M. Matlins, Publisher

Or phone, fax, mail or email to: **JEWISH LIGHTS Publishing**
Sunset Farm Offices, Route 4 • P.O. Box 237 • Woodstock, Vermont 05091
Tel: (802) 457-4000 • Fax: (802) 457-4004 • www.jewishlights.com
Credit card orders: (800) 962-4544 (8:30AM–5:30PM EST Monday–Friday)
Generous discounts on quantity orders. SATISFACTION GUARANTEED. Prices subject to change.

For more information about each book, visit our website at www.jewishlights.com